Copey of Harvard

OTHER BOOKS BY

J. Donald Adams

THE SHAPE OF BOOKS TO COME

LITERARY FRONTIERS

THE TREASURE CHEST: AN ANTHOLOGY

OF CONTEMPLATIVE PROSE

THE NEW TREASURE CHEST: AN ANTHOLOGY

OF REFLECTIVE PROSE

TRIUMPH OVER ODDS: AN ANTHOLOGY OF

MAN'S UNCONQUERABLE SPIRIT

Charles Townsend Copeland,
after the portrait by Charles Hopkinson
in the Harvard Club, New York

Copey of Harvard

A Biography of Charles Townsend Copeland

BY J. DONALD ADAMS

WITH ILLUSTRATIONS

The Riverside Press Cambridge

HOUGHTON MIFFLIN COMPANY BOSTON

1 9 6 0

TO CHARLES F. DUNBAR, NEPHEW OF

CHARLES TOWNSEND COPELAND, AND

TO HIS WIFE KATHARINE, THIS BOOK

IS DEDICATED IN TOKEN OF THEIR

UNSWERVING INTEREST AND HELP IN

ITS PREPARATION.

Contents

Illustrations

Copey of Harvard

Prologue

THIS IS the story of a man who became a legend in his life-time, which began in 1860. The legend had ample space for its growth, since his life spanned nearly a century, but it was already full-blown before he was fifty. He was one of the greatest teachers this country has produced, and the only one ever to have an alumni association of his own. He was also a wit, and one of the most remarkable public readers in the English tongue since Charles Dickens. Through the magic of his interpretations, thousands who heard him were first drawn to the love of reading for themselves, and by the force and illumination of his teaching, many of the best American writers of this century were moved to express their lasting indebtedness. More books were dedicated to him than to any other person of his time. But his influence went beyond instruction and the communication of delight. One of his friends was to say of him after his death that Charles Townsend Copeland had probably changed the course of more lives than any other American of his period.

To generations of Harvard men he was one of the unforgettable figures of their youth. Whether or not they had been among his students, most men who were at Harvard during his forty years of residence in the Yard remembered "Copey." Half a lifetime later, they could still see the strange figure pointed out to them as freshmen: a little man with a bulbous head, topped always by a derby (in summer, a stiff-brimmed straw), emerging from his eyrie in Hollis Hall, moving across the Yard as they had never seen anyone move before; you could not say merely that he walked; it was something between a march and a trudge, with the stiff-jointed motion of a wound-up toy.

The great teacher, as distinct from the great scholar — the contributor to knowledge — acts as a kind of catalyst upon the personalities that come into his sphere of influence. He helps them realize their potentialities, and brings out that dormant or retarded quality which may confer distinction. Sometimes the outstanding teacher and scholar are combined in the same person — as they were not in Copeland — and that is a wonderful conjunction indeed.

There is no mystery about what makes a great teacher, and it is easy falsely to endow him with some almost occult power. He is a man who possesses certain qualities which, when encountered separately, are by no means extraordinary. These qualities are human sympathy with and interest in others, especially the young; the gift for clarification and simplification of subtle matters; a strong desire to communicate what he knows, and the capacity to create enthusiasm in others; and lastly, the power to project his own personality, even to the point of being a showman, as Copeland unquestionably was.

Although all great teachers possess these qualities, not all use them in the same way. Copeland's qualities were his own, and he varied them to suit the diverse temperaments and capacities of his students. In certain cases he used a method which, as Dr. James Bryant Conant once pointed out, has its analogy in the world of sports, where it is frequently used by an effective coach. Selecting the best material he can, the coach badgers these men, often mercilessly, out of too easy satisfaction with themselves. Just as the football coach, be-

tween the halves of a game, may give his squad a brutal haul-
ing over the coals, in the same way the teacher can put his
students on their mettle and draw out from them the best
they have to give.

It was a method employed over and over again, as we
shall see, by Copeland, but he used it chiefly with students
whom he thought overconfident of their ability, and with
those rebellious against discipline. He had, to a degree
amounting to genius, the capacity to help men realize themselves, and find their own true bent. This ability was no
doubt partly the product of Copeland's own difficult and
lonely struggle to discover what he himself was best fitted to
do. He had conquered in that battle, after the sacrifice of
much he had wanted, and it was his dedication to the task of
helping other men to do likewise which, added to his natural
gifts of sharp perception and intuitive insight, made him the
great teacher he became.

CHAPTER ONE

The Son of Maine

THROUGHOUT his life Charles Townsend Copeland wanted to know where people were from, where they were born and had their roots. He was always interested in what these places meant to them. This was partly because much of his life was vicariously lived, but the interest stemmed also from the fact that the place and region of his own birth meant so much to him — so much, indeed, that for more than thirty years before he died, he never returned there. "Too many ghosts," he used to say, and chose to live with the memories he cherished.

He was born in what for most Americans is one of the least-known corners of their country — its easternmost edge, in the town of Calais, Maine. There the St. Croix River divides the United States from Canada; just below Calais the St. Croix broadens out into the reaches of Passamaquoddy Bay, which in turn loses itself in the Bay of Fundy. These waters, famed for their whirlpools, their powerful currents, and the unparalleled depth of ebb and flow in their tides, were known to the earliest voyagers who reached our eastern coast.

Charles Copeland loved them, and when he was a young newspaperman in Boston he wrote that

the scenery of the coasts of Nova Scotia, New Brunswick and Eastern Maine, but especially that of Maine and the neighboring province, has a picturesque and varied charm that is not to be found elsewhere on the Atlantic coast. The hills, the bold headlands, the mighty arms which the sea stretches up into the land, "the hard, glad weather," are all very dear to the dweller in that country. Its scenery gets a sort of personality — which is never forgotten by those who have once known it — from the great rushing tides of the Bay of Fundy, that make such wonderful changes in the outline of the coast from hour to hour, and also from the fogs and mists of the same bay, which, in the warmer months of the year, turn the landscape into a succession of dissolving views, and soften everything in a way which is surprising to eyes accustomed only to the somewhat hard light that shines over most of our coast scenery.

This land of the lovely river and its island-studded bay, set among low-lying wooded hills, is rich in the early history of the continent. Its part in the story of North American colonization has been somewhat scanted by historians, though its element of drama approaches that of Jamestown and Plymouth. After St. Augustine in Florida, the first white settlement on the Atlantic coast was made on an island in the St. Croix, about seven miles below where Calais was to stand; this was three years before Captain John Smith's settlement of Jamestown, and sixteen years before the Pilgrims landed at Plymouth.

It was in June of 1604 that a French expedition, led by the Sieur de Monts and piloted by Champlain, sailed up Passamaquoddy Bay and into the St. Croix. They were delighted by the surrounding country, and found a site much to their liking on the island named St. Croix by de Monts, later known as Dochet, but locally pronounced as Docher's Island. Where it lies the river is more than a mile wide, and the island, in midstream, offered a commanding position for their cannon.

The Frenchmen's hopes, however, were short-lived. The winter, of a severity they had not imagined, was disastrous.

Of the seventy-nine members of the expedition, thirty-five were dead before it was over. To continue there seemed to invite annihilation, and early in the summer of 1605 the survivors crossed the Bay of Fundy and settled at Port Royal (now Annapolis Royal) on the coast of Nova Scotia. At the exercises held on the island, on the three hundredth anniversary of the St. Croix settlement, in June of 1904, Charles Copeland read an ode written by another Calais man, Henry Milner Rideout, ending with the lines:

> Here flows the shining river endlessly,
> Here the isle echoes with their fortitude.

The settlers' defeat has its puzzling aspects. They might have fared better had they known how to build log cabins instead of frame houses and huts. But scurvy was reported as the reason for many of the deaths — and there was no lack of available fresh food. As Champlain himself noted, there was an abundance of shellfish about the settlement at low tide, the surrounding waters swarmed with fish, and the woods with game. Their relations with the Indians, who did not suffer from scurvy, were friendly, and one wonders whether Father Biard, a roving missionary who visited them, did not give a clue to the difficulty when he reported to his superiors in Paris: "Of all Sieur de Monts' people who wintered first at St. Croix only eleven remained well. These were a jolly company of hunters who preferred rabbit hunting to the air of the fireside, skating on the ponds to turning over in bed, making snowballs to bring down the game to sitting around the fire talking about Paris and its good cooks."

2

Nearly two centuries were to pass before Calais itself was founded. In 1779 Daniel Hill, who had been one of Rogers' Rangers, and one of sixteen men who had settled Machias,

Maine, in 1763, took up land where the International Bridge now spans the St. Croix between Calais and its New Brunswick neighbor, the town of St. Stephen. Three years later, with two other men, he built the first sawmill on the river. There were to be many more, and when Charles Copeland was born there on April 27, 1860, Calais had been for a generation a thriving center of the lumber business, and was busy as well building the barques, brigs and schooners employed in the trade.

As a child Charles Copeland knew the scent of sawed pine that was never absent from the Calais air until the forests of Maine had yielded up their best timber, and the smell of pine was replaced by that of spruce. Gradually, through the second half of the century, as the forests were gutted, the number of mills declined; in the '50's there had been as many as seventy-five. Gradually, too, the hammers of the shipwrights ceased to sound on the banks of the St. Croix. There are no shipyards now, and only a fraction of the lumbermills survive. Calais today is no larger than it was at Charles Copeland's birth — a town of about 5000 people, kept alive by what remains of its woodworking, its fruit and dairy processing and its activity as a market town for the surrounding countryside.

Yet it is an interesting town even now, if for nothing else but its unique relationship with St. Stephen. Their history and their life have been intertwined for a century and a half and the people of the two towns have lived in close proximity and unbroken amity. This relationship was cemented as far back as the War of 1812. At that time a veteran of Burgoyne's army, named Duncan MacColl, served as preacher to the settlers on both sides of the river. When war came MacColl, according to local legend, threatened to turn out of his church anyone who made a show of belligerence. "I've christened you and married you and buried you," he said, "and I'm not going to let you fight now." The story goes that in consequence, the gunpowder which had been allotted to St. Stephen for its defense was presented to Calais for its Fourth of July celebration. This feeling has persisted through the years, and on the Queen's birthday Calais flies its American flags, and Calais children sing:

> The 24th of May is the Queen's birthday.
> If they don't have a holiday I'll run away.

Similarly, on the Fourth, St. Stephen breaks out its Union Jacks, and when George VI was crowned, both towns paraded together to the tune of the Stein Song.

Nor are these bonds confined to sentiment. Calais takes its water from St. Stephen's supply — the only existing instance of the citizens of one country obtaining their water from those of another; St. Stephen gets its cooking gas from the Calais gas plant. The fire departments of both towns constantly co-operate; the St. Stephen department has been known to be first at a Calais fire, and vice versa. Calais residents are likely to buy their meat in St. Stephen, and this was usual practice during the meat-rationing days of World War II. A St. Stephen girl may come hatless across the International Bridge, and go back wearing a bonnet bought in Calais. There has always been much intermarriage, usually between Calais men and St. Stephen girls. And many Calais citizens have preferred to be buried, because of its beauty, in the St. Stephen cemetery.

Briefly, during the days of the Fenian rising in 1866, relations between the two towns became somewhat tense. The Irish Republic Brotherhood, whose headquarters were in New York, had more in mind than the freeing of Ireland from the British yoke; England was to be conquered, and Canada annexed to the United States. Perhaps because New Brunswick, proud of her status as a Crown colony, had voted down confederation with the rest of Canada in 1865, she was selected by the Fenians as the first province to be invaded. New Brunswick took the threat seriously, and defense preparations were made in all the little towns on the Canadian side of the St. Croix. As a boy of six, Charles Copeland doubtless watched the bonfires that an Irish sympathizer in Calais set blazing for two miles along the riverbank, hoping to make the Canadians think they marked the bivouac of an army. Actually, a band of Fenians did arrive at Eastport, Maine, in a schooner loaded with arms, but General Meade had been dispatched to the border to preserve neutrality, and after his enthusiastic reception in Calais, proceeded to Eastport, where the Fenians promptly took ship back to New York.

This flurry, however, had no lasting effect on the citizens of Calais and St. Stephen. No words have truer meaning for them than the inscription on the bronze plaque at the boundary mark on the International Bridge at Ferry Point: "This unfortified boundary line between the Dominion of Canada and the United States of America should quicken the remembrance of the more than century old friendship between these countries, a lesson of peace to all Nations."

In 1805 the country was aglow with gratitude to France, which no doubt had something to do with the choice of a name by the small village on the St. Croix. Calais was probably suggested by the fact that a stretch of low but steep riverbank on the Canadian side was somewhat magniloquently known as Dover Cliffs. Outlanders often need to be told that Calais is not to be pronounced as it is in French. It has always been "Callus" to the people along the St. Croix, and Charles Copeland, ever a stickler about such matters, never permitted any other pronunciation, any more than he overlooked the use of "up" for "down" in reference to the State of Maine.

3

When his maternal grandfather, Reuben Lowell, who had been born in Buckfield, Maine, came to Calais in 1825 at the age of thirty, the town's population was still numbered in the hundreds. These Maine Lowells, of whom there were already many, were descended from the younger son of that Perceval Lowell (or Lowle as it was originally spelled) who founded the Lowell line in this country. Although it was John, the elder son, from whom the more illustrious branch of the family derived, yet Richard Lowell's descendants were nevertheless of the same sturdy, tenacious and prolific stock.

The Copelands, like the Lowells, were New England to the bone. Charles Copeland's grandfather, Thomas Jefferson Copeland, arrived in Calais in the 1840's; Boston born, and a graduate of its ancient Latin School, he had gone to Norridgewock on the Kennebec, at the age of twenty-one, and there for ten years or more published and edited *The Somerset Journal*. While in Norridgewock he married the daughter of his cousin Dr. Amos Townsend, and when they moved on down to Calais, they brought with them their son Henry Clay, who in 1858 was to marry Reuben Lowell's daughter Sarah. Charles Townsend Copeland was the first-born child of this couple.

Most of the immediate ancestors of Charles Copeland were men of business, and took an active part in the affairs of the growing town on the St. Croix. His grandfather Thomas Copeland was elected alderman in 1852, and his father was to fill the same office thirty years later. Two of his Lowell kin also served as aldermen. Daniel Kimball Chase, who married Charles's Aunt Minerva Lowell, was in the 1850's mayor of the town, and at his death left his estate for the benefit of its "worthy poor." They were all people with a strong attachment to the region in which they lived, and with a few exceptions they died there. Two of Charles Copeland's Lowell uncles had a brief fling at the far West; George Albert and Reuben B. Lowell caught the gold fever in 1849 and sailed round the Horn to California, but both, after two years in the

West, returned to Calais, where in 1882 George was elected city treasurer. Of Reuben B. the only surviving story of interest is that he once killed a cow he discovered ambling through his corn by throwing a hatchet at her.

On the Copeland side, there is a family legend that one of Charles's eighteenth century forebears, Elizabeth Tupper of Sandwich, who married Abraham Copeland, was able to dance a hornpipe with a glass of wine on her head without spilling a drop — an accomplishment in which Charles, who was never physically adept, took great interest both as boy and man. Of her husband, who was a sea captain, it is told that he was of such a crabbed and disagreeable nature that his family were always delighted when he packed his sea chest for a voyage, and counted the days with foreboding when he was expected home. At the age of sixty, he had a change of heart; he was converted, joined the Methodist Church, and was ever after the pattern of amiability.

Charles Copeland, from childhood on, took the keenest interest in these ancestors. He delighted in the most trivial details about them, and he was pleased to discover in these details evidence of their gentility — for example the fact that his great-grandfather, Dr. Townsend, the Norridgewock physician and farmer, wore lace ruffles on his sleeves. He was concerned about whether the doctor wore his hair in a queue. On Washington's birthday, by his own account, Copeland always made a ritual of studying the silhouette of his grandfather Reuben Lowell, a lad of twenty in a ruffled shirt, and of taking out of its pewter box a miniature of George Washington which had belonged to Reuben. It was set in a small gold brooch, and Charles felt sure it had often been "pinned somewhere in the voluminous folds of that silhouetted shirt." Often he would produce such family mementos on his famous evenings "at home," when Harvard undergraduates flocked to his rooms in Hollis Hall, and or-

dinarily the boys gave them their polite interest; once, however, an uninhibited young man who was to become well
known as the painter Waldo Peirce took one of these tokens
in his hands and blandly remarked, "Yes, Copey, I will now
admire for the third and last time your grandfather's watch."
At the age of seventy-five Copeland wrote to his cousin Agnes Lowell, about his Lowell grandfather:

> I never thought of saying to you that my chief motive, al-
> though there were others, in having photostats of the old
> deed — my chief motive was in order that the designation
> as "gentleman" of our grandfather in contradistinction to
> Gibson as a "yeoman," the designation being, of course, not
> by the men themselves but by the judge, might be per-
> petuated. This is a sentence almost as long as from Reuben
> Lowell's time to mine, but I think you have got the heart
> of it, which is that I'm a bit of a snob, and you, although
> my first cousin and a woman — supposed to be given to
> snobbery because you are a woman — didn't even think,
> apparently, of that social distinction in the deed. I showed
> that and other documents a number of years ago to Presi-
> dent Lowell, who agreed with me that it was very odd in
> so democratic a community as Maine, especially Eastern
> Maine, to have those social distinctions publicly proclaimed
> at so late a date. Have you by chance any such relics of
> our past?
>   Almost as much as ancestor worship was my interest in
> all the lands and waters down there belonging to the Low-
> ell farm or near it. I wish we had some good photo-
> graphs of the meadow and the bridge over it, and Maguer-
> rowock and sich. I haven't been down home since 1918,
> and in my last sight of the farm and the meadow, I saw a
> man with a scythe slowly cutting meadow hay, a pictur-
> esque object in that beautiful scene. I enjoy the cards you

send me very much, but am sorry they don't correspond
with reality today.

No more now from

Your affectionate cousin,

CHARLES

Many of his forebears lived to a great age, a fact by which
Copeland was at once fascinated, and as time went on and
his disabilities increased, more and more repelled. If he could
say, as he frequently did in middle age, "I expect to live to be
a hundred, and then, like Manuel Garcia, turn into a cigar,"
he could also, in letter after letter, and in conversation after
conversation, bewail the new milestone he had reached. But
he delighted in copying out from old records such an entry
as this: "Jan. 15 1699/1700. This day fortnight Lawrence
Copeland of Braintry was buried; 'tis counted that he liv'd to
be at least one hundred and ten years old, *Teste Arnaldo
octogenario olim ejusdem vicino*." He took careful note of
the fact that Japhet Robinson, father of his great-grand-
mother Smith, "was killed by a falling tree at the tender age
of seventy-nine," and that his grandfather Lowell died at
forty-three "only because he had been hit in the chest with a
heavy timber, and thus driven into what was called, in those
days, quick consumption."

All this longevity (his father and mother lived to be
eighty-two and eighty-three respectively) brought close the
distant past, as when Copey recalled hearing his grandmother
Lowell tell how as a child of four, in 1799, she saw her father come into the house in Gardiner, Maine, and say to her
mother, with grief upon his face, "My dear, General Washington is dead." Whenever he told this story, Copey seldom
failed to remind his listeners that the general was never referred to as President Washington by his contemporaries.

Copey's grandfather, Thomas Jefferson Copeland, the edi-

tor of *The Somerset Journal,* turned to the lumber business
when he came to Calais, and prospered in it; he was, too, one
of the organizers of a local railroad which later went into
bankruptcy. Charles's father, as a member of the firm of
Copeland, Kelley and Duren, also fared well for a time in
the lumber trade, but shortly after the panic of 1873 the firm
failed, and Henry Copeland never recovered his financial
footing. About the time his fortunes began to ebb, the big
house on Lowell Street in which Charles, his younger brother
Lowell, and his sister Katherine were born was burned to the
ground and the family moved to a smaller house on Main
Street, which still stands. Henry Copeland was fond of horses,
and in his more prosperous days kept several, but they were
destroyed in the fire, and he was never able to replace them
by more than one. Charles was about fourteen at the time of
the fire, and years later his brother Lowell recalled having
heard some of the neighbors say that while the rest of the
Copeland family were frantically trying to get the animals
out of their stalls, Charles was seen calmly emerging from the
house, a bird cage clutched in one hand and a pair of kid
gloves in the other. Whenever, as a grown man, Copeland
referred to this incident, it was always with tragic overtones,
and he would lament the loss of his Messenger mare.

In his later years Henry Copeland was rather a pathetic
figure, though still much respected in the town as a man whose
word could always be counted on, who was meticulous in
money matters, as he was in his dress (an uncommon trait in
the Calais of those days), and always ready to contribute
what he could to the town's needs. Though he had a reputation for closefistedness, he is reputed once to have said that
whatever a certain "old skinflint" gave toward the new
school, he would give fifty dollars more. When to everyone's
surprise the old skinflint made a donation of $100, Henry
Copeland kept his word. As an old man he held a minor post

in the Customs House, Calais being then, as now, a port of entry.

4

Although the bonds between Charles and his father were never close, and they shared few of the same interests, the two were alike in abruptness of manner, a scrupulous attitude toward their obligations, and in a constant concern about their personal appearance. As a youngster returning to Calais on vacations from college, Charles dazzled his townsmen's eyes by the flamboyance of his dress, and as an old man past ninety whose mind had failed, he never appeared unshaven or with clothes disordered. His failure to reach a more intimate relationship with his father was the result, perhaps, of the elder Copeland's ornery manner, a recurrent Copeland characteristic, and one often exhibited by Charles himself. This, and their lack of common interests, added to Henry's deep reserve, tended to keep a very sensitive and unsure boy from that closer union he doubtless craved.

That the elder Copeland was not wholly unsympathetic is shown by the help he extended in the matter of Charles's education. When his son's fame as a teacher and a public reader began to grow, Mr. Copeland, though loath to show the fact, was very proud. That he was not insensitive is clearly apparent in a recollection of his childhood which Charles wrote for the *Harvard Advocate* when, at the age of twenty, he became one of its editors. The story was touching; it was also revealing to an extent, perhaps, that its young author did not realize as he set it down.

As a small boy, Charles had often been attracted by some bright red berries which grew beside the fence outside the house of an old lady "with corkscrew curls," he remembered, who lived down the street from the Copeland home. One day as the boy came by, the blinds were drawn, and the opportunity to indulge his longing seemed at hand. He plucked a berry and ate it, but its taste was bitter, and he took no more. As he was about to turn away, the blinds of a window flew open, the old lady leaned out and cried, "Now, you naughty boy, you have found your reward. Those berries are deadly poison, which I keep especially for naughty boys. Tomorrow you will be dead!"

Charles's heart leaped in his breast. Reflecting on how sad a fate it was to die when his life had scarcely begun, he hurried, panic-stricken, to his home. There he found his brother Lowell in the hall, and poured out the dreadful story, begging his brother's forgiveness for all injuries he had done him, exacting a promise that he would attend the funeral, and telling him of certain prized possessions he would leave to him. Charles then kissed his brother, who was by this time in tears, told him he would see him once more, and went out of the house. In the garden he found his father, and told him all that had happened. His father, he remembered, seemed to smile, took him by the hand, and led him back to the scene of his crime. Quivering before the old lady, Charles implored her forgiveness and begged her to give him something which would forestall his imminent end. She exacted his eager promise that never again would he molest her property, whereupon she produced a gumdrop and plopped it in his mouth. Thus comforted, he took his father's hand and left for home.

That childish panic was to be repeated more than once in his later life, for hypochondria and the dread of death were always with him. Walking with Harvard's historian, Samuel Eliot Morison, the bell of Memorial Hall tolling above them, and Copeland not yet sixty, he sighed and said, "Sam, do you know what it says? It says, 'death, death, death.'" And there was the day when Morison came to see him, up the three narrow flights of time-worn stairs in Hollis, and was greeted by a deeply perturbed voice, quavering, "Sam, I've just had a terrible shock — a terrible shock. Jones [the janitor of Hollis] said to me this morning, 'Mr. Copeland, I was just thinking that it's going to be an awful job getting a coffin down these stairs.' " How much of this was said with tongue in cheek is hard to know; Copeland loved to tell the story afterward, as he liked to say that it was his intention to leave Hollis feet first. And there was the day when he sat with Malcolm MacNair on the front steps of Hollis, and suddenly asked, "Do you think there is anything after death?" and before MacNair could reply, burst out, "Oh Mac, I *hope* there isn't, I *hope* there isn't." Graveyards always fascinated him, and when, on his walks, he came to the one in St. Andrew's, he was sure to ask of the caretaker, "How are your dead this morning?" Just as invariably, the answer would be, "Haven't heard any complaints, sir."

Rollo Walter Brown has written how he called on Copeland one day when he was having a year of leave from university work, but living as usual in his Hollis Hall quarters.

He lay upon a couch with a heavy towel that had been dipped in ice water on his forehead, and with his hands folded so neatly that he looked like a corpse.

"Do you suppose I am ever to be well again?" he asked.

"Of course you are — just as soon as you get away from here and quit thinking about students and lectures and themes and conferences."

"But you must remember that I am sixty-three years old."

"Now let me see," I replied in an effort to be comforting: "that is just twenty-six years younger than President Eliot, isn't it?"

The corpse sprang up, full of furious life. "My God! Don't you dare mention that man to me! The Lord just made him to show to people."

CHAPTER TWO

Beside the Tides of Fundy

COPELAND's lack of rapport with his father was no doubt intensified by his very deep attachment to his mother — one which she lavishly returned, creating a bond between them which lasted until she died. All those who knew Sarah Copeland have spoken of her as a remarkable woman, and she was no doubt the strongest formative influence in the life of her son. She shared fully in his literary interests and did all she could to encourage and foster them. Her letters speak constantly of her pride in him, and she was delighted, in her reading, often to find that her favorite passages or characters were his also. From his boyhood on, their correspondence was continuous, and it is a matter for great regret that while many of her letters to him survive, not a single letter from Charles to his mother has been found, although he must have written her thousands. Apparently she destroyed them at his insistence, as they were received. There is evidence of this in her letters to him as far back as 1903, for early in that year she wrote:

> I thank you for frequent and most original telegrams, and now a fine letter has come. If you have shortcomings, neglect of your mother cannot be counted among them — but I say in truth, that if you will confine your communications from now until the first of June, or later, to post-cards

and telegrams, you will add largely to my peace of mind.
The thought of you wielding a pen for me is quite upset-
ting. [It is evident from earlier letters that he had confessed
the manual difficulty he had in using pen or pencil for any
length of time.]

I can recall nothing of the ink-copied scrawl except the
B.S. Sketches, and I cannot account for your interest in it
— but why, let me ask, when at your request, I have to destroy your dear and entertaining and precious letters, so
dear to my heart — do you claim the right to possess my
commonplace ones? This matter is worth considering.

At her death in Cambridge in 1916, two years after her
daughter Katherine had brought her there from Calais, the
published tributes to her memory were of extraordinary
warmth. Though the strength of her personality had never
been exerted outside the circle of her family and friends, she
had touched and affected many lives. She was a semi-invalid
for years, and did not go about, but people came to her con-
tinuously both in Calais and Cambridge, irresistibly drawn by
the radiance she gave.

In the *Boston Transcript* for January 12, 1916, Fanny
Quincy Howe, wife of the biographer Mark Antony DeWolfe
Howe, wrote of her:

> She was much more than "a sweet old lady" — her keen
> and kindly humor, her mental agility and lightness of
> touch, her sympathy with people rather than for them,
> make it impossible to compress her vivid and delicate per-
> sonality into a stereotyped phrase. She had that wonderful
> reconciling touch which distinguishes the best, not only in
> the age she represented, but also in the bewildering one
> that pressed upon her later years — and through sickness,
> sadness, change, and death, her wit and humor played their

saving parts, and enabled her to keep her interest alert and her courage undaunted to the end. . . .

All who knew Mrs. Copeland could echo, with devout enthusiasm, the words written to her a few days before her death by one of the young men who loved and appreciated her: "Every time I have seen you, you have made me forget my cares and cheerlessness and lay aside my roughness of heart — which makes me wish to see you again soon, and many times." Such words were not a tribute which Youth can often truthfully pay to Age, but all felt themselves contemporaries of the wise and gracious friend, who, with feminine flexibility, shared the point of view of young and old alike. . . .

And Byron S. Hurlbut, then Dean of Harvard College, wrote:

To those who saw her in her home in Calais, before the delicate body had become as fragile as some winter blossom, to those who sat with her among her books and flowers, warming alike hands and hearts at her kindly fire, she was the embodiment of that womanhood which men who think set as their ideal for a mother of sons. She had the gift, bestowed upon comparatively few women, of sympathetic understanding of the boy's and the man's point of view, so that into her friendships there entered no thought of discrepancy in age; it was like the friendship of man to man, with the added blessing, which the man realized only after he had thought thereon, of a woman's subtle intuition and "mothering.". . .

Her wit was like the finest steel: but she never left a wound or a scar. Her humor was a bubbling spring at every turning of life's twisted, dusty road: it was true humor, for it often trembled on the verge of tears. If only she had

set her pen to paper, — if only she had written down the
stories she could tell so well, or even a tithe thereof, the
all too slender gallery of pictures which Rowland Robinson
and Sarah Jewett limned would have gained worthy companions, and the inheritance of the fast vanishing descendants of a vanished New England would have been so much
the richer. . . .

In the *Calais Advertiser*, Henry Milner Rideout wrote:

When we talked with her, we knew the world was better than we feared, because she took us into a chamber
that was peace, where every window looked toward the
sun. It is impossible to tell, impossible to forget with what
a play of intelligence, keen but gentle, she entertained us;
with what interest she clothed for us the little facts of our
own lives; above all, with what incomparable sense of fun
she made us laugh, always at things that "give delight and
hurt not."

It was small wonder, then, that Charles Copeland adored
her. Not only did she give him the courage to make the most
of himself; she responded with equal interest to everything
which interested or concerned him, just as he was to do in his
relations with his students and his older friends. She fed, too,
his insatiable interest in the background out of which he came,
as is charmingly shown in a letter she wrote him two years
before her death:

My dear Charles: —
    In the house where I was born more than eighty years ago,
built by my father, there was a bed-room, back of the sit-
ting-room, which I shared with my mother. Memorably
in this room was a high, carved four-poster — a bed with

curtains of copper-plate, printed with flowers and other figures, between which it was my delight, when I was stowed away for the night in winter, to see pictures in the glowing fire on the hearth. Two windows at the back looked out upon a green sloping down to the beginning of a long row of thrifty damson trees that reached to the stone wall at the back of our land, and to the edge of our garden with much grassland adjoining.

At the time of this story which I am trying to tell, it was decided that I must go away to school, as I was in my 17th year. Our room was given up to preparations for this event, and your card-table, which your grandmother — but that is not to be told here — was spread in the centre to hold my outfit as it was made ready, — all laid in order so that confusion was impossible. There were boxes for gloves, laces, and so on — many bags of different sizes, all labeled to hold buttons, tape, thread, silk, pieces, etc., etc. — and an attractive work-basket, furnished with implements to keep my clothes in repair. Chairs and the bed held my larger garments. I distinctly recall two frocks of muslin, a pink and a white, looking so cool and fluffy on the bed, with gloves and slippers to match, but at that time I cared little for clothes. Maguerrewock with its fields, meadow, water and mountain had greater charms for me. I wondered when I viewed this array, how it was to be got into a medium-sized trunk, and then I would turn to the windows and wonder still more, how I could live a year without my dear mother, and away from all that I loved so much.

The morning came at last, when we were taken to the boat, but by what conveyance I cannot remember, nor of our stay at Eastport, if any, but our steaming into Portland harbour "near the night's pale end," — landing in a crowd, and such noise — finding a coach — the like of which cannot be in your recollection, a roomy vehicle, high up from the ground, with back and front seats, and one in the middle to fold away when not in use — all this is vividly before me. . . .

In the hour or so before the Waterville train-time, we went forth into the town. At Lowell and Senter's, leading silversmiths and jewelers Lizzie [an aunt of Charles's who was to be his mother's roommate] and I made choice from a bewildering show of pretty things, of chased silver combs. We were greatly pleased with them. The silver was very effective in my dark wavy hair. They were quite the fashion at that time. A few years later your grandmother held a brief genealogical correspondence with the Lowell member of the firm — it was interesting and sometimes amusing.

The school year was far pleasanter than I had dared to hope, and the home-coming was happiness without alloy, — a time for rejoicing! Even the old well sweep seemed to creak a glad welcome when I lowered the bucket. [As an old woman she was often to say, when trying to recall some incident of the distant past, "Wait till I lower the bucket."]

I have condensed this sketch with all my might — I have not written freely, and still what a spread I have made with all my trying not to.

Your affectionate
MOTHER

Bandboxes and baskets were much in use those days for traveling purposes. I was provided with a fine basket, lined with cambric of a light-brown color, and encased in a bag of the same with a draw-string at the top — so my packing was not crowded.

In January of 1912, four years before her death, she wrote an entry in her diary, of which Charles later made many copies, as he did of so many things of personal interest. It read:

My mother often comes to me in dreams, but only twice has she come in my waking hours. The first time was one evening in the early part of August, 1893. I was sitting on the front step in the twilight, when she walked slowly back and forth near me a number of times. A hazy figure, but distinctly my mother.

The second visit was about two o'clock this morning. I had been fully awake for a brief time, when I became conscious of a presence in the room, and soon my mother was standing by my bed, extending her hand to me, with what appeared to be leaves from a small diary in it. It was so real that I exclaimed, "Oh mother, what is it?" Then the thin mist which had before veiled only her face gradually enveloped her figure, and carried it away from me. I grieved for a touch of her hand, for the sound of her voice, but not in this life can I ever have them.

I do not know what it all means — but this I do know, that I was awake, well, sane in mind, and that my mother came to me.

Interesting too, for quite different reasons, is a letter she wrote to Charles in the summer of 1910, from the old Loyalist town of St. Andrews, some twenty miles down the river and bay from Calais. St. Andrews, so much closer to the sea, with its lingering aura of more glamorous days than Calais ever knew, had been for many years a favorite vacation spot of the Copeland family, as it was and still is of many Calais people. It is the letter's opening paragraph which is of interest now:

Through a cold, dense fog on Saturday [she wrote], that serene old prostitute — you can not take exception to the noun because it is just what she has been — came to see me — that creature who, born with all the grace and charm of a beautiful woman, has lived a life of shame.

Who can wonder that she fears to be alone? She was profuse in urging me to visit her, and "would I kindly carry her wish to my son to call upon her. It would give her so much pleasure to meet him" etc., etc. Why does she thrust herself upon those who have never asked her, and do not want her near them? She is still fascinating, and if you should go to see her it might cause even greater suspicion than fell upon Dr. Johnson when "he wanted to know where the old woman, in the hut, slept."

2

There would be more to tell about Charles Copeland's boyhood if he had not so long survived his Calais contemporaries. And since he was to remain a bachelor all his life, there were no children to pass on such stories as he might have told them. When I visited his birthplace in 1958, six years after his death, there was but one person living who had known him as a boy, and he had been an intimate, not of Charles, but of his younger brother Lowell. This was Frank Beckett, then ninety-six, who was still making with his own hands, and selling at something like fifty cents a pound, the old-fashioned country-store chocolates for which there was a brisk demand in his grocery shop on Main Street. "I didn't see much of Charles," he said with a wry smile. "He was always with the girls." He left the implication that Charles, in his estimation, had been something of a sissy.

Certainly the Calais of Charles's boyhood, its wharves crowded with shipping, its schooners tempting a venturesome lad to climb their rigging if he could wangle the chance, its exciting lumber mills, offered endless opportunities for adventure, but Charles, physically awkward and frail, probably never attempted any mizzentops. There is no doubt that he was a shy boy, and somewhat withdrawn. When Van Wyck Brooks, who had been one of Copeland's students at Harvard, was in Calais some years before my own visit, he talked with an old druggist who, like Frank Beckett, had been one of Charles's schoolmates, and a member of his class at the Calais Academy. He produced a photograph taken at their graduation, and there, standing five paces apart from all the other boys and girls, was Charles. His old classmate pointed him out and said, "He was like that always." But the trouble was not wholly one of shyness, and the timidity a boy may feel who is smaller and less robust than others of his years; he was, through the intellectual interests of his mother and his Lowell grandmother, more mature in thought than other boys of his age in that remote community, and he found more of the mental nourishment he craved in the society of his elders; particularly, because of the inadequacy he must have felt as a boy among boys, he was to seek solace and support, even when he was older, among women.

Withdrawn though he was, he had a lively sense of fun and a large capacity for mischief. This is evident in his relations with his Aunt Mary Kelley, who had married one of his father's partners, and to whom he was devoted. Her granddaughter, Mrs. Richard Wait, from the memories of her mother, Alice Kelley, who was about the same age as Charles, and one of his favorite companions, has made that abundantly clear. Charles liked to tease his Aunt Mary; she was very nearsighted, and when he walked with her he would tell her to jump over puddles, which she trustingly did, although the ground was perfectly dry. Like many women of her generation, she was terrified of tramps, and young Charles, aware of this weakness, once hid himself under her library sofa, whence, as she came into the house at dusk, issued sounds which put her in a panic.

In this spirit of mischief it occurred to him one day that it might be fun to promote a match between Miss Alice Pike, an eminently respectable maiden lady who lived opposite the Kelleys on Main Street, and Mr. Washburn, an equally respectable widower whose house was in the neighborhood. Conspiring with his cousin Alice, he concocted a note, purporting to be from Miss Pike, which invited Mr. Washburn for supper that same day. He signed it "A. Pike," explaining later that this use of an initial removed any possible taint of forgery. But the betraying factor proved to be the postscript, which luringly read, "I shall be alone." He and his cousin Alice delivered the note at the Washburn house and impatiently waited for developments. Presently a Washburn daughter came out and headed in the direction of Miss Pike's home. The young conspirators learned nothing more until Alice's mother was told by one of the Washburn girls that her father had been greatly pleased by the message until he came to the postscript. Then, he at once said, he knew that a respectable woman like Miss Pike would never have written it, and immediately sent one of his daughters over to inquire.

The house in which the Copelands lived after their home in Lowell Street burned down had no direct access to the river, but Charles had a rowboat which he kept at a dock below Mrs. Kelley's house, the grounds of which sloped down to the St. Croix. Its care must have been something of a problem for a small boy, for even on the river as far up as Calais the rise in tide exceeds twenty feet. Often he took his Aunt Mary or his cousin Alice out on the river, but occasionally his companion was another boy, and according to local legend, when they got down to the dock Charles would say, "Look, I'll give you ten cents if you will do the rowing." This, if true, was the earliest indication of what was to become a highly developed capacity to relieve himself of any work which others might do for him. He treasured his conversations with his Aunt Mary on these river jaunts, and of-

ten told how she once said to him, "Charles, don't you think
it strange that the good Lord never took the trouble to bring
more good-looking people into this world?" Her nephew no
doubt agreed, for he would, throughout his life, never fail to
remark on a pretty or a handsome face.

Like other Calais boys, he had the chore of taking the family cow out to pasture, and bringing her back, but his method
of performing this task was singular in that or any other lo-
cality, for he devised a bridle for the animal and rode her
back and forth each day. And once, at least, he managed to
equip a pig with his mother's sidesaddle, and rode the porker
too. Down the street lived one of those typical Victorian in-
valids who passed her life in a darkened room, with a mattress
spread on the porch roof outside, to deaden the sound of rain.
Every evening, after dark, her husband got between the shafts
of a buggy and took her out for an airing; this spectacle, naturally, fascinated Charles, and he was not content until, after repeated pleading, he was permitted to pull the buggy
himself. Of this invalid it may be added that after her husband's death she joined the Christian Science Church, recovered entirely from her imagined complaint, and was happily
wed to the trombone player in a circus band.

Charles was never adept at games, and cared little for them;
his pronounced lack of physical co-ordination, persisting
through his life, would have made him ridiculous had he attempted baseball or tennis, or almost any other sport, and he
was painfully aware of this handicap. His one physical out-
let was to be walking, and though even in that his manner
was singular, he forced himself, even in old age, to walk
several miles each day; otherwise, he always said, he would
never sleep at all. As a child — and the fact argues against a
complete physical timidity — he was fond of mounting the
steep gabled roof of his Aunt Mary's house and sliding down
until his heels clicked against the gutter and stopped his fall.

3

By the time he was big enough to attend the Calais Academy, Charles's chief delight was to go down to the livery stable and hire a rig to take his mother for a drive. Their favorite destination was Clendinnin's Hill, on the Canadian side of the river, a height from which, he never tired of telling in later years, could be had the most embracing view of the border country, and always, whenever he returned to Calais, he was sure to go there. On longer excursions the objective was usually St. Andrews, which Calais people, in those days, customarily reached by little steamers which touched there on the way to Eastport, Maine. Charles loved the old Tory town, whose principal streets had been named for the children of George III, and as he grew older, liked to talk with its characters, particularly with the old Indian Nicholas who held his piece of land by royal grant. In 1884 he would write of the St. Andrews people that they were greatly addicted to drink. "If you make a morning call upon people of a certain rank, you are offered port wine and cake. At a sufficient descent in the social scale your visit would be rewarded with Irish whiskey. All classes are bibulous to an extent, and with a publicity, which in New England is most unusual. Even on the other side of the border a man must drink in bad company or in none."

But he was never, unlike his Lowell uncles and his seafaring forebears, to respond to the call of far places; always he urged his students to knock about the world before they settled down to write; as for himself, in spite of his unflagging interest in what was going on the world over, he made but one trip abroad, and that confined to England and Scotland. In his own country he was not to venture farther west than Chicago, and his deepest south, he used to say, was Philadelphia. It distressed him not to return at night to his own bed, and a long journey anywhere was an undertaking which he dreaded.

He entered the Calais Academy — by then the Calais High School — when he was thirteen. His "deportment," which at that time took the place of "adjustment" on school report cards, was excellent, and his grades equally high. Separate marks were then given for punctuation (this was long before it became one of the lost arts), and in this he particularly excelled. In his second year he became an editor of the Calais High School *Herald*, which ceased publication before he was graduated, but during 1874 he contributed several essays, written in remarkably good prose for a boy of fourteen. Their subjects included "Cremation," an account of an imagined visit to Hades, the life of King James I of Scotland, "Observations During a Rainstorm," and "Is It wrong to Play Cards?" — a question which Charles decided in the negative.

One passage from these pieces has some bearing on his future development:

I could see no boundaries to the place I was in; the perfectly level surface stretched away on all sides for an immeasurable distance. Everything was dust-colored; the place had a general air of waiting. After recovering from my amazement at being in so strange a place, my curiosity prevailed and I began to look about me. There were groups of beings in human shape all around. I had heard that Hades is the place where people, after leaving this world, go to wait for the judgment day, and being interested in public and political characters, I tried to find some. In my search, I saw Napoleon. His features looked like those in his pictures, handsome, vicious, and smart; but here they were smoothed out into a sort of passiveness, and the impatient Bonaparte seemed to have caught the spirit of the place, — a peaceful waiting. I could not find Abraham Lincoln, perhaps because I did not search sufficiently, but it was my opinion then, and is now, that the soul of Abraham Lincoln needed no certificate to pass the heavenly gates, that it went straight in. I was startled in my meanderings by seeing some of the characters that had figured in books I had read; Rochester's crazy wife, but with all the wildness and turbulence gone; she was peaceful as the rest; and old Krock, but with all the traces of the internal fire which had consumed him, gone. The seeing of these persons of fiction confirmed my theory, that all the characters mentioned in books must exist, or must have existed somewhere.

Charles Copeland was to read a great many more books than he had then, but something of his boyhood theory about the characters in them must have survived, for one of the factors which contributed so much to his effectiveness as a public reader was the conviction of reality he brought to any character that figured in his readings. For the time being, he was that person, just as Dickens had been to the point of nervous exhaustion and collapse, and this made part of the spell by which Copeland's audiences were bound.

There was one teacher by whom he was especially affected. This was Laura Burns, who taught him English in high school. Later he was to credit her with having made college a goal for many of her students. Throughout her life, he was deeply attached to her and even began to weave a kind of legend about her. Miss Burns's photographs show her to have been an attractive young woman, but not, as he was fond of making her, a rival to Helen of Troy. She painted many pleasant water colors of the border countryside which were always among his most loved possessions.

Copeland had early set his heart on going to college, and had made his choice at the age of twelve. This is apparent in a brief preview of his future, written in 1872. He called it "When I'm a Man," and reading it, one wishes one might have had similarly serious, acute and candid forecasts of other illustrious careers by those who were to have them.

> To be a man, or a woman [wrote this young analyst of himself] is the highest aspiration of almost all boys, and girls; but for my part, I'd rather be a child always. If I could grow right up, to be a rich man, without any work, I should like it, for I hate work; *but I do not hate the things that proceed from work.* (Italics mine.) I am going to Harvard College when I am old enough, and after that, I suppose I shall have to be a doctor, lawyer, or something of that kind. I think I shall teach school, a little while, right after I leave college; for I think school-teaching improves patience. If I get stamps enough, in my profession, I shall build a splendid house, and have everything to match. Then, after I have lived long enough, I shall die, and I hope to go to heaven. I believe that last part puts an end to the story.

When he was graduated from the Calais High School in June of 1878, the family's financial situation was such that even the continuation of one boy's schooling was difficult enough. He was two years older than his brother Lowell, whom he was to outlive by seventeen years, and thus the opportunity came to him. It was an advantage he was never to forget; and Lowell, a capable and attractive man with a wit as lively as that of Charles, spoke of him as "the most generous brother in the world."

In September of 1878 the young "tidewater countryman," as he later liked to call himself, left his spectacular border waters for the college on the placid Charles, where no Calais boys had ever preceded him (though two had attended the Harvard Law School), unaware that he was leaving for the place where the greater part of his long life was to be passed, and his measure of fame secured.

CHAPTER THREE

Cambridge on the Charles

IT WAS a lonely, apprehensive boy who came from Calais to Cambridge in the fall of 1878. Before his arrival he knew no other boy in his entering class, and his freshman year would no doubt have been far lonelier without one fortunate point of contact waiting for him. It was to provide an anchorage and a haven throughout his college years. For he carried with him the address of his father's first cousin, Julia Ruggles Copeland, who by a chance which was to be fruitful for Charles Copeland's future had married Charles F. Dunbar, Dean of Harvard College and the first professor in the United States to hold a chair of political economy.

Charles Dunbar, as editor of the *Boston Advertiser*, had already won a wide reputation as a student of finance when he came to the Harvard faculty in 1871. He was to become right-hand man to President Eliot whose administration had begun only two years before, and it is told of him that he was the only person ever to address that most austere of American public figures by his first name. Luckily for young Copeland, Professor Dunbar, who was graduated from Harvard in 1851, had two sons in Charles's class. They were George Bradford and William Harrison Dunbar. William, twenty years later, was to marry Charles's sister Katherine.

The Dunbar family lived in a big house at 64 Highland Street in Cambridge, which was full always of people both from the college community and from Boston. A few days after his arrival in Cambridge, Charles Copeland called there, and was received with warmth — and some puzzlement. He was an odd youngster, his cousins concluded, but appealing; they took him into their circle, and did their best to make him feel at home. As usual, he found it easier to meet on intimate terms with the feminine members of the family, and soon Anna Lowell Dunbar, next to the youngest of the four children, became his special friend and confidante. She encouraged him to come often, and he would sit with her on a huge icebox in the Dunbar pantry, sip a glass of sherry, pour out his troubles and confide his hopes.

Charles greatly admired Professor Dunbar, of whom he afterwards often used to say that he was the only man he had ever known with truly blue eyes. As time went on, he became a close friend of the youngest son, William, who was to be a leading figure at the Boston bar and a partner of the future Justice Brandeis. Charles's sister Katherine was to follow him to Cambridge in 1893; coming first to Miss Hersey's School in Boston, she spent a year at Radcliffe, and like her brother, turned to her cousins in Cambridge. She married William Dunbar in Calais, in 1898.

The Harvard to which Charles Copeland came had just begun the great expansion which was to make it truly a university. Dr. Eliot, still in his forties, was rapidly changing the face and the character of the institution which he directed so forcefully until his retirement in 1909. Rare indeed were the firsthand contacts between that unbending, stately figure and the boys who came to Harvard then or later. To them he was chiefly a presence, striding across the Yard like Zeus on Olympus, and just about as approachable. He wore his great birthmark like a badge of honor, and during the years when I used to see him, when he walked down the aisle of Samuel McChord Crothers's church in Cambridge, there was an invisible ramrod under his black coat. Those few who did find themselves, on rare occasions, alone in his company discovered that he could be considerate, courteous and kind, but the voice that most of them heard was that of the public speaker, arresting in its delivery, sounding, as Charles Copeland was later to say, "as if it had issued from channels which had been warmed by old port wine."

As a freshman in 1878, awed like the rest of his classmates, Copeland could not have foreseen that fifteen years later, when he came to teach at Harvard College, he would suffer the disfavor of Dr. Eliot, who held in high esteem all the conventional virtues, of which this young instructor with his evident disdain for the drudgery of graduate scholarship seemed by no means the pattern. Nor could he foresee the day when, on a visit to the Harvard Club of New York, he would stand looking up at the newly installed heads of African game, glare at the impala and the elephant, and exclaim to his host, "When President Eliot dies, they will stuff *him* and put him up there!" But he was also to say of the President, in a public tribute on Eliot's ninetieth birthday, "Charles William Eliot found Harvard a select little New England college. After forty years he left it the most important seat of learning in the Western Hemisphere."

The college in 1878 was still small, with an enrollment of some eight hundred students, and little more than half that number in the other departments of the university. There were seventy-four men teaching in the college, and a handful more in the allied schools. Today the university's enrollment exceeds 11,000, with a teaching staff of about 3500. There were 234 boys in Charles's entering class, of whom forty-three left during their freshman year; by Commencement in 1882, they numbered 181. More than half were New England born, and all but fifteen of these were residents of Massachusetts. One was of foreign birth, and the remaining fifty came from the Middle West, the far West, or the South. Harvard College was still, essentially, a provincial school.

Boston itself contained only 350,000 people, and Cambridge, certainly, had less appeal for the eye than the bustling
and handsomely situated town which Charles Copeland had
left behind him. Its center in Harvard Square was either
dusty or muddy, and sleepy and dull, with few buildings of
charm or beauty except the oldest structures in the college
Yard. Horsecars rattled through its streets, and the college,
which when founded two and a half centuries before had been
offered a spacious tract facing on the Atlantic near Marble-
head, was crowded chiefly in its ancient Yard, its back to the
meandering and slowly flowing river. Yet it had its relieving
features: handsome little Holden Chapel, of pure Georgian
design, Hollis Hall, where Revolutionary soldiers had barracked, with its simple but classically Georgian lines, Stoughton, a not quite perfect duplicate, and Harvard, Massachusetts, and Holworthy, none of which, in their mellowed
brick, was unpleasing to the eye. University, then as now, the
only white structure, had simplicity of line. Of the newer
buildings, unfortunate in the period of their construction, the
less said the better. Most of them were eyesores, and some
of them still remain.

When Charles Copeland first saw the Yard, Sever Hall,
whose little amphitheater was to be the scene of countless triumphs of his as a public reader, was no more than a hole in the
ground. Just completed was the Hemenway Gymnasium, a
building he would spend as little time in as possible, although
he did speak afterward of having watched with enjoyment a
side-whiskered senior named Theodore Roosevelt, tenaciously
taking a thrashing. The sports of that era, in which he had
no part, were confined to football, baseball, rowing, lacrosse,
and one no longer played at Harvard, cricket. Bicycling, always a favorite Cambridge pastime, gathered to it a large
club of undergraduates, but Charles was not one of them. He
would, as always, trust to shanks' mare.

2

Socially, the college was then, as it always had been, and still remains, more a replica of the world outside than college communities in general. There was, and is, no large flock of fraternities, so widely embracing in their membership that those boys who failed to be taken into one were to feel themselves outcasts. Harvard had then, as now, a number of purely social clubs — a few of them with special interests — most of them small in membership, so that through Harvard's later history, at least, the unchosen had never to feel that they were merely clinging to the outer fringes of college life. This duplication of the world they were later to encounter has always been one of the college's strongest assets.

As for young Copeland, coming from a backwoods town, unaccompanied by friends, the product of a country high school, by nature shy, timid and retiring, by condition poor as the proverbial church mouse, by physique and inclination unfitted for sports, and by slight exposure to the world of sophistication awkward and uneasy in mixed company, it is not surprising that he was not taken into the big preliminary social club, the Institute of 1770, to be passed on from there into the Hasty Pudding. Yet he did, before his graduation, become a member of the O.K. Society, whose roster included such socially prominent youngsters as Owen Wister (also a member of Harvard's most exclusive club, the Porcellian), William C. Wait, John Eliot Bullard, Joseph Peabody Gardner, and Stephen Van Renssalaer Townsend. All these men were in Copeland's class, as was the club's president, George Lyman Kittredge, the foremost scholar of '82, who was to soar like a rocket to academic eminence within a few years of his graduation.

Copeland also, in his junior year, became one of the editors of the *Harvard Advocate*, the literary magazine of the college. There too, he was to be outdistanced, for a time, by Kittredge, who became its editor in chief and contributed to its contents in a ratio of ten to Copeland's one. We have already sampled Copeland's touching little piece about his childhood misadventures. He also wrote a sketch about "Our Waiter" — a college character — an essay on "Eating in English Books," and another on Dean Swift's "Modest Proposal," for the theme of which he was, as he grew older, to exhibit even stronger sympathy, for he could not abide "the infant puling in its mother's arms," or the sight of the toddler. Years afterward, he distressed the wife of one of his favorite pupils, the late Maxwell Perkins, by his impatience with the behavior of the very young. The little son of one of several women present was making ineffectual efforts to walk, while the ladies cooed delightedly. Copeland bore with this performance as long as he could, and then crustily exclaimed, "This is the most revolting exhibition of ineptitude that I have ever watched!"

He was, however, always hopeful that his former pupils might name a child after him. Professor Frederick C. Packard, Jr., who recorded Copeland's voice for posterity, tells of a graduate who, on a visit to Cambridge, encountered Copey in Harvard Square, stopped him and introduced himself as a former student. "What is your name?" asked Copey. The graduate gave his name and class. Then, COPELAND (sucking in his breath rather dolefully): "I don't remember you at all!" An embarrassed pause. "Are you married?" GRADUATE: "Yes, very happily, thank you, sir." COPELAND: "Have you any children?" GRADUATE: "Yes sir, I'm happy to say we have three wonderful children." COPELAND: "I suppose you named one of them after me?" GRADUATE (swallowing hard): "Well — uh — no sir, I'm afraid I didn't." COPELAND: "Oh, I see, all girls, eh?" All this, you may be sure, Copey enjoyed more than did his victim.

Some of the physical characteristics of Copeland's class-mates, who were representative in that respect at least of college men in general at that time, are not uninteresting to us now, as we look at the giants of the current generation. The average height of the boys of '82 was only five feet eight, and their average weight but 137 pounds. The tallest man in the class was an even six feet, and the shortest, who stood but a little below Charles Copeland, was five feet one and a half. Their average age at graduation was just about what it is now, twenty-two years and a half. And they were making almost the same proportionate choices among the vocations they would follow as their successors do today. Of the 181 seniors who, with Copeland, were admitted "to the fellow-ship of educated men," fifty-four had decided to enter busi-ness, forty-six planned to be lawyers, twenty would study medicine, eleven intended to teach, six would prepare for the ministry, and only seven would seek a career in science, a proportion which today would be considerably greater. Five meant to become journalists, and now that choice also would be more frequent. Twenty-one had not yet made up their minds. Eight years after graduation, the number of those who had turned to business had considerably increased, and twice as many were teaching as had made that choice before leaving college.

Copeland's was an average class in the account it gave of it-self in the world outside; it produced no great galaxy of dis-tinguished men, but not a few established national, and few in-ternational reputations. George Lyman Kittredge became one of the world's foremost Shakesperean scholars and, of course, one of the most brightly shining stars in that dazzling constel-lation of great college professors which distinguished the Harvard in which Copeland was to find his place. Copeland's brother-in-law, William Dunbar, as we have already noted, pursued a brilliant career in the law. Charles Eliot, the son of Harvard's president, who was one of the men toward whom Copeland was drawn, became the leading landscape architect of the country and was memorialized after his untimely death by his father in that most unusual literary phenomenon, a biography by a father of his son. Owen Wister, after some difficulty in finding himself — a purgatory through which Copeland was also to go — went on to write *The Virginian*, and to become, in his time, one of the country's leading authors. These, with Copeland's, were to be, perhaps the most spectacular successes in this group of young men, but there were others who left a mark on their time.

There was Asaph Hall, son of an astronomer, who was himself to head the Naval Observatory, and be appointed to a lifetime professorship in the Navy, in a commission signed by Theodore Roosevelt. There was Arthur McArthur, who was to create the Chicago World's Fair of 1893, build many miles of western railroad, help to construct the Chicago Drainage Canal, New York's Cross River Dam, and the Soo Channel connecting Lakes Huron and Superior. Albert Elliot became Secretary of what was until recently the Territory of Alaska. Harold Sewall served as our consul general in Samoa, hobnobbed there with Robert Louis Stevenson, and, as Minister Plenipotentiary to Hawaii, presided over the transfer of Hawaiian sovereignty from Queen Liliuokalani to the United States. Evert Jansen Wendell, another man to whom the young Copeland was attracted, became a well-known philanthropist. Sherman Hoar, of the old Concord family, was regarded by his classmates as the most highly gifted of their company. They chose him their Class Orator, and he made for himself a distinguished career in Congress; he was to pose for his fellow townsman, the sculptor Daniel Chester French, for the figure of the Minute Man on Concord's ancient bridge, as he did also for the statue of John Harvard, the benefactor from whom the college took its name — that seated figure which graces the front of University Hall and has, on occasion, been disgraced by irreverent undergraduates. Samuel

Williston, another of Copeland's preferred companions, lived on to become a mainstay of the Harvard Law School, and an authority on contracts.

One, and one only, of this heterogeneous group, was to outlive Charles Townsend Copeland. This was Godfrey Lowell Cabot. He and Charles Copeland, with his Maine background — and you have to understand the separation between Boston and its frontiers fully to appreciate the gulf between them — could not abide each other's shadow. At this writing, Mr. Cabot is the oldest living graduate of Harvard; in the not uncharacteristic Lowell fashion he amassed a great fortune, some of which went to his brother-in-law, Abbott Lawrence Lowell, President Eliot's successor, for the further expansion of Harvard University.

3

The college to which young Copeland came was in the throes of a transition which was to be severe and far-reaching. Nine years before, Charles William Eliot, aged thirty-five, who had been (unlike one distinguished successor) an indifferent chemist, but had already proved himself a masterly administrator, was elected President of Harvard. The times called for a vigorous and daring leader; the country itself was in the grip of deep-seated change; materialism was in the saddle, industrial growth was proceeding at breakneck speed, and, as Samuel Eliot Morison wrote in his *Three Centuries of Harvard*, the university "must expand with the country, must save something for the advancement of learning out of this scramble for wealth, or the age would pass her by, and the ghosts of Dunster, Leverett and Kirkland would rise to reproach her." Other and younger universities were pressing her hard. At Harvard the college itself lumbered in the ruts of tradition; the Law School had premature hardening of the arteries, the Medical School needed a complete overhauling,

and the Lawrence Scientific School had won itself the reputation of being "the resort of shirks and stragglers." Far in the
future were the world's largest university library, the School
of Business Administration, the country's foremost law and
medical schools and the Fogg Art Museum as we know it
now.

Eliot provided the impetus that was implicit in the last sentence of his inaugural address: "The future of the university
will not be unworthy of its past." By the time Charles Copeland arrived there, Eliot was not only revitalizing the graduate
schools; he had begun to put into practice a revolutionary
theory about higher education. It was his belief, backed by a
dominant and persuasive personality, that the undergraduate
should be free to choose those subjects of study toward which
he was most attracted. It is difficult today, in our own educational quandary, bedeviled as we are by the crackpot theorists
who have dominated American education and who have mis-
applied to the point of absurdity the liberating ideas of Eliot
and of John Dewey, to appreciate how radical a change was
being effected by Harvard's young president. This revolution, to be known as the elective system, had not run its full
course when Copeland was enrolled as a freshman. Like so
many revolutions, it went too far. In its later and less restricted development, it became possible for students at Harvard to follow so far their natural inclinations, however immature and unconsidered they might be, that their course of
study had no balance whatever. Most of them could not be
truly called "educated men." They might, if of scholarly inclination, know much in the field of their special interest, and
be at the same time ignorant as a contemporary high school
senior about the thoughts and actions which have raised man
to his present pinnacle in the world he inhabits.

The Eliot revolution was at its initiation, in part, at least, a
reaction against the narrow basis upon which Harvard's instruction had been originally founded, and upon which she

had built for generations. She had begun as a training school for young men who aimed at becoming members of that clerical group who for a time controlled, as no other segment of the American population in any other region has since done, the tone and temper of society in New England's earliest settlements. And Eliot, even if the weaknesses of the elective system finally became so evident that modifications were made by his successor, did more to widen the horizons of Harvard than any man who came before or after him.

Small though the faculty was which gave instruction to Copeland and his classmates, it contained, besides its president, several figures of outstanding ability and interest. I have already mentioned Professor Dunbar, who, with Eliot, was one of the makers of the modern Harvard. There was also Francis James Child, whose course in Shakespeare Copeland attended; it was to become, under Child, and later, under George Lyman Kittredge, who was also his pupil, one of the most famous courses given at Harvard. The son of a sailmaker, "Stubby" Child, as he was known in Cambridge for half a century, got his first education on the Boston waterfront; through the efforts of Epes S. Dixwell, principal of the Boston Latin School, came his chance to go to Harvard, where he began to teach immediately after his graduation with the class of 1846. Curly-headed, zestful, and humorous, he was one of the best-loved teachers of his time, and one of the country's most eminent scholars. He was the leading authority on the old Scottish and English ballads, and for years he held one of Harvard's oldest chairs, the Boylston Professorship of Rhetoric and Oratory, first occupied by John Quincy Adams. A century later it passed to Professor Child's young pupil from Calais, and when he first appeared before his students with that hallowed title he calmly observed, as he began his first lecture: "Gentlemen, I would have you know that I am now warming the chair once occupied by the cold, correct bottom of John Quincy Adams."

There were also Nathaniel Southgate Shaler and Charles Eliot Norton. Shaler was the leading American geologist of his time, and a greatly beloved teacher; young Copeland probably visited his classes, for he was an eloquent speaker on many matters besides schists and tertiary deposits, but the boy from Calais had only the slightest scientific curiosity, and studied no science beyond the mathematics, physics and chemistry required of him in his freshman year. Shaler was known to some undergraduates as "the Confederate general," although they knew he had fought in the Union Army; but he was a Kentuckian, with a Kentucky colonel's goatee, and wore a wide-brimmed hat. Dedicated scientist though he was, he astonished Cambridge, three years before his death, by producing a five-volume "dramatic romance" called *Elizabeth of England*. The story goes that when Shaler heard that certain members of the English department had spoken slightingly of his poetic drama, he remarked with some heat, "It's better than they have done — to date," and was delighted when it won the praise of William James and George Herbert Palmer. With a few others of Harvard's favorite figures, he was caricatured in the drawings and verse of *Harvard Celebrities*, in which Henry Ware Eliot, brother of T. S. Eliot, wrote:

> This is Shaler,
> Fairy-taler,
> Scientific mountain-scaler,
> Penetrator
> Of each crater
> From the poles to the equator,
> Tamer of the hurricane,
> Prophet of the wind and rain,
> Hypnotizer
> Of the geyser,
> Wizard of the frozen plain.

Copeland did not study under Charles Eliot Norton, the translator of Dante, who was then Harvard's exponent of the fine arts, and professor of their history. He did have a course in psychology under young William James, later to be one of the chief luminaries of the university; he took Dunbar's course in political economy — and barely squeaked through it; he studied Greek under one of Harvard's most famous characters, Evangelinus Apostolides Sophocles, who, when he came to this country, had added the surname by which he was to be known because an early teacher of his in Greece had called him his "little Sophocles." Professor Sophocles was a magnificent-looking old man; fiery-eyed and lushly bearded, with an imposing head, he could have posed for a statue of Zeus himself. He liked to play tricks on his classes, and once he asked suddenly, "What was done to the Persians who were killed at the battle of Thermopylae?" The boys floundered, and made ingenious guesses — until one sturdily answered, "I don't know," whereupon the old man shouted, "That's right. Nobody knows!" He raised chickens, and kept one in his rooms in Holworthy Hall, where it would come at his call and perch on his shoulder. "My chicken," he once told a friend, "likes Greek better than some of my freshmen," and when he was dying, and was brought some chicken broth, he refused it, saying to George Herbert Palmer, "You do not devour someone you love."

4

Copeland's scholarship as an undergraduate was no more distinguished than it was when he became a college teacher. His colleagues were to say of him that he was an extremely well-read man, but not truly a scholar. He was always impatient with the burrowing of candidates for the Ph.D. degree in English, which he was never tempted to try for. He liked to speak of the "Ph.D. death-rattle," and when the president of Bryn Mawr, Miss Carey Thomas, asked him to suggest some promising young men whom he thought eligible for her English staff, making the proviso that they have their doctorates, Copeland sarcastically replied that it was unfortunate she could not avail herself of the services of such men as George Lyman Kittredge, Barrett Wendell, Bliss Perry, and "your humble servant," none of whom had slaved over a thesis on the use of the conjunction "and" in Chaucer. The outburst was typical of a man who, although always an inveterate reader, was proud of having once remarked, "A man is always better than a book."

Scholastically, he made a most unpromising beginning as a freshman, for whom at that time the course of study was wholly prescribed. His subjects were Greek, Latin, German, mathematics, physics, and chemistry; of these he did best in Greek, with a percentage of 79 in one course and 62 in the other. In Latin he got but 54, and in German 64. In mathematics and physics, he made his worst performance — 43 and 36 in the one, and 40 in the other. In chemistry he was almost equally bad, with 50 per cent. All in all, it must have been touch and go whether the first entry from Calais at Harvard College would be permitted to continue there.

In his sophomore year he did considerably better, and this was to be true of his record, both as a junior and a senior. With sophomore Greek, he advanced from grappling with grammar to the reading of Plato, Sophocles and Euripides, in which he was graded 70, and to a course in Herodotus in which he got 78. His Latin — he was now reading Terence, Cicero and Tacitus — got him a mark of 82, and his German improved to 75. In rhetoric he did quite well, with 83; in the writing of themes, not as well as one would expect — 76. In medieval and modern history he was given 83, and in a course on constitutional government in England and the United States, 79.

As a junior he attended Professor Child's classes in Shakespeare, but since this was an extra course, voluntarily added, he received no grade in it. In Professor Adams Sherman Hill's course in English literature of the eighteenth and nineteenth centuries, he made the best grade he received in college, 90. In theme writing he advanced to 83 per cent; in forensics, he got 74. He did not do very well in psychology under William James, for his grade was 62, which was what he received also in Professor Dunbar's course in political economy. In late Roman and medieval history he scored 71, and in European history from the beginning of the seventeenth century through 1750, he got but 69.

During senior year, he studied oral discussion with Professor Hill, for a mark of 78, while in forensics he got 86. In the translation and reading at sight of French, his mark was 69. He took three courses in history that year, one of which dealt with the constitutional and political history of the United States, and in these his marks were 83, 80, and 81. At graduation he stood just about midway in his class, ranking eighty-eighth in an enrollment of 181.

The first-ranking scholar in the class of 1882 was George Lyman Kittredge, who also marched off with a handsome collection of honors and awards. Copeland, as a sophomore, won a $30 prize for reading, but strangely enough, he never captured the Boylston prize for elocution, nor did he win, as Kittredge twice did, one of the awards for the Bowdoin dissertations. He received an honorable mention in history, and at Commencement, with Kittredge shining as Ivy Orator, Copeland had to be content with a dissertation which he read in Sanders Theater; still, he was one of the four out of forty-six to whom Commencement parts were awarded, whose essays were actually delivered. Copeland's topic was a comparison of the novels of Jane Austen with those of Emily Brontë; his classmate Henry M. Sewall read an essay on American government, Frederick R. Burton discussed Wagner's theory of the opera, and Frank E. Fuller dealt with Swift and Sterne.

Commencements at that time were more formal for the seniors than they are today. It was required of them that both on Class Day and Commencement Day they appear "in dress suits, white cravats and silk hats." Seniors were officially warned that they "should avoid any absurdity of dress at the exercises around the Tree" — a class ceremony no longer observed because the Tree no longer exists, though there is still the "Tree Spread." The Class Day exercises were not yet held outdoors in good weather, but like those of Commencement itself, always took place in Sanders Theater. The confetti battles of more recent years were to wait for the building of the Stadium. There was then, as now, music in the Yard and dancing in Memorial Hall, and for the seniors, on the Sunday of Commencement week, the Baccalaureate Sermon.

It was delivered in June of 1882 by the Reverend Francis G. Peabody, who told the young men assembled in Appleton Chapel: "Here, then, is the most serious question one can ask himself when he faces the choice of a vocation: Is it likely, on the whole and in its general sweep, to enlarge life or to stunt it? Do its lines converge to narrowness or open into breadth? Is it to be a constant addition of permanent resources, or a slow impoverishment of the soul?" It was an extremely godly sermon, even for the period of its delivery, and unrelieved by any lightness of touch.

Nine years later, Mr. Peabody was to write to one of his listeners that day, who had begun to attract audiences by the skill and beauty of his reading;

My dear Mr. Copeland:
    Will you allow me to send you a word of cordial thanks for your Bible readings? It would be superfluous for me to say how well they are done, so restrained, lucid and inter-

pretative; but I may congratulate the university on this most interesting and novel undertaking to disclose the literary power of the Bible. It is a distinct contribution to our religious life as well as to our literary judgments.

At the Class Day exercises there was music by the Germania Band, and the prayer was delivered by the Reverend Dr. Charles Carroll Everett. The serious orator of the day was Sherman Hoar, who urged his classmates to go forth and reflect credit on the college which had nurtured them. The Class Poem was read by John McGaw Foster, who later entered the Congregational ministry; his poem, which alternated between resounding rhetoric and a not too graceful playfulness, ran on for several hundred lines, and one now hears in imagination the shuffling of restless feet on the floor. The class ode was read by Frank Edward Fuller.

The bright particular star of the occasion, one gathers, was George Lyman Kittredge, who, as Ivy Orator, held forth in high spirits, and managed to be at least as amusing as Ivy Orators at Harvard ordinarily are. Robert Benchleys are not produced in every class, but Kittredge was, I imagine, better than average, for he could flourish a pretty wit, as on the day years later when he lost his balance on the lecture platform, stumbled and fell. Picking himself up, he imperturbedly faced the class, and before the laughter could grow, quietly observed: "For the first time, gentlemen, I find myself on a level with my audience." This quick turning of the tables has been attributed to his rival Copeland, but the jibe was "Kitty's."

On that Class Day he began with a reference to a superstition new to me: that odd-numbered classes were always superior to even-numbered ones. The superstition was absurd, argued Kittredge, because when the Class of '82 arrived in Cambridge, Harvard was "a howling wilderness." There were no lamps on the corners of the buildings to light the student home; there were no steam radiators; there were no brick paths and plank walks in the Yard — all was mud. Sever Hall consisted of two sticks to mark its foundations. The Library was not open Sundays, the Co-Op did not exist, and the Total Abstinence Alliance was as yet unfounded. There was no gymnasium worthy of the name. Nor were '82's achievements limited to parochial affairs: "We set ourselves against the Chinese Bill. President Arthur was vacillating. He waited for some clarion voice of public opinion." This was provided by '82, for did not one of its members, William C. Wait, preside at the Harvard Union meeting which voted the Chinese Bill "an outrage on human rights," and did not the Presidential veto follow? Foreshadowing somewhat Sir Winston Churchill, he worked up to his peroration: "Who can fill our places? We are going — going. We shall be missed (shall we) at prayers; we shall be missed on the river; we shall be missed on the ball-field. They will miss us at Carlo's, at Adam's, and at Memorial Hall."

Four years afterward, in an editorial written for the *Boston Post*, Copeland would say of Harvard Commencements:

Grave Fellows come in their gowns to hear some half-dozen or more of the graduating class pronounce the various orations, dissertations and disquisitions for which they have been chosen. The speakers are also in gowns — alone among their class — but not, as many persons suppose, the gowns of Oxford. Those are short and without dignity: the speakers of commencement parts at Harvard wear ampler, more flowing robes, borrowed for the occasion from resident clergymen. And when the young men are first invested with their gowns, they are so far like angels that they fear to tread, lest they step on the hem of the unaccustomed garment and meet an ignominious fall. It is well known in what may be called "academic circles" that many rehearsals are needed to acquire the grace and propriety requisite for wearing a gown without accident. . . . [History sayeth not whether young Mr. Copeland tripped and fell.]

After the somewhat trying exercises in the theatre are over comes the "alumni dinner" in Memorial Hall, when speeches are made and sentiments expressed at which John Winthrop and his companion worthies may be seen to shudder in their places on the wall. In the afternoon the classic punchbowl is set out, and if some deep potations are the result, remember what the Autocrat sang years ago:

> Hast thou a drunken soul?
> The fault is in thy shallow brain,
> Not in my silver bowl.

They filed out, these youngsters, to exchange their chatter about the days immediately ahead. We have already caught glimpses of what the future was to hold for some of them. None, perhaps, was more uncertain of what was waiting for him, more unsure of what he most wanted to do, than the shy and still withdrawn little senior from Calais, Maine. At twenty-two he was better-looking, as his class photograph attests, than he was to be as a man of middle age, or in his closing years. The disappointments and frustrations, the belated official recognition, the essential loneliness and the deep yearning to be loved, had not yet been etched on his young features: the brow was smooth and wide, the hair abundant on the head he was later to view as "monstrous": the eyes bespoke the observer who knew himself observed, but had not yet acquired the penetration they would have. The well-shaped, generous mouth was still without the sardonic lines of grimness it would assume. For all the turmoil that must have seethed within him, it was a serene young face, and not unhandsome. He bade farewell to the Dunbar family and a few others of his friends, and took the train for his border home.

CHAPTER FOUR

The Twig Is Bent

PART OF that summer of 1882 Charles spent in New York, a city he was rarely to visit afterward, except for his annual spring excursions, beginning in 1906, when he came down from Cambridge to be feted at the Harvard Club of New York, and to read there before the members of the Charles Townsend Copeland Association and their distinguished guests. It was not that he shared the average Bostonian's or Cantabrigian's distaste for the metropolis; it was simply his lifelong aversion to travel.

Actually, he was always fascinated by the differences between New York and Boston, and particularly by their separate mores in the matter of transportation. Even today, a Boston taxidriver will get out of his cab when your destination is reached, and carry your luggage to the door, an attention in which only the most exceptional of their New York brethren ever indulge. On one of his visits, Copeland was much interested in the newly instituted regulation requiring all New York taxidrivers to display in easy view of his passengers a photograph of himself. He was lunching with Maxwell Perkins, editor for the publishing house of Scribner, and on the way to the speakeasy Copeland took note of the fact that the required picture was not in its accustomed place. Their driver was a villainous-looking character, who seemed capable of cutting a throat on the slightest provocation. As they arrived at their destination, Copeland leaned forward and inquired of the driver, in that emphatic and insistent tone he could assume, "*Where* is your photograph?" The driver, an excitable Italian, bounded out of the cab, and gesticulating madly, explained that the frame in which it was ordinarily held needed to be replaced, and that temporarily he had pasted the photograph on the roof of the cab. Copeland, by now in the street, poked his head inside and craned upward. "Ah," said he, "just like the ceiling of the Sistine Chapel!"

In late September, 1882, he received a letter from his mother, addressed to him at 17 West 11th Street, which throws a little light on the difficulties he was encountering. Apparently he had decided to try, for the time being, at least, a teaching job, thus fulfilling the forecast he had written at the age of twelve, and possibly still bearing in mind his belief at that time in the value of a spell of schoolteaching for the improvement of patience. His mother wrote:

Got a letter from you this morning from 17 West 11th Street and no date, and another tonight from Ithaca dated the 17th and mailed the 21st. As you will see by the delay of the Ithaca letter I was saved the suspense of the Cornell decision. In spite of my advice to the contrary you did the wisest thing to take what you could get, and I hope all things will work in your favor. You know they most always do. I shall have no conversation with anyone outside of our immediate family about your doings in New York, further than to tell them you have made a temporary engagement as an assistant in a private school in Englewood, N. J. Your father seems quite pleased that you should have taken the situation, and thinks, as I do, that the trip to N.Y. and among strangers will be of benefit to you. Two missives have come to you which I did not think it worth while to forward. One from the President of Colby to the effect that they were supplied for this year but would keep your name in mind and your papers for reference. . . .

My splendid boy, I do not think you have been out of my thoughts for an hour since you left me, and I miss you sadly. I fully realize you have much to bother and perplex you, but when you are inclined to be downhearted, just think of the little study, and your cheery, sunny room, and the hearts filled with love for you awaiting you here at home, and be happy. The old Professor (and may Heaven bless him for his kindness to you) has the right of it. You will succeed, but you must have patience.

To these words of encouragement Sarah Copeland added a postscript: "Please burn this letter, and after this one, knowing your carelessness about letters, I cannot write with any freedom unless you promise to burn them all." He could not have made this promise, for he preserved, apparently, every word he ever had from her. She also spoke of his teacher Laura Burns, who "has just looked in long enough to hear that you are not coming at present, and she says 'tell Charles I am forlorn and inconsolable.' "

A few days later she wrote again to tell him his clothes and books were being forwarded to him, and asking him "to answer all my questions about how you are situated [he had by this time gone to his post at the Englewood school]. School, boarding place, and all. You know detail is pleasing to me. Louise King came to me yesterday to know about you and if you were coming home this winter. She wants to begin her studies at once. I am glad you are not teaching in Calais. What shall I say if anyone asks about your salary?" [It was $700 for the year, of which board represented $300.]

On the same day, October 11, Copeland heard from his father, who began, "Dear Chas. I have been intending to write to you for some time and now proceed to do so. And first of all I am more than pleased with your success in getting the situation. I was getting about discouraged in regard to money matters, as it has been nothing but pay out, and we were living ahead of our income, which is not the thing to do, and when you wrote that you had let yourself for $400 per year outside your board I felt quite independent, and encouraged, and think you made an excellent beginning."

Through the fall and winter months Charles's mother continued to send him cheerful and chatty letters about Calais happenings, trying to lift his spirits by repeating complimentary references to him: "Quotation from Mary Lambe — 'I want to live to see Charles a literary critic.' Miss Rounds — 'Charlie Copeland is the most entertaining person I ever knew and I am sorry he has gone away.' Are these sweets enough for one letter?" But once or twice she gave way to her feelings, as when she wrote him in later October: "I am sitting in the study, all alone, and I never miss you so much as when I am here. Everything reminds me so of you. When I look up from my papers, and see the little French picture on the wall, the candlesticks, the cup and saucer marked for George, the bunch of sea-weed hanging just where you left it, and O! so many other things of yours, I get dreary and think I will never come here again. I am tired and cannot write a cheerful word."

Now and then she would draw a little picture for him of the town he loved:

The morning is fine and cool, and so invigorating, that many people are walking to church who oftener drive. They go by in twos and threes, in droves, and singly, and it is entertaining to watch them. First went the choir, early — for they have to practice, not only hymns to praise the Lord with, but funeral hymns to be wailed over a dead

man this afternoon: — Later comes the disjointed proces-
sion of churchgoers, and, here and there, I catch quick
glimpses of a familiar face or article of dress. Conspicuous
is Mrs. N —— n with a row of full blown roses across the
front of her bonnet. And there is a proud old face, with
puffs of white hair above it, topped with a stylish, sombre
bonnet which "Cami — who has exquisite taste — sent from
New York." Here is the incomparable Laura with Nellie
Hunt effervescing beside her — both (though appearing to
listen to Capt. Lord who is earnestly talking, it may be,
about their sanctuary, purified by fire) with a little longing
in their hearts to be as young as the two fair damsels who
are following closely behind them, and hoping that the Rev.
Merkle, and eligible Mr. Murclin will not see any difference in the freshness of their youth. The fairer and younger
maidens are lovely to look upon: — The fashion of their
garments is graceful and the colors are suited to the season.
Louise King comes tripping and skipping along — and Julia,
with a flapping green hat, a light-colored shooting jacket,
and her long legs, is simply grotesque. She is hanging on,
and over her bosom friend Kate W., whose raiment is
nondescript. At a distinguished distance behind, treads a
stately lady, clad in costly robes of velvet and satin. Money
can buy such clothes but not the royal air with which she
wears them. Your father, who has been reading, starts up
and exclaims, "I declare I shall be late for church!" And
just as he goes across the street your Aunt Mary appears,
looking red and making a great show of speed, for she
knows that she is behind time. Your father speaks to her.
She anxiously consults her watch, gets redder, and goes
bumping along from side to side at a faster pace than ever.
Then your father goes slowly for a minute — evidently not
liking to leave her alone, as they are the only persons on
the street at this hour — then hastens on — hesitates again,

but finally his dread of being late overcomes all else and he dashes off, and the poor "Lady Mary" is left to bear her disgrace alone.

2

There is no doubt that Charles was discontented in his work, and lonely as well. He had tried without success to get a college teaching job, and he was the last youngster likely to bear with boys only a little younger than himself, nor is it probable that they were pleased with him. He was physically not imposing, and could have taken no interest in their sports. With all his salt and vinegar he was not cut in the pattern of Mr. Chips, and a boys' school was definitely not the place for him. Apparently he made few if any friends during his stay in Englewood. "It is my opinion," wrote his mother, "that you have not found one person in Englewood whom you can really enjoy. Cambridge society can not be found in many places." He was to say afterward, however, that several people had been "very kind" to him there.

He had been in correspondence, too, with Professor Dunbar, whom he so greatly admired, and it is evident from a letter which Dunbar wrote him from Florence in October of 1882, that he was considering the study of law, but was having difficulty in making up his mind whether that was the proper course for him.

My dear Charlie,
I have thought many times of your letter since it came and wondered what I could reply to it. Not to dwell upon the delay implied in this statement, — you are in a frame of mind which I recognize and indeed recollect, having once written one or two quite similar letters, after graduating with no special leaning towards any professional pursuit in

particular and with a burning desire to be about something and no special opening visible. A good many unhappy months passed before I seemed to find my place, and then as it was, I made a false start. I really think then that it is with some reason that I advise you not to let yourself be discouraged but to keep up a good heart. At any rate, do not let your time go for nothing. If you expect to study law or even doubt whether to do so or not, read some law now; you can manage to borrow the books for a start. If you can do no better, write to Frank and ask him to send by express my Blackstone's *Commentaries* and Parsons on *Contracts*, — perhaps not a modern way of beginning, still you will have a chance to see a little what the law is like. Read some of the lives of the Chancellors by Lord Campbell and see how men have begun the road to success and fame. If you are set against the law and are waiting for something else, write something which shall take up your mind and keep it active. That is, keep yourself busy as the best thing for your spirits and do so to avoid losing precious time before you find yourself settled at last. I take it for granted in this that you will find yourself settled at last. Everybody does who has anything in him and I know that you answer that description; but it is not an uncommon misfortune to pass some time feeling that you could do something if only the chance were given. I am well aware that this seems to advance you but little. You want someone to tell you what to do, but, my boy, nobody in the world can do that with any effect and I do not seem able to do it at all. I think I should advise you as before to aim for the law, but in the meantime, you will have to find your way yourself and I can only advise you to keep up your mental health by work, not to be cast down, to keep your eyes open and on the alert for any point of light on the horizon. Is your case after all much worse than poor George's? [Professor Dunbar's elder son, and Charles's classmate.]

He is on the wide ocean now, with no idea how he shall strike land, with something awry inside him which makes every chance doubtful, and with the strongest reason for impatience which a man can possibly have. It makes me pretty sober when I think of him and his chances for doing the best with his pure gold. It is not time for us to hear from him at the West yet; we only remember that in addition to other troubles, his old rheumatism seems to threaten him again. However, there is nothing for it but to wait and hope for the best.

I hope that by the time you get this, your affairs will have cleared up somewhat. At any rate, write and let me know what you are doing. I note what you say as to no longer dependence on your father. Of course you cannot be indifferent to that and ought to take care of yourself as soon as possible, and a delay of a year or two in getting at your profession is not to be weighed in comparison with his interest. But after all, if worst comes to worst, I think that you will find in his opinion even longer dependence is not so bad as a misstep and that if the time is used in work of some kind, it is not all loss to him. At all events, remember that we all want to know about your welfare and that you stand among the very few about whom we feel anxious. And I assure you that although I am so poor a comforter, there is nobody outside of your own circle more concerned about your success than

Yours very truly,
CHARLES F. DUNBAR

As you desired, I have not shown or mentioned your letter to me to anybody.

By December, Charles had made his decision to quit teaching and to try the law, for on January 3rd his father wrote him:

Dear C.

Yours came in due season, and I have duly considered what you say in regard to going to the law school next yr, and yr. request for a little assistance in getting through the first yr.

I do not see any objection to your plan, as you intend to read one year at home out of the three year course, and if you prefer taking the first year at Cambridge I have no objection, and I will furnish the $250, if you need as much which I hope you will not, as all I let you have now will have to be taken out of our principal as it is all we can do to get along on our income, etc. We shall have to be economical to do that, as everything is so high these times, but perhaps it will be better to invest a little of our principal on your brain in hope of getting more than 5 per cent out of it, the latter being all you can now be sure of in making safe investments. As you will have $300 to start on you will not have to call on me until the spring of 1884, perhaps the summer will be as soon as you will need some portion of it.

On the same day his mother wrote:

It pleases me to have you remember my birthday. Your father promises a speedy answer to your communication.

I mentioned to your Aunt Mary the fact that young Evans [an Englewood acquaintance of Charles's] had been stricken down with a fever. She observed, "There is more or less malaria in all those towns about New York." I said, "Charles has such a repellent will that it is more than probable he will escape." And then Alice piped up, "That is a fact, Auntie! He would just say that he would not catch a fever and that would end it." But for all my courageous assertion — and Alice's assurance, my heart quakes with fear lest some fearful thing will come to you, and if you should die, how could I bear to live?

3

Of Charles's year at the Harvard Law School there are no traces, except for the notebooks he kept there. Some of these he later used for other purposes which pleased him more, for over the pages devoted to riparian rights and other legal matters, he pasted the clippings of the contributions he made to the *Boston Advertiser* and the *Boston Post* during his seven years of active journalism, thus achieving a comforting piece of New England thrift, and at the same time obliterating, or at least obscuring, these reminders of what must have been for him rather a tedious year.

When the spring term at Law School was over, he left for Calais, where he was to stay from June of 1884 until his departure for Boston some time in 1885. Through the interest of Professor Dunbar he made the acquaintance of Daniel Singleton, a part owner of the *Boston Advertiser,* who got him placed on the editorial staff. While still in Calais, where he had gone to read law, in accordance with the deal he had made with his father, he had begun to contribute book reviews to the Boston paper. That year in his native town appears to have been a rather secluded one; he kept much to his room in the Main Street house, and liked to encourage the local rumor that he was exiled from the family dining table because in the fall of 1884 he had cast his first presidential vote for Grover Cleveland. In those days a Democratic vote in Maine was as scarce as liquor sold anywhere but in the "blind pigs" — some of them elaborate forerunners of our later speakeasies — which abounded in the Pine Tree State.

Daniel Singleton was something of a character. Copeland

was a frequent visitor at his home after he came up to Boston, and it was there he met the first woman younger than himself by whom he was strongly attracted. Singleton's grandson, Eugene F. McCarthy, a writer on scientific subjects who was later one of Copeland's students at Harvard, recalls that Daniel, who sported sideburns and was always impeccably dressed, usually had in his jacket pockets an Epictetus or Suetonius in battered tooled leather. He was ostensibly a designer of men's clothes (he was strongly to influence Copeland's taste in dress), but had a finger in many pies, of which the *Advertiser* was one.

Copeland was also often a guest at the Commonwealth Avenue flat of the second eldest Singleton daughter, Adela, who had studied at the Sorbonne, and was set up by her father as a wholesale dealer in Chinese and Japanese *objets d'art*, and the young newspaperman was fascinated by the apartment's décor, which was Oriental to the last detail. But he was still more fascinated by Adela's young sister, a roguish girl of sixteen by whom he was teased unmercifully. They were to exchange many letters, and there was a packet from Copeland which Adela's sister burned just before her death, having previously shown them to her son Eugene, who remembers that they were ardent in the best Victorian manner.

Through Daniel Singleton, Copeland met Edwin M. Bacon, proprietor of the *Boston Post*, and after a few months with the *Advertiser* he transferred there to a better opportunity. He remained on the staff of the *Post* until the fall of 1892. With Singleton and his son John, a student of the classics and the fine arts, and a concert singer of local repute, and Edwin Bacon, Copeland became much better acquainted with Boston's drinking places than he had been as an undergraduate. Though he spent most of his time in reading and study — for he reviewed books and the theater for the *Post*, writing also an occasional editorial, he enjoyed climbing about Beacon Hill with John Singleton, and was fascinated by the houses where Prescott, Motley, Thomas Bailey Aldrich and Edwin Booth had lived or were living. The younger Singleton liked to recall the night of a blizzard when he, his father and Copeland were trekking home afoot — for no cabs were available and the last horsecar had gone to the barns — over the old Warren Bridge to Charlestown. All three well mulled, with Copeland held between the two Singletons, they plodded through the drifts in a howling wind, Copeland in terror lest they be blown into the Charles.

In his early newspaper days he used to eat at noon in a place in Spring Lane. Here one could scoop one's baked beans out of a big and glossy brown earthenware pot, and if the customer did not arrive too late, he could manage to snaffle a few pieces of pork to go with his beans and brownbread. This substantial fare, including a generous wedge of apple pie, plus milk or tea, could be had for a quarter, a sum well within the reach of even a fledgling newspaperman. Copeland sorrowed audibly and often when this haven went out of business.

He worried much over the pieces he wrote for the *Post*, which had established a tradition for good writing, and his editors — like those he dealt with in his later life — were frequently in anguish over the time he took in meeting deadlines. Often he would beg for an extension of time, and demand more space than could be allotted him. Even then, he had contracted his lifelong concern with the *sound*, as well as the sense and style, of what he was writing, a point he was to hammer home insistently with the students in his writing courses. It was his conviction that if a sentence does not come smoothly on the tongue, it is not well constructed, and in everything he wrote he aimed at its fitness for oral delivery. He even went so far, as a young reviewer, to argue that people quoted him to booksellers and to their friends, and that if what he had written was readily quotable aloud, it must help to sell books and theater tickets.

During his years on the *Post* he saw much of Mark Antony DeWolfe Howe, who became his most intimate friend in Boston. Copeland's junior by four years, Howe, a Rhode Island boy, had come to Harvard from Lehigh University, and received a second A.B. in 1887. In 1888, when Copeland met him, Howe was associate editor of *Youth's Companion*, and then, from 1899 to 1913, assistant editor of *The Atlantic Monthly*. Ninety-four at this writing, he has behind him a long list of distinguished biographies, and still revolves new projects in a mind which, unlike that of his friend from youth, has never failed him. Their friendship remained unbroken until Copeland's death in 1952.

In 1953, at the age of ninety, Howe published these verses in commemoration of their days together:

In threescore years of friendship there is time
To note the morning, noon, and evening lights
On both the friendship and the friend.
As night drew near he seemed to lose his way
In a blurred shadowland of memories,
Yet through the obscuring dimness
One pictured him at noon — the little man
With magisterial voice and speech
That added inches to his stature,
Too avid, if you will, of admiration,
Nursing unblushingly the vanities
One could not suffer had he tried to hide them,
But turning even these to quick account
With friends in nimble talk,
With crowded halls of happy listeners.
Thus for the separate and the multiplied,
Talking of books and men who made them,

He planted in a thousand minds
Interpretations and inspiritings
That fed the springs of youth
With freshened waters for a lifelong draught.
Small wonder that a host of grateful hearts
Still blesses such a teacher at his noon!
Before that time of day his path and mine
First crossed. The morning light was on us both —
For me he made it brighter with a strain
Of wit unknown to me before.
Nor was it wit alone
That marked this new-found friend,
But a warm flow of sympathy
That promised friendship through the waiting years.
The fabled "Copey," gifted equally to annoy
And fascinate the few and many,
Stood even then prefigured.
Happy my lot to have seen the crowns
Of honor, fame, and love
Wherewith his world has crowned him —
The selfsame person in the various lights
From morning, noon, and evening skies.

Of their early days Mark Howe has written in his *Adventures in Remembrance:*

One of the happy accidents of this period resulted from
Copeland's addiction to making his younger friends known
to his older. It was he who first led me to the hospitable
door of Mrs. James T. Fields, the widow of the publisher
whose generous ways promoted the cohesion that made the
"New England group" of writers so definite a unit. Fields
himself had died about ten years before I first entered the
house on Charles Street in which Mrs. Fields was continu-

ing, in what Henry James called her "waterside museum," the hospitalities for which it had long been famous. Copeland used to call her "Clytie" — not to her autumnal face which kept much of its springtime beauty — and indeed there was in her personality and its setting something of the Grecian quality which gave one to understand why Boston used to be called the American Athens. . . .

For Copeland, as a son of Maine, — the Mrs. Knowlton, of whom I have spoken, used to call him a "bit of Machias delft," and for many others, the house in Charles Street held a second magnet in the person of Sarah Orne Jewett — who spent, with her *alter ego* Mrs. Fields, either in Boston or at Manchester-by-the-Sea, all the months in which she could separate herself from her own abode in South Berwick, Maine. In these two ladies the charms of the classical and the continuing New England were singularly united. Old England also was largely present in the books and manuscripts, the pictures on the walls, the dining-room chairs that once belonged to the Duke of Ormonde and were bought in London under the guidance of Charles Dickens. The American past was brought into what was then the present by Mrs. Fields's habitual references to her friends of former days as "Mr. Emerson," "Mr. Longfellow," and all the rest — excepting possibly Hawthorne, whose name, as I recall her use of it, seemed never to need a handle. Besides these ghosts there were many living presences — Louise Imogen Guiney, Willa Cather, Mme. Blanc ("Th. Bentzon"), George Edward Woodberry, Thomas Bailey Aldrich, and such relative ancients as Charles Dudley Warner and that vigorous old Chicago parson, Robert Collyer. The femine segment of the circle may have been a little excessive, and there were grounds for a feeling that the precious and the rarefied did something to the atmosphere. Long before meeting Mrs. Fields I had heard from a Harvard classmate the profane breakfast-table story of her saying to her husband when a crumb of toast lodged in his abundant beard, "Jamie, there is a gazelle in the garden." It would be a pity to lose such an anecdote, apocryphal as my later knowledge of Mrs. Fields, with her surely saving grace of humor, compels me to believe it. For whatever of the feminine and the esoteric there may have been in all thse surroundings, there was a full appreciation of masculine likings for the best of substantial food and pleasant wines, and above all there was the heartiest of constant, generous friendship.

Writing about these days to Samuel Eliot Morison in November of 1918, Copeland observed:

> Peace hath its atrocities as well as its victories. I was walking through Charles Street in Boston the other day, and came to a great, dismal heap of bricks where once (and for many years) stood a dignified old house. It was much nearer Cambridge Street than "anybody that is anybody" lives now. Mrs. Fields was the last of them. She was the beautiful, variously gifted second wife of the famous publisher, James T. Fields, whom she long survived. Miss Sarah Jewett, exquisite writer of New England life, used to pass much of every winter at 148 Charles Street, and together these ladies maintained the last of the salons.
>
> In Mrs. Fields's drawing-room — its tall windows looking far up the bay and river — I met much of the American world and a little of the foreign. I'm not going to stifle you with catalogues of people who never remembered me, because I was only a cub newspaper critic, there chiefly because Miss Jewett, a Maine woman, encouraged my presence.
>
> But it won't bore you to hear that on a shining morn in April, 1895 — where were you then? — I had breakfast at Mrs. Fields's with Joseph Jefferson. His "Autobiography"

talks as he did. Light it up with his comedian face and blue, starry eyes (they were literally like stars, old as he was, and shone kindly on us), and you will realize something of my memory of him. Jefferson, our gracious hostesses, Mrs. Bell (a great wit, and daughter of Rufus Choate), and Russell Sullivan. They were all there, and they are all gone except your friend and servant. The long garden, which, until the embankment was built, ran to the water's edge, is turned into a tennis-court for the pampered children of Charles River Square; and the house, with its clustered memories, is an abhorrent pile of bricks and mortar. But below my chimney-piece hangs a photograph of Mr. Jefferson as Bob Acres, which he gave me in his dressing-room, on the evening of that great morning. On the back he wrote from "The Rivals," "Dress does make a difference, don't it, David?"

I won't conceal from you that, because time and energy fail me, I am sending this same bit of the past to a few soldier and sailor men, hoping it will beguile them for five minutes from the horrors of war.

If you care for other memories, or for a word about the university standing on its head, write instantly — and at length, I beg — to

Your faithful old friend,
C. T. Copeland

This "form" of mine is a desperate bid for a long, honest-to-God letter to go into my war books, now five volumes strong. [He refers to the letters written him by former students who were in the armed services.] Please leave a very wide margin to the left.

Dear Sam, I am very anxious about you. Your notes and cards have been extraordinary. Mayn't I have a letter, and have it now? [Morison, who was to be commissioned a rear admiral in World War II, was at the time of this letter serving as a private in the infantry.]

4

Howe and Copeland were frequenters of a little restaurant known as the Hole-in-the-Ground, situated in a basement under an apartment house on Mt. Vernon Street near Charles, "where," Howe recalled, "William Dixon, a Negro, magnified in our eyes as the brother of a prize-fighting 'Coffee-Cooler,' provided what Calverley called 'light and salutary meals.' They ate also, a little later, at a Holmesian boardinghouse on Chestnut Street, which was kept by the Mrs. Knowlton already referred to. Her daughter, Mrs. Arthur Foote, the composer's wife, called forth from Copeland an early *mot* which concerned both her and 'the beautiful Mrs. Inches,' best known to Copeland through Sargent's portrait. 'It takes twelve Mrs. Inches,' said he, 'to make a Mrs. Foote.' "

At the Hole-in-the-Ground where Howe and Copeland first met, there was an occasional patron who seemed as far away then from the Supreme Court of the United States as Copeland from the Boylston Professorship of Rhetoric and Oratory at Harvard. He was Louis D. Brandeis. "It was Copeland, however," Howe remembered, "who seemed most nearly unique. Perhaps he would have been a revelation to anyone in his twenties whose friends had conformed in general with conventional patterns. Certainly he was a revelation to me, falling heir as I did to an intimacy he established first with my brother Wallis. 'Babble on, sweet child,' he used to say to that beginner in architecture whose witty observations were the more amusing to him for the hesitating speech which made brothers of us in more than the common sense."

At this time Howe fell in love with an eighteen-year-old

Boston girl named Fanny Huntington Quincy, whom he was to marry in 1899, and to live happily with until she died thirty-three years later. His friend Copeland was greatly attracted by her too, and often she was his companion at the first nights he covered as the *Post's* dramatic critic. So strong, indeed, was this attraction that when Fanny Quincy consented to marry him, Mark Howe felt with foreboding that the first person he must tell of her decision was Copeland. Nevertheless he sensed that their attachment was basically platonic, and so it proved, for the three remained fast friends always.

There is an amusing note written by Fanny to Copeland, which takes its flavor partly from the circumspect manners of Boston young people of that period. She wrote from 82 Charles Street, in November, 1892:

My dear Mr. Copeland

I was sorry not to see you last night, but if you will choose the middle of my night for your visits what can you expect? On your arrival I was engaged in my usual evening pastime of crying! This time for no better reason than that I had to begin another week in this vale of tears. However, I had something to cry for when I heard that you were downstairs, & that I was unable to see you. I really was sorry not to use the ticket to Mrs. Winslow's reading, but I truly had engagements which I ought not to break. I have been so depressed lately, that the other day I was on the point of writing to you that I would go to the theatre with you so often as you would take me & let 'what people say' be d——d. But I have now come to a final decision which I regret to say is *No,* — though you know how much I have enjoyed the little sprees — All my lady friends are married, & almost all my gentlemen friends are engaged, so I am utterly deserted. I am in a Boy's Club

& play games with the horrid little brats every Tuesday evening — That's what it is to be really charitable. If you had a grain of charity in your composition you would tell me what afternoon you would go to walk with me, or at least you would come to see some time before 10 P.M. If my depression continues, you will see 'A Tragedy in High Life' in the Morning Post soon, & you can go to identify me at the Morgue — It will be my last wile.

Yours de profundis
FANNY H. Q.

Fanny Quincy was the third and last, if we include his teacher Laura Burns, of Copeland's early loves. In early middle age he became the devoted friend, and she his, of Minnie Maddern Fiske. Always, when she came to Boston to play, she would go out to Cambridge to see him, and there is the often repeated story of how, when she was being entertained in the offices of the *Harvard Advocate*, Copeland dispatched a messenger bearing the oral command, "Minnie, come over to Copey's." "She'll laugh," he predicted, "and then she'll come." And so it was.

There is also a story, told by Eugene McCarthy, and perhaps attributable to a youthful romantic imagination, to the effect that when as an undergraduate, he lived in the same entry of Hollis as Copeland, he once mounted the stairs a little after midnight and encountered the great lady of the theater descending, "with that look about her of a woman who has just been made love to." Copeland's relatives and other intimates doubt the story's foundation in fact, believing that C.T.C. would never have so far transgressed university regulations or would have put Mrs. Fiske in such a situation. If the two ever went beyond the bounds of pleasurable conversation, they contend, some other locale than Copeland's quarters would have been chosen.

The basic facts about Copeland's amatory life would seem to be these: He never, from childhood on, had any excess vitality, and it was necessary for him always to husband carefully his physical resources. He had the genes requisite to long life, but never an abundance of animal spirits. Then too, he had strong convictions regarding the responsibilities of marriage; having finally chosen a career in which the monetary rewards were small, he felt that he had no right to ask a woman to share his meager resources. Often he advised his students, "If you feel you must teach, then remain a bachelor as I have, for you have no right to ask a girl to share the thin financial future of a teacher." Or, he would say, "Don't marry for money, but go where money is." There was no question, ever, of any sexual deviation in Copeland; his attitude toward the young men who flocked about him was always that of a father, uncle, or older friend. He could be bawdy with them on occasion, but never was there a hint of any homosexual relationship. He admired good looks in men as well as in women, but that was the sum of his physical attraction to those of his own sex.

Once the mother of a student in one of Copeland's courses protested against the assignment for reading of Defoe's *Moll Flanders*, and other books which she regarded as "improper." Copey, without mentioning her name, of course, told the class about it, and snorted, "A man who is not aware of the primary relation between the sexes doesn't know enough to be in Harvard College."

It was in the course of these Boston years that he renounced a strong desire for a career on the stage. He saw, during his years on the *Post*, all the foremost performers of his time, for they all came to Boston, and he would dearly have liked to be one of their profession, for which, in some ways, he was splendidly equipped. However, as he confided to at least two people — Robert Frost and William James, the artist son of the psychologist and philosopher — he did not make the attempt because he felt himself physically inadequate, in stature, in presence, and in freedom of motion. The voice he unquestionably had, as he was to prove in his readings, and he had, too, the actor's sense, and the sympathetic understanding through which to interpret a part which might be alien to his own temperament and character.

5

It was during this period that he began to try out his ability to hold an audience by his reading. His first appearances in this role seem to have been made in Calais, where he always returned for at least part of his vacations, and where his fellow townsman Guy Murchie, a lawyer who was to write the story of their region in *Saint Croix: The Sentinel River*, remembered seeing the young Boston journalist appear at summer picnics, and hearing him read to the assembled boys and girls. And it was through Fanny Quincy, who had early discovered Copeland's gift, that his first Boston audiences gathered at her parents' house in Charles Street. Mark Howe recalls that

he read aloud to me, within the four walls of my lodging, much prose in which he found beauty, and much poetry, especially Shakespeare. From his companionship I derived also a stimulus to good reading in general, and a provision of criteria, to which I suspect I have owed more in my commerce with books and writing for some fifty years than I can ascribe to any other single teacher. When I hear some of those "former pupils" of whom Copeland is so proud acknowledge their debt to him, I am tempted to interject, "But I was a private pupil before you were born."

In 1930, that unique organization, the "Charles Town-

send Copeland Association," celebrated the seventieth birthday of this old friend at a dinner in the New York Harvard
Club. Unable to attend it, I sent from Washington, where I
was spending a winter at the Library of Congress, some
verses for the occasion. They were called "A Former Pupil
of Mine." There has been no change in the feeling they
sought to express. Two stanzas may speak for all the original four: —

> Was I a pupil of his? Would the *custos rotulorum*
> Find name of mine on the lists of the fortunate
>   beings he taught?
> What does it matter? Who cares about counting an
>   adequate quorum
> At meeings with Copeland? What counts is the
>   lucky infection one caught!

> Catch it we did, whether sitting like empty pails in
>   his classes,
> Soon to be filled with a lavish outpouring of wisdom
>   and wit,
> Or talking alone with the master and quickening
>   friend that surpasses
> The rest, as the candles of Hollis surpass the lights
>   otherwhere lit.

It was, however [continued Howe in his *Venture in Remembrance*] the wholehearted friend and good companion
of Copeland's journalistic days that I liked best to recall.
Late at night my name would sometimes ring out from
the sidewalk below the window of my lodging on Mt.
Vernon Street. When I thrust out my head the voice which
has so often — and often so badly — been imitated would
issue its summons: "Come down to the Adams House and

eat things." To my reply, "Too late, Cope, I must go to bed," I can hear now the melancholy rejoinder, "You do not love me any more!" There was good reason to wonder what the neighborhood made of this tragic parting word. His desire to "eat things," especially at hours impossible for any worker at an office desk, won him my nickname of *"Edax Rerum."* Perhaps some of the neighbors, even in Boston, would have wondered at that also. Nor could they have guessed what capacities of friendship, what wells of feeling, moved about Beacon Hill in the person of the slowly perambulating Copeland.

CHAPTER FIVE

Mr. Copeland Goes to the Play

THE BOSTON theater of Copeland's newspaper days set forth heady fare. During his years with the *Advertiser* and the *Post* he listened to all the greatest performers, at home and abroad, who flourished in the late years of the nineteenth century. Thither came Edwin Booth and Lawrence Barrett, Joseph Jefferson, Bernhardt and Modjeska, Adelaide Neilson, Rose Coghlan and Lily Langtry, Viola Allen, Salvini, Clara Morris, J. K. Emmett, Wilson Barrett, Fanny Kemble, E. H. Sothern, Julia Marlowe, Richard Mansfield, Ada Rehan, John Drew, Tyrone Power (the first), Henry Irving, Dion Boucicault, Edward Harrigan, Robert Mantell, Coquelin, Nat Goodwin, Mme. Janauschek, and many others whom the young critic singled out for praise, but whose reputations have not survived into our time.

Both in his book reviews and his dramatic criticism, Copeland displayed a keen and balanced judgment, and many of the hundreds of columns he wrote for the *Advertiser* and the *Post* stand the test of reading now. The style, naturally, was more formal than is the contemporary fashion, but it was not stilted, and it was often enlivened by humor and salted with wit. Many of the writers, as well as the players, whose work he considered have faded from view and are long since gone into the literary dustbin, but one can with much interest observe his comments on the performance of such stars as Booth and Jefferson, Bernhardt, Modjeska, Marlowe and Salvini, and take note of his shrewd appraisal of such already established writers as Emerson, Lowell, Holmes, Howells, Meredith, Wilde, and Matthew Arnold, his appreciation of newly introduced foreign authors like Turgenev and Tolstoy, and his discerning estimate of the newly rising figure of Rudyard Kipling.

For Edwin Booth he had the greatest admiration, and shortly after his newspaper days ended, wrote a brief life of the actor, in which he told of their one encounter outside the theater:

The scene was Park Street in Boston; the time, a very cold and very bright winter morning. The street lay white under the sun, and the Common stretched white beyond. Doubtless there were other people about. I don't remember seeing any; I remember only that I caught sight of Booth at some distance, coming down the hill toward me. As he drew near, walking slow, I watched him intently; and even when we came face to face, it is to be feared that I still gazed. There was no harm — Mr. Booth must long before have formed the habit of being stared at! And it was a reverential stare. Such was my deep respect for him and all he had done that, not knowing then the fate of Charles Lamb's "merry friend," Jem White, I came near taking off my hat to a gentleman I had never "met." It is a question whether, at that moment, Booth would have perceived even such an attack, for he seemed to be looking in, not out, with the curious, introverted gaze of his own Hamlet. Let no one suppose that his expression was subdued to a professional melancholy, or that he had the consciously unconscious air which so often marks the celebrity in his walks abroad. But as he came toward me on that glittering, bitter day — stepping lightly though not quickly, his head a little bent and his hands in his pockets — he looked like Hamlet in a great-coat. I thought then that I had never seen so sad a face, and I have never yet beheld a sadder one.

Many years later, at the suggestion of his former student, Paul Hollister, Copeland was made one of the few honorary members of The Players, the club Booth founded, and lived in during his last years.

Of Booth's Hamlet, which he saw numerous times, he wrote that "it is strangely hard to write intelligently, or even intelligibly, for persons who never saw him, because there is no actor on the American or English stage with whom he can reasonably be compared." Long afterward, he was to speak of his friend John Barrymore's performance in the same role as a "great" one. One of the things Copeland admired most in Booth was his voice, and he reminded his readers of the unanimous opinion of the Greeks that a voice is the actor's chief gift. Booth, he wrote:

had by nature a beautiful and eloquent voice. Listening at the keyhole to his father, years of association with his father, and constant self-training, with the aid of his own intellect, taste, and aptitude, brought Booth's delivery — especially of blank verse — to such excellence that, during the last twenty-five years of his career, when he was without an English-speaking rival in heroic parts in tragedy, his speech was a recognized model. It was as far as possible from an artificial or external elocution, which is a vain thing. It was equally far from the laborious diction of pedants. Booth did not mouth, or recite, or — except in bad moments, declaim, as it is to be feared the old actors often did. Nor did he croon or chant. He was simply a clear medium for the poet; and, with a perfect adherence to metre, he yet brought out the meaning as easily as if he had first learned to talk in iambic pentameter, unrhymed.

It was to his advantage, Copeland pointed out, that Booth actually looked like Hamlet as we think of him, with "his pale face lighted with darkly bright, melancholy eyes. As he looked when he followed the Ghost, when he spoke the brooding phrases of 'To be or not to be,' when he took his wild farewell of Ophelia — at almost any juncture of the play, indeed, Booth's picture would have made a portrait of the Prince of Denmark." And over his whole characterization, it seemed to Copeland, "hung, like a dark vapor, the sense of tragic fate."

Of Booth's Shylock, he remarked that

it is hard to carry the mind back from such a performance to any period when the part was deemed one for a low comedian. It is easy, on the contrary, to imagine that some such performance might have raised the character in a single night from its low estate to the height and dignity of tragedy. Mr. Booth, as playgoers well know, gives the Jew in Shylock with picturesque intensity; he has Abraham to his father; and he hates those who rail against the sacred nation. Nor does our great actor make the mistake of interpreting Shylock with nineteenth-century refinement.

But the young critic could be cutting too, as when he let fly at that sentimental piece, *East Lynne,* so beloved in the eighties and nineties: "The play is drearily lachrymose, and Miss Gray accentuates the woe, and makes it, 'like Niobe, all tears.' Criticism of such a performance is really out of the question. The lady's method is unpleasingly compounded of prose and rant; the members of the supporting company had chiefly prose to offer, but there was enough rant left to leaven the whole lump."

2

It is interesting in a period when we have had several fine characterizations of Joan of Arc to read Copeland's report on a playing of the role which few living persons can have seen — Sarah Bernhardt's. The play was Jules Barbier's *Jeanne d'Arc*, written in Alexandrine verse, which Copeland termed "one of the most artificial modes of expression known to man," and by means of which M. Barbier "put in Joan's mouth long speeches of the most conventional declamation about glory and all that sort of thing," — a criticism which our contemporary reviewers would no doubt duplicate. He nevertheless gave Barbier some credit for his interpretation of the theme, though noting that, as in all writing about the Maid since the chronicles of her time, it failed to reflect "the absolute simplicity to which those who had known and seen her testified." He found Bernhardt's impersonation "very beautiful."

It may now be freely owned that the remembrance of this actress's repertoire and of the style of character in which her fame has been won, made it seem not altogether a pleasant thing that she should act Joan of Arc. Artifice — however artistic — was to be feared, and a failure to strike or at all events, to keep the note of exaltation. But every fear of this kind was removed at Mme. Bernhardt's first appearance on the scene. The peasant garb and arrangement of the hair were not more faithfully rendered than the feeling of the character. In the first act, of course, at Domremy, Joan is the dreamer and mystic the consciousness of whose mission is gradually coming upon her. The music given by M. Gounod to the "voices" that called Joan to the salvation of France was sung behind the scenes sweetly, but too loudly, with too little compromise between this world and the next. But it was impossible to think of anything but the solitary figure on the stage. Mme. Bernhardt's up-turned face, the look as of a person in a trance, the expression of purity and devotion, gave a quality to the scene which marked it out from all ordinary experiences of the theatre. It was like Bastien Lepage's portrait come to life. . . . The final appearance at the stake had more symbolism than pathos, but this was probably intended, and indeed the music drowned out all articulate speech. For the rest Mme. Bernhardt realized to a remarkable degree the received ideal of Joan of Arc. The very spirit of purity and devotion was in her voice — which in its remoteness from earthly passion was almost the *vox infantilis* which the old chroniclers ascribe to Joan — and the fervor of the exhortations to the king and his armies surpassed, without doubt, any utterance of French patriotism on our stage since Rachel chanted the Marseillaise at the Boston Theater.

Another star of the European theater for whom Copeland had high praise was Signor Salvini, especially in his playing of Othello. His rendition of the part, said Copeland:

reminds one of the saying that art is nature seen through a temperament: it is Shakespeare's Moor seen through the temperament of Southern Europe, and — softened as this conception of Othello has become with the years — it is still more savage, more carnal, than the lines of Shakespeare give warrant. But it is only after such a performance as that of last evening and not during it that intelligence and emotion can be kept so far separate as to consider the question with entire coolness, for whatever may be thought of Signor Salvini's scheme of the character, there can be no two opinions in regard to his execution of it. Perfection is

scarcely too high a word for an art so graduated and meas-
ured that even after the most passionate outbursts there is
no suspicion of anti-climax — an art, moreover, re-enforced
with such physical and temperamental strength, that there
seems always to be a reserve even when most has been
lavished to meet the demands of the scene.

He dealt kindly but firmly with young Julia Marlowe in her
playing of Juliet. He found her much improved over her first
effort of three years before, but the impersonation

lacked passion in the beginning and it lacks it now. Miss
Marlowe's Juliet has in a higher degree than ever the
charms of beauty, grace, sentiment, even tender affection,
nor has it lost in any degree the charm of youth; but the
keynote of ardent passion is struck faintly and then only for
moments and phrases. The

> high and passionate thought
> To their own music chanted

were for the more part last night little but sweet echoes of
the poet, in the play which is "Shakespeare all over, and
Shakespeare when he was young."

It is not meant that much pleasure may not be had from
Miss Marlowe's impersonation — a cultivated and very
large audience testified eagerly to the contrary — and up to
and even through the balcony scene her acting is almost
constantly close to Shakespeare. But from that point on-
ward the greatest actress in the world, whoever she may
be, would find her genius sorely taxed to render unto
Shakespeare the things that are Shakespeare's. Miss Marlowe's tribute, as has been said, is an imperfect one, and —
whether or not her temperament ever adapts itself to the
character — the hard saying is not likely to be gallant
enough to relax itself in her favor, that an actress who is

old enough to act Juliet is too old to look Juliet. At one and the same moment that these words are written, memory is haunted by the vision of Miss Marlowe and Mr. Taber in the balcony scene; and the recollection of their beauty and their untouched youth is alone enough to make it worth while that we should now and then see a Juliet who is Romeo's contemporary, and is not playing to her grandson. Mr. Taber brings the essential requirement of passion to his part, which he executes with only a few characteristic faults.

3

"Readings" were very popular in the Boston of those days. In Copeland's newspaper writing there are frequent reports on what was soon to become a lost art until it was revived in very recent years, owing chiefly to the initiative of Charles Laughton. Those who saw his fine performance in Harry Leon Wilson's *Ruggles of Red Gap* (Wilson, with Robert Benchley — another Copeland pupil — was one of the last of the true humorists, before the need to be smart, knowing, or completely cock-eyed had distorted what should be a natural upwelling, a sense of the incongruous), and heard Laughton's superb reading of the Gettysburg Address, were not surprised when with Tyrone Power, Judith Anderson and Raymond Massey, he staged that remarkable rendition of Stephen Vincent Benét's *John Brown's Body*, and went on to successive triumphs as a reader from the Bible and other literature similarly suitable for reading aloud.

In Copeland's Boston days there was a flock of these practitioners. He commented on the performances of George Riddle, Mrs. Erving Winslow, J. J. Hayes, Sidney Woollett, Annie Elizabeth French, W. C. Lawton, Arthur Falkland,

Adolphe Cohn and George Washington Cable, all of whom read repeatedly to Boston audiences. In his standards for the art, Copeland was in advance of his time, and bore down hard on mere elocution. George Riddle was his favorite, and of him he remarked that "Mr. Riddle's qualities are precisely of a sort to distinguish him from the awkward squad of 'elocutionists' who are always displaying their imperfect drill before a long-suffering public."

It is for this reason that one resents George Santayana's patronizing references to Copeland in that volume of his autobiography called *The Middle Span,* in which he spoke of Copeland:

> A more pathetic servant of popular joys, humbler than Barrett Wendell and more openly sentimental, was my neighbor for years in the Yard, and although I seldom saw him, I was always vaguely aware of his beneficent existence round the corner. He was known as Charley Copeland. An artist rather than a scholar, he was a public reader by profession, an elocutionist; he could move his audiences by declaiming, with disciplined voice and restrained emotion, all the most touching or thrilling popular selections from the Bible to Kipling. This was a spiritual debauch for the hungry souls of the many well-disposed waifs at Harvard living under difficult conditions; and these Copeland made his special friends.

But it is only fair to add that Santayana went on to say: "Apart from his readings, he took pains to thaw out the most timid and warm them at his fire, materially and morally. He was the poor boys' providential host and inspirer, doing for the forlorn and disinherited what Norton did for those who were, or ought to have been, already somewhat cultivated, or what Palmer did, more speculatively, for the intellectual proletariat."

4

Copeland's literary appraisals were forthright and independent. These attitudes were extended even to those sacrosanct figures of the New England pantheon with whom, as Mark Twain had found to his confusion and dismay at a dinner in the seventies, it was impossible to treat jocosely in Boston. In reply to a writer who was disposed to exalt Dr. Holmes's humor over that of any other American writer, Copeland observed that "there are those who find the humor of the 'Biglow Papers' and 'The Courtin',' and 'A Few Words on a Certain Condescension in Foreigners,' and the humorous halflights of Hawthorne's marvellous tales, to be sprung from the soil — like the Athenians — and thus to have a peculiarly national and characteristic quality which is seldom found in the humor of Dr. Holmes."

About William Dean Howells he had his reservations also; he was not very much impressed by Howells's brand of realism. Copeland found it inferior to the realistic approach of a Turgenev or Tolstoy — writers who were in the eighties just becoming known to American readers, and who had in this young Boston journalist a strong admirer. It was Copeland's repeated conviction that "Mr. Howells would keep his reader down upon too dead a level, both of incident and character," and that he defeated his purpose by "making fiction too uniformly commonplace for a fair copy of life." He objected to Howells's deprecation of passion of any and every kind as being unnatural and distorted. "Now the truth of the matter is," wrote Copeland in a review of Howells's criticism, "that this world has been a passionate one ever since it began, else Cain would never have killed Abel, Menelaus would never have joined with the jealous divinity in laying siege to Troy, Sappho would not have cast herself into the wine-dark sea." Nor could he find in Howells's writing "the fruits of a generous study of books," as they do appear in that "of the best and most inspiring critics."

A little later he wrote a supposititious estimate of Howells, such as might be expected to appear in a literary manual to be published "about 1950." It might, Copeland thought, read something like this:

William Dean Howells, a clever American novelist of the second half of the nineteenth century, united criticism with his craft, and expounded the doctrines of the realistic school with much gentle violence. It should be said, before glancing at his work, that Howells himself was one of the most agreeable, charming and best of men, for whom his friends always expressed admiration in the same breath with regretful apologies for his opinions. What they especially deplored was not his praise of the school to which he himself belonged — for much useful work was done within its narrow limits — but his patronizing disparise of far greater and stronger novelists who had preceded him. The incomparable Thackeray seemed to him theatrical; Sir Walter Scott, childish; Balzac, distorted; and Dickens, impossible. What poor Howells could not see was that the world is appealed to not by any school or method but by absolute force of talent, in whatever way it is exercised. Nor did he ever understand that the only thorough-going realist in English — in his restricted meaning of the word realist — who reached the first rank among novelists, was George Eliot. . . .

In the course of one of these curious little onslaughts upon the mighty dead, Howells announced as his motto, "Beauty is truth; truth beauty"; but "the new, the good, and the beautiful" would be a fairer statement of his principles. For having, early in his critical career, curtly dismissed

Fielding (that stalwart realist) as coarse, he afterward found many good words to say for Zola, who as we all know, wallowed in depths of nastiness which Fielding's manly nature could not have conceived. . . . Howells did not prize virility.

Copeland went on to make this percipient observation:

It is not worth our while, in this more enlightened day, to sum up all of Howells's vagaries, but one or two more of them may be instructive as well as amusing. The typical character, for example, was always odious to him. He contended for the individual as opposed to the type, not seeing that a peculiar strength and permanence comes to a character in which the individual and the typical are happily joined, somewhat as the greatest art has known how to join the ideal and the real. Howells could not see that Lapham, the only one of his own creations who is now remembered, owed much of his vitality to the fact of being not only individual but typical. Silas Lapham will not live forever, but the odds are in favor of the immortality of Don Quixote, and not least because he is the highest example of this union in prose fiction. Critics as a class fared badly at the hands of Howells, and he made himself truly absurd in his hysterical protest against anonymous critics as masked bravos.

On the other side of the water, Matthew Arnold came in for a severe dusting off, in connection with an article about his American impressions which had appeared in the *Nineteenth Century Review:*

Not only man is vile to Mr. Arnold, but the prospect does not please him [he had found Lincoln without distinction], and even our much admired scenery does not appeal to him. We are conceited and boast of our country, and to cut the matter short — the only gracious statement in Mr. Arnold's pages seems to be the concession that, although Americans as a class are to be despised, there are among them many cultivated, judicious and delightful individuals. The tone of the article is absurdly splenetic, and its method and details almost incredibly trivial and unjust. Mr. Arnold could never become a common scold; he would be distinguished even in his degeneration. But if he goes on in the shrill and fretful manner of which this American article is but one of several recent instances, the apostle of sweetness and light will soon be little better than a Xantippe touched to finer issues.

Copeland knew why George Meredith would become one of the least read of the Victorians: brilliant though he could be, he allowed himself to write "whole pages of rubbish." He found in him also a "repellent cynicism" which would work against him — "Not a soft-hearted cynicism — 'the younger brother of sentiment' like Thackeray's — but a kind which sometimes has the effect, fatal in a novelist, of putting him out of touch with humanity. To our mind, Mr. Meredith's defects must keep him out of the first rank of novelists; his high qualities, of which we should like to speak at far greater length, give him every dignity short of that, and make his best work — by a rare combination — both impressive and exhilarating." Copeland's favorites in Meredith were *The Ordeal of Richard Feverel* and *Diana of the Crossways*.

5

Kipling made his debut while Copeland was writing for the *Boston Post*. In later years many selections from his verse and prose were to be in Copeland's repertory as a reader, and he delighted generations of undergraduates with his rendering of "The Truce of the Bear," "Mandalay," "The Man Who Would be King," and "The Taking of Lung-tung-pen." The young reviewer gave the new star of English letters — Kipling was five years his junior — unreserved praise for his three musketeers — Ortheris, Learoyd and Mulvaney, and saw in him "the now very rare gift of the born story-teller," adding that "he often relies, with a justified confidence almost equally rare, upon humor alone or pathos alone — with little or no background of circumstances or scene — to achieve an effect. An unpleasant crudeness is too often the unavoidable accompaniment of this latter practice." Copeland cared little for the stories about children (perhaps because he was uninterested in them himself?) and found the tales of garrison flirtations too often unreal and immature. "To those persons who fervently wish that Mr. Kipling would write a novel, it may be said by way of caution, that his Irish soldier is almost the only evidence he has given of an ability to draw character, that the disregard of detail and environment not amiss in a short story would have to be amended, and that pathos is apt to muddle itself into sentimentality." His misgivings were to be confirmed when Kipling published *Captains Courageous*. He was more deeply impressed when "Without Benefit of Clergy" appeared in *The Courting of Dinah Shadd and Other Stories*. This tale, thought Copeland, has a sweetness and maturity seldom visible before in Mr. Kipling's work, and the little romance, heartbreaking itself, shows the great gulf that is fixed between Englishman and native, between Christian and Mussulman. It would only, he imagined, be by developing the qualities shown in "Without Benefit of Clergy" that Kipling could excel in the novel, "for it is evident here that a writer who has heretofore seemed open only to the extraordinary in life may sometime be keenly alive to the ordinary as well."

Copeland sounded a note contemporary to ourselves in what he had to say about American realism in general — not merely that of Howells. "A particular form of art," he wrote:

> can only commend itself by the strength and success with which it is practiced. American fiction of the most charac-teristic sort is in the main occupied with incidents measur-ably less important than the fall of a sparrow. A woman smiles, a man looks out of the window, or a letter is mis-laid — there is seldom much more than that; although one of our chief writers did lately, in a moment of frenzy, over-turn a carriage at the end of one of his books. Two causes conspire to keep American realism, in the hands of its most admired masters, from being impressive. One of these is the prevailing triviality just spoken of, the apparent belief that the trifles of life are its only realities, to which there is, however, a notable exception in the largely conceived and largely executed figure of Silas Lapham. And the other cause is the well-known coyness of the Anglo-Saxon muse, which need not be dwelt upon further than to say that it keeps a great part of life out of novels in the English lan-guage, as being written for boys and maidens, and leaves some of the deepest and most passionate notes of humanity unsounded. Thackeray felt this limitation when he said — as he is reported to have said — that, if he had dared, he would have written another "Tom Jones." . . .
>
> To romanticism there can be no return, and we, for our part, do not wish for a return. . . . Realism, then, is the best thing we have, but it should be recognized as transitory, like all literary movements. It is but a phase in the develop-ment of the novel; it may even be its last phase, and a signal for the more or less speedy revival of some other form of literature as the most vital expression of thought and artistic impulse. But, recognizing the realistic novel as

the best now within our reach, we must also recognize that only in Russia and France is it now really strong.

6

In 1892 the *Boston Post* suffered a change in ownership. The new publisher, for reasons undetermined, decided to drop Copeland from the staff. And he, by this time, had tired somewhat of his reviewing chores, and never took them up again, although years later Robert Lincoln O'Brien, then editor of the *Boston Herald*, tried to enlist Copeland's services as literary critic at a generous salary. By then his fame was firmly established, but O'Brien's plea, although it pleased Copeland greatly, fell upon ears that were reluctant to the point of deafness.

Once again upon leaving the *Post*, this devoted son of the border country turned his face in the direction of Calais — always his refuge in time of trouble. Once again he was puzzled and disturbed about the future course of his life. His dearest love, the theater, he had long since concluded, was closed to him, except as an observer, and he knew — for he had much self-knowledge — that he had not the abundant nervous energy necessary for a distinguished career in writing. His standards were severe and high, and he judged himself as he judged others. Yet ambition burned in him, and he would make no truce with mediocrity; he must be foremost in something. Perhaps his future lay in teaching, for he already knew that he could light lamps in the minds of others, and communicate to them his enthusiasms for what was great and enduring in the written word. He went home, to the enchanting river and the restless, powerful tides which were absent in himself, thinking that maybe there he could chart his course and find his guiding star.

His closest friend, Mark Howe, wrote of that departure in the *Harvard Crimson* for April 27, 1950 — Copeland's ninetieth birthday: "Many letters have come to me in recent years signed, 'Your oldest friend, C.T.C.' I believe I could have used the same words in answering them. The Old Friends of Octogenarians dwindle away in number. Occasionally one of them turns Nonogenarian. Then indeed it is time to look back over the years." Howe went on to recall Copeland's newspaper days:

> When he walked the streets between my brother and me who had become his playmates he used to commend us as "Two props of virtue for a Christian prince." He enjoyed his own witticisms and liked to repeat them to others, usually with a culminating "whereupon he laughed." What he valued most in his social relations was "talk — good talk," in which indeed he bore his own memorable part.
>
> In 1892 he left Boston for a year in his native Calais, Maine, having added the Atlantic Monthly to the Boston Post as a medium for his critical writings, and having demonstrated to friends of a young friend who assembled them in her Boston parlor, his power to hold an audience of more than two or three. This foreshadowed but dimly the future of the "Copeland Readings," and all the happiness they created.
>
> Yet it was none too happy a little man whose trunk I helped him pack in his Pinckney Street room late in the night before his departure for Calais.

Copeland would take stock of himself during the year that followed, and then make the step by which he would cross the threshold of his true career. He had written superior journalism, but he was to find still another means of communicating his literary enthusiasms and his attitude toward life.

CHAPTER SIX

Harvard in the Nineties

THE HARVARD and Cambridge to which Copeland returned
in 1893 did not outwardly differ greatly from the scene he
had left eleven years before. It was still a millennium away
from the Harvard and Cambridge of the present; one still
journeyed between Boston and Harvard Square by streetcar,
unless, in temporary or permanent affluence, one hired a cab
or had one's own carriage. There had been, for the time being, a lull in the building ferment in and about the Harvard
Yard, though by now the Gold Coast — that scattering of
luxurious private dormitories which arose to supplement the
Spartan accommodations then provided by the university itself
— was beginning to take shape, and profoundly to influence,
for more than three decades, the social structure of Harvard
College. There congregated the boys from well-to-do Boston
and New York families, graduates, usually, of the fashionable
Episcopalian private schools — Groton, St. Mark's, Pomfret,
St. Paul's and the like, with a sprinkling from the older and
more democratic New England academies, Andover and Exe-
ter. The graduates of public high schools, even of such a ven-
erable and honored one as the Boston Latin School, whose
boys had once been socially acceptable both in Boston and
Cambridge, and in the college clubs, did not frequent the
Gold Coast, and rarely made the clubs, though, as we have already noted, their college life was far from crippled by these

exclusions. They could, and did, if they were able, have a full share in undergraduate activities, and unless they were socially supersensitive and ambitious, they suffered little sense of being outsiders in the college community.

Harvard had begun to broaden the geographical base of its enrollment, though it by no means yet approached the wide distribution which has been increasingly characteristic during the past half century. In one respect — as regards one region — the Harvard of the eighteenth and early nineteenth centuries was more inclusive than it is today; for more than a century the South sent many of its sons to Cambridge, and while some still come, the proportion is not as large. Their numbers sharply decreased after the Civil War. This was due partly to the poverty of so many old Southern families, but the decline proceeded also from Harvard's tradition of racial tolerance. Negro boys could play on the Crimson's teams, and did, nor were they barred from eating in the college dining halls. They were never numerous, but there were always some Negroes at Harvard from the latter years of the nineteenth century down, and they were never made to feel unwelcome.

The teaching body of which Copeland now became a part was steadily and rapidly enlarging. It had not yet attained the pre-eminence it was to have during the opening years of this century, but already many of the names which were to give increasing luster to what has been called "Harvard's Golden Age" were to be found on the university roster. William James, who had been called to the university in 1872 by President Eliot to teach anatomy and physiology, then psychology, and finally philosophy, was now a man of fifty; his reputation as a psychologist had been won, and his restless mind and spirit were seeking new fields to conquer. George Herbert Palmer was already there; indeed, in 1884 he had launched what was to become one of the most celebrated of Harvard courses, Philosophy Four, in which he continued to teach ethics until his retirement in 1913. Palmer, incidentally, who was one of the most felicitous writers and speakers of his period at Harvard, and whose nobility of mind and character his students would always remember, was one of Copeland's greatest admirers, and spoke of him as "doing the work of God." Josiah Royce, that modern Socrates, whom he physically resembled, had begun his interminable friendly arguments with William James, for they much admired each other and were completely at odds in their philosophical positions. George Santayana, too, had begun to teach at Harvard in 1889; he of the glowing liquid eyes and the delicately chosen speech. Never before, perhaps, had there been such a congregation of eminent philosophers. And in the year before Copeland's arrival there came to this department from Germany the brilliant young psychologist Hugo Münsterberg; within three months he mastered English sufficiently to deliver his lectures in a language he had never before spoken. He became a storm center twenty-two years later, amid public clamor for his resignation during World War I. President Lowell met it with resolute disregard, and thus once more upheld Harvard's championing of freedom of expression.

Assembling also was the remarkable department Copeland had come to join; the English faculty, like that in philosophy, became unparalleled in the country. No man, whatever his field, could have entered stiffer competition. Already there was his college rival, Kittredge, who had begun to teach at Harvard in 1888; by 1892 he was an assistant professor, and a year later became a full professor and head of the department. The rivalry was to be long continued, with Copeland lagging in official recognition, but forging ahead even of Kittredge in popularity. Both were to become legendary characters, both to be celebrated for their wit and their occasional ferocity. Copeland was to envy Kittredge's rapid academic advancement, and his classmate to realize, somewhat wistfully, perhaps, that he was admired and held in awe, but not cherished and loved like the little man from Maine. Yet both showed generosity of spirit toward each other: Copeland praised the learning of his rival and disclaimed credit for one witticism commonly attributed to Copeland, but which was really Kittredge's — the one about falling from the platform and finding himself for the first time on a level with his audience; Kittredge was to yield at last to pressure for Copeland's promotion. Both became known throughout the university by their nicknames, Copey and Kitty. Copey would dine in Boston, at Marliave's or the Parker House, or other favorite haunts, with his young student friends, for a mildly bibulous evening, and Mark Howe's brother Wallis recalls that on one of these, at Marliave's, the waitress regaled Howe and Copeland with the story of a customer who had expressed unbounded admiration for her breasts. One of them he had named Fortress Monroe, but she could not recall what he had christened the other. "Doubtless Old Point Comfort," said Copeland. Kitty, maintaining a more Olympian attitude, commanded undergraduate sympathy and interest by his reputed visits to the burlesque shows at the Old Howard, where, upon occasion, were to be seen Cora Livingston and her "lady wrestlers." Kitty had the presence an unkind Providence had denied to Copey; physically vigorous, a furious smoker of cigars (whereas Copey permitted himself only Richmond Straight Cut cigarettes), he flaunted a dazzlingly white beard which proclaimed his coming a hundred yards away. This contrast was to be pathetically deepened as the two grew older, for Kitty remained mentally and physically active and alert up to his retirement, years after Copey's. Both were men of intense contradictions; in them the bitter and the sweet were inextricably commingled; Copey could be woundingly harsh at one moment and gentle as a mother at the next; Kitty could terrorize his class in Shakespeare and show the utmost consideration toward a nervous candidate for honors in English.

2

Nobody could write about the Harvard of yesterday without mention of Le Baron Russell Briggs. He too was a member of the English department when Copeland joined it. In 1883, after a few years of teaching Greek, he had transferred to the English faculty, and a year before Copeland's arrival had been made Dean of Harvard College, a post in which he was to become the most beloved of Harvard personalities. He too, and before Copeland, won renown as a teacher of writing; and, indeed, among those Harvard graduates who distinguished themselves in the field of letters there has always been a minority who preferred the gentler and more whimsical methods of Briggs to those of Copeland. The two had high regard for each other, and between them there was none of the acrimony which often muddied the relations between Copeland and Kittredge. Copeland referred to him always in conversation as "dear Briggs," for nobody could bear a grudge or feel antagonistic toward the Dean. The kindest and most self-effacing of men, he inspired only affection and respect, and was so tactful and sympathetic that he could fire a boy from college and make it seem like a benediction.

Nor does the roll of these exceptional teachers end with Briggs. There was Fred N. ("Fritz") Robinson, who taught Anglo-Saxon and Chaucer, and could make those ancient forms of the English tongue seem palatable and interesting even to his undergraduate students. There was the Boston Brahmin, Barrett Wendell, who in 1884 began the course in English composition which Copeland was to make still more famous — English 12. Wendell had his limitations: he was rabidly an Anglophile, and was to write and speak condescendingly of American literature. Nevertheless he was an excellent teacher and wrote one of the best textbooks of English composition. Clarity, force and elegance were Wendell's criteria for good prose, and he hammered them home to his classes. But it was not for his exposition of such matters that he was an undergraduate favorite: the boys in his courses were in the first place fascinated by his obvious and unmistakable role as a man of the world; he exuded sophistication and elegance of dress and manner. They were fascinated, too, by his little mannerisms; his constant twirling, as he lectured, of his watch chain, like President Eliot's twirling of his thumbs. Above all, they were captured by his bawdiness, and sat forward on their seats, expectantly waiting for one more departure from the accepted norm of academic behavior. Indeed, one former student of his recalls that Wendell was pleased whenever someone turned in a theme on a broad subject like the mores of those ladies of an ancient profession who adorned the houses on Bulfinch Street. Compositions like these were likely to receive an A.

Wendell too, was a favorite target for the Harvard *Lampoon's* fun makers, and Henry Ware Eliot wrote of him:

> Please make a careful study of this truthful illustration,
> And take especial notice of the subtle connotation.
> The atmosphere of London is so well suggested there,
> You'd think you were in "Rotten Row" instead of
>   Harvard Square.
> How palpably inadequate my feeble talents are
> To tell what Harvard culture owes to this, its guiding
>   star!
> Coherence, mass, and unity in Barrett are combined,
> To edify the vulgar, and abash the unrefined.

Four years before Copeland, came George Pierce Baker, that pioneer in teaching the history of drama and its composition, whom Harvard, in one of its least perceptive and understanding moments, was to lose to Yale in 1925. He was to father a flock of successful playwrights, among whom were numbered Edward Sheldon, author of *Salvation Nell* and *Romance*, Eugene O'Neill, Robert Sherwood, S. N. Behrman, and other figures of importance in the theater like Kenneth Macgowan and Robert Edmond Jones.

It was, truly, a great English department, later to be augmented by such outstanding men as William Allan Neilson, Bliss Perry and John Livingston Lowes. And though Harvard College was then strongest in the humanities, which also included such distinguished scholars as Irving Babbitt, Hans von Jagemann and Kuno Francke, and, for a few years more, Charles Eliot Norton, there were, in the sciences, men like Shaler in geology, Thomas C. Pickering in astronomy, and Theodore C. Richards in chemistry.

Henry Ware Eliot sang of Norton:

And ever and anon the far-off cry
From Shady Hill — "Back! back!" it calls in wrath,
"To Ruskin and Rossetti!" But the herd,
Entranced with brutal sports, hears not the word,
To Soldiers' Field pursues its downward path,
And Art is left to languish and to die.

Copeland's mentor and helpful friend, Professor Dunbar, died in 1900; had he lived longer, it is conceivable, considering the weight he carried with President Eliot, that Copeland's advancement might have proceeded at a faster pace. Yet this is unlikely, for Dunbar was no man to throw his weight around. Albert Bushnell Hart was teaching history, and had begun his classes in government, in which he was in a few years to be joined by a young Boston lawyer named Abbott Lawrence Lowell. Edward Channing, who was to delight the undergraduates by his emphasis on the importance of rum and the slave trade in building many New England fortunes, and also by his insistence on the fact that General Washington never actually took command of the Continental Army under the so-called Washington Elm in Cambridge, had started his teaching of American history.

3

When the young man from Calais, now thirty-three, began his teaching with the rank of instructor — the official level on which he was to remain for seventeen years — he occupied a room in Grays Hall, one of the most dismal-looking buildings in the Yard. He faced the drudgery which was, and is, the lot of young college teachers of English; one of his duties was to bear a share of the burden imposed on the instructors in Freshman English, with the reading, correction and appraisal of the daily themes which were a required part of that course. The habits of his newspaper years were still with him, and were, indeed, never completely to leave him. He was a night owl, living among people — undergraduates apart — whose lives were, for the most part, set in a more conventional and rigid pattern. In these early teaching years his Boston forays were more frequent than they were in later years though he never abandoned them until age raised a forbidding finger. His potations were deeper, too, and some of his near-contemporaries still remember that there were occasions when the young instructor, after a night on the town, was ready to accept a helping hand in mounting the stairs to his room. Copeland was never an alcoholic, though in his final years the friends who lunched with him knew that the talk he loved could not really get under way until there had been a jolt of brandy under the Copeland belt. Tales of indecorous proceedings no doubt came to President Eliot's ears, and this fact, together with other academic peculiarities of the young man from Calais, and what Eliot regarded as his lamentable laziness, unquestionably played their part in the tardiness of his academic advancement, for the virtues Eliot most admired were the conventional ones.

To Copeland, Henry Ware Eliot soon addressed himself as follows:

> If wit and madness be as like as Pope and others tell,
> Then Copey by the merest squeak escapes the padded cell.
> Those merry quips, those airy jests he springs in
>   English 8
> Mean spinal meningitis at no very distant date.
> And is it all spontaneous, or is it (hush!) a bluff?
> And does he make them up o' nights and crib them on his
>   cuff?
> Oh, wicked, clever cynic! How dare you be so sly?
> How dare you read "Peg Woffington" and make the
>   Freshmen cry?
> You bold, delicious joker! You know it, yes you do!
> There's but one clever, clever Copey — and that one is
>   you!

Copeland arrived on the Cambridge scene like a current of fresh air. There had been, and were, characters in the faculty as pronounced as his; some of them have already been named. But he brought something new into the college atmosphere. Perhaps Walter Lippmann, one of his students, put it most succinctly when he said, in the 90th Copeland birthday issue of the *Crimson*, "Copey was not a professor teaching a crowd in a classroom. He was a very distinct person in a unique relationship with each individual who interested him." As the *Crimson* editorially observed that day, "he personalized Harvard education."

CHAPTER SEVEN

The Legend Strikes Root

NEITHER faculty nor undergraduates were long in realizing that there was a new ferment at work in the Yard. Copeland was not content with his official role as a Freshman English theme corrector; he sought and obtained permission to lecture informally to whoever would take the trouble to come; word of his interesting talks about Dr. Johnson and his circle, Jane Austen, Scott, Stevenson, and others of his favorite writers spread beyond the college community; people frequently came out from Boston when a Copeland lecture was announced. Also, he set about doing something for the improvement of oral expression among the students; "Mr. Copeland's voluntary reading classes" in Sever Hall rapidly gained popularity. At these Copeland would read aloud himself, and criticize the diction and delivery of those who attended. Soon, too, he began to assist those seniors who had been chosen to deliver Commencement parts, or who were competing for the Boylston prizes in oratory. One man's chances of winning a Boylston prize were nearly squashed when, in the midst of delivering his speech, he became aware of Copeland, in the front row of the balcony, gazing at him fixedly through a big pair of binoculars.

It was at one of the meetings in Sever 11 — the little amphitheater memories of which Copeland would cherish in later years — that his voluntary students gathered one morning and

waited expectantly for the little man in the somewhat emphatic clothes (checks and plaids designed to increase his
bulk), and the rigid derby — never cocked at an angle —
with a bundle of books clutched under one arm and like as
not umbrella in hand. But he did not appear, though they
waited beyond the seven or eight minutes of grace accorded
to teachers. Two mornings later, at the appointed hour, they
found Copeland at his desk before they arrived. "Gentlemen,"
said he, "I suppose you noticed that I was not present at the
last meeting of this class. It was not, I assure you, that I love
you less, but because I love breakfast more."

In all this work he made himself approachable and acces-
sible to a degree hitherto unknown among the teaching staff
at Harvard College; it was the nearest thing to what President Garfield had envisaged when he said, "A log cabin in the
woods with a pine bench in it, with Mark Hopkins at one end
and me at the other, is a good enough college for me." There
were those who thought Copeland was not sufficiently up-
holding the dignity of academic position, and others who
looked down their noses at his scholarship, unadorned as it
was by a doctorate or its equivalent in the form of a period
of residence at a German university, German methods and
standards of scholarship being at that time regarded as the
most admirable in the western world.

It was true that Copeland was lacking in the equipment of
formal scholarship, and that he detested the drudgery which it
entailed. But he was already a very well-read man in the English classics, especially in the eighteenth and early nineteenth
centuries, and he was well versed in French literature also.
In the drama he was probably better informed than any member of the Harvard faculty with the exception of George
Pierce Baker. It was the Copeland of these years who made
his bow in college fiction in the guise of Mr. Fleetwood of
Charles Macomb Flandrau's *The Diary of a Freshman*, a Har-

vard classic which was published in 1901. He makes his entrance at a Harvard Square restaurant known as the Holly
Tree. Approaching his accustomed table — for Copeland was
one of the most habit-bound of men — Mr. Fleetwood in-
quires of the freshman, "in a slow, tremulous, reproachful
voice," "Who's been sitting in my chair!" "I jumped up, of
course," the narrative continues, "and after he had set down
and leaned back, he murmured feebly, 'I'm an old man, but I
know my place.'

" 'I'm a young man, but I seem to know your place, too,'
I laughed, as I looked around for another chair.

" 'You boys chaff me so,' he replied mournfully. 'You
mustn't chaff me; I'm only a simple villager.' "

And then the diarist recalled that this was the odd figure he
had encountered on the day of registration, the little man
who looked so bored with the proceedings, and who now and
then made some comment filched from Shakespeare.

The freshman was to see more of Mr. Fleetwood, and was
indeed, with a classmate, to dine with him in Boston and then
carry him off, protesting that he must go home to bed — to
the theater. There, after the first act, he was approached by
an acquaintance who talked earnestly with him for a few moments, and then departed. Fleetwood informed the boys that
his friend was a journalist who had begged him to write his
review of the play, and that he had consented. They accom-
panied Fleetwood to the newspaper office after the final curtain, and observed all that ensued with great interest. Mr.
Fleetwood, they noted, "spent more time in groaning, 'My
facility is gone — my hand has lost its cunning,' than in writing."

Copeland occupied first the room in Grays, and then
moved to Stoughton, where he was to be for several years before he obtained the rooms in Hollis which were forever to
be associated with his name. The habits which were to be cel-

ebrated in undergraduate verse were rapidly forming: there was the famous sponge, immortalized by Henry Webster Palmer, who wrote in the Harvard *Lampoon:*

> See that funny porous thing
> Hanging on a piece of string,
> Ever there from Fall to Spring,
> Decorating Stoughton Hall.
>
> Copey dear, can't you remember
> Where you hung it last September,
> Or have you become a member
> Of the Never Wash at ALL?

The author of these verses had an uneasy moment when he encountered Copey in the Yard a few days after the *Lampoon's* appearance, and was halted by him. Much to his surprise — and relief — Copey forthwith, and in his best manner, declaimed the verses, and then asked Palmer if he might have the original manuscript. The delighted youngster of course complied, and it was presently framed and hung among numerous other mementos in Copey's quarters.

2

In these years also, Copeland began to journey farther afield to be heard as a reader. He was much in demand in the New England preparatory schools, and in the preliminary correspondence leading up to these engagements, as well as in his manner of filling them, he soon established the reputation of being decidedly eccentric. Always reluctant to spend a night away from his own bed, he would make it clear in answering an invitation to read that if it were impossible for him to return to Cambridge on the night of the reading, his fee must be doubled. There were, if he accepted, detailed and strict instructions as to what arrangements must be made for the reading itself. The table must be of solid construction, and so draped that his legs would not be visible. (This injunction had been adopted at the suggestion of Barrett Wendell, who maintained that to an audience, "the appearance of the bisected man is not attractive.") The lamp must give a satisfactory light, and all heating and ventilating matters must be looked after by the janitor or other custodian before the scheduled hour. If he must stay overnight, he must not be expected to appear at breakfast, and so on.

Several times he was asked to come out to Groton, where the boys became his enthusiastic admirers. On one of these occasions he wrote to the school's celebrated headmaster, the Rev. Dr. Endicott Peabody:

My dear Mr. Peabody:
I did indeed send you a letter which you never received. But all is right now. I shall be very glad, indeed, to read from the Bible on our first Friday evening, from Shakespeare on the second, and from Dickens on the third. Glad also to pass the night, as I know that I am not to be billeted on some one for breakfast.
Believe me, with kindest regards,
Yours truly,
C. T. COPELAND

In this exchange — or apparent lack of one — Dr. Peabody's comments to a friend are of interest:

My dear ——:
I have already written to your eccentric friend telling him that selections from the Bible, Shakespeare and Dickens

would be entirely acceptable to us. It was quite incidentally that I discovered that he proposed this programme,
for so far as I know, he got no farther than thinking he
would write to me. No letter of his has crossed my threshold for several months.

It seems a pity that he should stay at Groton Inn. The
one and only time that he was here, he partook of faculty
supper in a cheerful frame of mind and came down to
breakfast the next morning like a little man. We can, however, very easily keep breakfast for him when he comes
down at a late hour, or my butler, Tommy, can carry the
food to him on a silver tray. If you dare approach the gentleman with these suggestions, I shall be much obliged to
you, and still more grateful if you will let me know how
they strike him.

The late Walter S. Hinchman, one of the most celebrated
of the Groton masters, recorded in his autobiography, *The
Only Paradise*, that once when Copeland came to read at
Groton, "he stayed with us and was apparently much impressed by my wife's clear enunciation and well-placed voice
— in contrast to the slovenly speech of girls in his Radcliffe
classes. In addition, my wife had been primed as to his peculiar needs, the raw apple and the poached eggs; and as she was
going to Boston, she gave him a lift to the station and sat with
him in the train. A few days later, when Thayer Addison
saw him in Cambridge, Addison said, 'I hear you have been
reading at Groton and stayed with Hinchman.' 'No, not
Hinchman,' replied Copey; 'with Mrs. Hinchman!' Incidentally, during that reading at Groton, he remarked: 'The next
selection is rather long. Perhaps the younger boys will go to
bed. During the last piece there was a distinct *susurrus* of the
feet.' "

Another school in which Copeland gave readings was Thayer

Academy in Braintree (where one of the Copelands had lived
to be 110), and David T. Pottinger, who once taught there,
remembers having heard from Dr. William Gallagher, then
headmaster, that when Copeland's reading was warmly received by his audience, and Dr. Gallagher told him so, Copeland said wistfully, "I wish you would write all that to Mr.
Eliot." Privately, Copeland would sometimes rail at the university's failure to advance him academically, but always adding at the end: "Who am I to complain? No other university
would have me."

He brought his own brand of individuality to Harvard and
Cambridge, but it was not, and never had been, an unknown
quantity in what may with fairness be called the most individ-
ualistic of our seats of learning. In greater or less degree, this
capacity to differ from the norm has left its mark on every
Harvard graduate, and is one of the university's proudest titles
to eminence (especially now, in our age of conformity).
Emphatic individuality has never been characteristic of the
university throughout, for Harvard was never a madhouse,
but its atmosphere of individual freedom has been carried
on unfalteringly from administration to administration. Two
graduates named Emerson and Thoreau had left an indelible
mark upon it; let it not be forgotten that it was before the
Phi Beta Kappa Society in Cambridge that Emerson in August
of 1837 delivered his address on "The American Scholar," our
second Declaration of Independence, and in July of the following year, the address before the senior class of the Divinity
School which rocked even the Unitarian Church to its foundations.

3

We have noted that Copeland was not alone among the
teaching body in possessing a pronounced individuality; in

that respect he had predecessors, contemporaries and successors. But this characteristic was observable also outside the Harvard Yard. In Copeland's early years there, one of the most familiar and affectionately regarded figures in Harvard Square was that of John the Orangeman — not so named because of his Irish inheritance — "God forbid!" he undoubtedly would have said — but because he dealt in fruits and candy, with which he used to call at students' rooms, carrying a laden basket. In their junior year the class of 1901 gave him a donkey and a two-wheeled cart; his picture, with his new equipment, adorned their 25th Anniversary report. It was John who was asked by a Yard visitor what the motto "Veritas" meant, and who replied in his velvety brogue, "I don't know for sure, sir, but I think it means "Ter hell wid Yale." Also there was Poco, the old clothes man, later to be succeeded by Max Keezer; both these gentlemen came eagerly to the assistance of strapped undergraduates, who might later want to reclaim their garments, and perhaps could do so, at something more than what they had been paid for them.

A special niche in the Harvard pantheon must be reserved for "the Widow Nolen" — William W. Nolen, graduated two years after Copeland — an American genius who has remained unsung outside the annals of Harvard, "The Widow" — as he was customarily referred to — was a brilliant student of almost everything, who graduated *summa cum laude*, and taught for two years at Harvard as an assistant in biology. For many college generations he was probably the most skillful and successful "crammer" who ever undertook to enable deficient boys to pass their entrance examinations or to overcome "conditions" imposed upon them by a relentless dean. Nolen had only just begun his spectacular career when Copeland arrived in Cambridge to teach. The man had an uncanny gift for the simplification of difficult matters; he could make a proposition in geometry intelligible to a boy who could scarcely multiply seven times seven; not only that, he had studied so carefully and perceptively the examination questions asked in Harvard courses that he could unerringly drill his often desperate pupils in just those matters in history, English, physics or what not by which, without his aid, at a handsome fee, they might have been floored. There must have been hundreds, perhaps thousands of Harvard graduates who owed their admittance or their continuance in the college to his efficient ministrations. His intelligence and skill reaped him a handsome fortune, and when he died he not only left Harvard indebted to him for the existence of some afterward distinguished alumni, but enriched its library by his great collection of Lincoln books, portraits, and memorabilia. His will also established "The William Whiting Nolen Loan Fund" for the benefit of "needy, diligent and deserving students" in Harvard College, and provided for two "William Whiting Nolen Scholarships."

He was the subject of two portraits in verse, one by William Bond Wheelwright, which appeared in the *Lampoon* in January 1900, and the other in Henry Ware Eliot's *Harvard Celebrities*. The nickname, by the way, resulted from his custom of buying for his student boarders on Saturday evening of each week the first two rows of orchestra seats at one of the Boston shows. On one of these happy occasions, the leading character in the play was named the Widow Nolen, and from this coincidence the boys took their cue.

Wheelwright's verses follow:

> When Mid-Years come our joys to rout,
> Who sends the postal cards about?
> >   The Widow.
> Who gathers in the careless sport
> And other students of the sort?
> >   The Widow.

Who gives a crowded seminar
(A thing we don't explain to Pa)?
                    The Widow.
And when we get the longed-for "C,"
What man has pocketed the fee?
                    The Widow.
Stand up, ye sports who owe him most,
For, fellows, I propose a toast:
                    The Widow.

These verses produced a kindly and appreciative letter from
Nolen to Wheelwright, together with an invitation to dine
with him the next day at the University Club in Boston. One
wonders whether a similar invitation was extended to Henry
Ware Eliot, who wrote:

No observer would suppose,
From his unassuming clothes,
This to be the famous Widow whom the student
     body knows;
A man of wealth immense,
Yet lacking all pretense,
He makes the Cyclopaedia resemble thirty cents.
He can give the whole of Mill
In one concentrated pill,
Or discourse at moment's notice on the Freedom
     of the Will;
He will translate Voltaire
With the greatest *savoir faire*,
And will read Indo-Iranian and never turn a hair.
Dead or dreaming, drunk or sleeping, Nolen puts
     you through,
But gratitude takes early wing when Nolen's bill
     is due.

The Widow was a phenomenon unmatched in the history of American education when he died in 1923.

4

The Copeland legend began really to grow after he moved from Grays to Stoughton in January of 1896. There he remained until his removal to Hollis in the fall of 1904. In Stoughton he began the practice of giving readings for the boys in his entry, and also of exercising a determined and yet generous control over their behavior. The poet Witter Bynner roomed in Copeland's entry of Stoughton, and recalls that

> Copey used to walk at more or less regular intervals from our hallway entrance in Stoughton, directly next to my room, which was No. 3, and under his, which was No. 7. My great friend Arthur Franklin Johnson had the room above him, so that Copeland used to say he "lived between the devil and the deep sea." That is why, after moving to Hollis, he called upstairs a gain.
>
> He would constantly come up and knock at Arthur's door, asking for less noise, and sometimes there was the same procedure at my door. At any rate, he finally complained to the Dean, who summoned us for reprimand and told us that Mr. Copeland was more important to the university than we were. I judge that we quieted down since we were not summoned again — or perhaps it was because I dared to ask Copey what in the world he was doing night after night when he would, for hours at a time, tap on the floor endless beats in a repetitive rhythm with what sounded like a cane or the end of a poker. He used to take potions by himself and I think that he would then lapse into a

happy trance in which his pleasure was to tap these rhythms. I think he saw my point: that this sound was harder to bear than any of ours.

Bynner remembers also that although Copeland frequently showed annoyance at their late and noisy hours

our relations remained grounded in friendliness and though we were not members of his special circle of undergraduates, we were frequently bidden to his room, and almost always guests there when he entertained notables. I well remember one afternoon when he co-starred as his guests the novelist Mary Wilkins Freeman and the actress Mrs. Fiske. Most of those present gathered round the novelist, who was very popular in her day, but I clung throughout the afternoon as close as I could to Mrs. Fiske, for whom my admiration was almost idolatry. At the time of our first meeting, I think she was playing *Tess of the D'Urbervilles* — whatever it was I had seen it repeatedly and with increasing awe. Mrs. Fiske must have felt the genuineness of my fervor, since later, when I was in my room and heard her leaving through the main door just outside my own, my letter slot clicked and in dropped a bunch of violets which she had been wearing through the afternoon.

At times these boys were a thorn in Copey's side. Bynner tells of hearing him

shout at a high pitch in that resonant voice of his, "Mrs. Sauers! Mrs. Sauers!" (the name of the "goody" on his floor). The cry was repeated until both Arthur Johnson and I ran to his room just in time to enter with Mrs. Sauers and see him standing on a chair, from which he pointed to a corner of the room and cried with anguish, "Mrs. Sauers

— a mouse!" He was of course annoyed when Mrs. Sauers could not help joining us in laughter. On another occasion his summons of her was better warranted. In the little room off his main room he had a large round metal tub in which he bathed, and outside the window always hung his sponge by a string from a nail, to dry it. One day from Johnson's room above, the two of us squirted into the sponge red ink from a syringe. Copey's wail this time, from the rosy water in his bath, when all three of us assembled to answer the call, was, "Mrs. Sauers, I am bleeding to death!" He was, however, so relieved by our confession that he gave us a wry smile.

There was the day Copeland introduced Mrs. Fiske to a large audience in Sanders Theater. In his brief remarks he bestowed upon her glowing praise, to the end that when she rose to speak her first words were, "I have known Mr. Copeland many years, but I can tell you truthfully that this is the first time he has paid me a compliment." For the setting that day let me turn to Aubrey Bowser, '07, who was present.

The place [he writes] was filled with wide-eyed students awaiting their first sight of a famous actress off the stage — no mere kicker-up of a soubrette, but a real personage. In came Copey in his sand-crab suit with a hand in his pocket. Then entered the handsome, indeed the gorgeous Mrs. Fiske. The place was rather chilly, and as they seated themselves Copey began hunching and shaking his shoulders. Then in disregard of all propriety, he turned up his coat collar, folded in the lapels, and sat hugging himself. We all snickered, of course. I fancy it was that kind of antic that grated on Eliot's nerves.

The "sand-crab" suit, Mr. Bowser explains, was "what we all called it. In all my four years Copey seemed to be wearing the same suit. The cloth was of an ugly pattern — tan-colored, with small black checks. It was rumored that years before he had bought several bolts of it, and had since used it for all his suits. Surmounted by his big black derby it made him look uncomfortably like a center-field bleacherite or a race-track tout."

The boys who lived in his entry played upon his apprehensions in other ways. He lived in fear of fire, and would from time to time predict the headline which would be read one day in the Boston papers — COPEY A CRISP. This was the basis, probably, of his acute distrust of the Yard squirrels; he feared that climbing the ivy of Hollis they might, coming through an open window, swing his curtains within range of the oil lamps he preferred for lighting. Robeson Bailey recalls that he and his roommate made a practice of leaving food for the squirrels on their window sills. Another of Copeland's phobias was the raucous behavior of the plumbing in the old Yard buildings, and the likelihood of these noises distressed him particularly when he was expecting women guests. Bailey remembers being approached by him early one afternoon with one of his odd requests. "Bailey," he said, "I am being paid a most singular honor this afternoon. The glorious Minnie Maddern Fiske is having tea with me in my study." Why, thought Bailey, the old dear is going to ask me to the party. But Copeland calmly proceeded, "As you know, Bailey, the water pipes in this building make a horrid noise, especially within the walls of my study. Will you do me the kindness of guarding the washroom between four-thirty and six, and permitting no one to take a shower or use the toilet? You could take a chair and a book just inside the door, and read there." "I was so astonished," Bailey writes, "I could hardly make reply. Unfortunately I had another engagement that afternoon and could not do Copey the favor he asked. I remember telling this story to Robert Hillyer a year or two

later, and saying that I thought it a bit absurd to have to pro-
tect Mrs. Fiske's and Copey's sensitivities to quite that extent. Hillyer said to me, 'But you know, that is an echo of
another world, a world it is very hard for us to understand.
Copey and Mrs. Fiske send each other violets.' "

Meeting Copeland once in the Yard, toting a large Bible,
Witter Bynner made bold to ask him what he was doing with
it. "I am reading from it," said Copey, "to the ladies of
Malden," and when I inquired which part, he answered, "I
wanted to read from the Old Testament, but the ladies of
Malden preferred the New Testament. They have their
doubts about the God of the Old Testament — but as for me,
I think the God of the Old Testament was a corker!"

At this time Copeland had begun to give his course on the
English Letter Writers. At the first meeting of the class, as
he called out the names of those who had enrolled, he came
to the name Bell, and the boy's response was so faint that
Copeland, ever ready with an apt quotation, rolled out the
line, "Bells of elfland, faintly tinkling —" by which, Bynner
recalls, everybody was much pleased except the unfortunate
Mr. Bell. And when Harvey Hull, of Bynner's class, arrived
late for a lecture, he was greeted, "It is good of you, Mr.
Hull, to give us a little of your time." The tales of such
greetings by Copey have had long currency at Harvard and
exist in endless variations: such stories as the one which Ector
O. Munn tells on himself. He had been repeatedly late in arriving at Copey's lectures, and one day he was slithering into
his seat just after Copey had begun. When he saw the luckless Munn, he pointed a finger at him, and declaimed, "What
is your name, sir?" "Munn," replied Ector. "Munn, MUNN?
M-U-N-N?" "Yes, sir." Copey exploded: "Mr. Munn, if this
occurs once more, it will be a simple instance of *Sic transit
gloria mundi.*"

Against this tale it is pleasant to balance another. It concerns a Summer School student who was paying his way by working nights at the Associated Press office in Boston; sometimes he overslept and had difficulty in getting to Copeland's class on time. One day he arrived quite late, and was bidden to come up to the desk when the lecture was over. Copey began to rake him over the coals with chilling ferocity. "But I work nights, Mr. Copeland," he explained. "What do you do, and where?" asked Copey. The answers given, he said, "Sir" — he somewhat fancied himself as, and indeed he was, a modern-pocket-sized edition of Dr. Johnson — "Sir, this puts an entirely different face on the matter —" remembering, no doubt, his own old difficulties in meeting deadlines. "You have my permission to be late *any* time — just come in as quietly as possible. Furthermore," he added, "I have done you a grave injustice and I shall apologize publicly at the next meeting of the class." This he did, taking care, however, to warn the others that this special indulgence did not extend to them.

5

If there were those who did not take kindly to the little man's peccadilloes, and who thought him merely an exhibitionist, they might have changed their opinion had they shared the experience of A. V. Kidder:

It was late in the spring, and having been playing tennis, I wore sneakers. I mounted the three flights to the top of the staircase of Hollis and sat on the bench which Copey had put there in order that visitors could recover their breath before entering his room. He used to say, "I can't have you people coming to me puffing like grampuses." As I sat there recovering my wind, a little spike-tailed kitten came walking out of Copey's open door, through which light was beginning to show. After the cat came Copey in his old red dressing gown, with his hands behind his back. He stood looking down at the animal: "Cat," said he, "if you are of the female sex — a question not easily determined in the case of felines — and did you know the entirely unjustified opinion of my morals that is entertained by certain of the more prurient-minded wives of faculty members, you would hesitate to invade my quarters at this hour of the night." Although I was devoted to Copey, I had been (this was my sophomore year) a little ashamed of him because I felt that he showed off somewhat unnecessarily. Now I thought to myself, if he talks this way when he thinks himself entirely alone, that makes everything all right, and his showing off is as much for his own pleasure as to impress anyone else.

One or two more classroom stories: the first is told by John J. Ingle, who on one occasion reached the lecture hall at what his watch told him was the zero hour. Through a glass panel he could see that Copeland was adjusting his spectacles, preparatory to reading from a book. Ingle glanced at the proctor, who signed that it was all right for him to enter. He did, and just then, Copey, having drawn breath to start his reading, saw him, and glared at him with customary intensity. "Does not the gentleman from North Carolina," he inquired, "know that it is against the rules of this class for him to enter this room later than five minutes past the hour?" Ingle answered, "Yes, sir, I know the rules, but according to my watch it is just now five minutes past the hour."

"No doubt," exclaimed Copey, "but that is a slo-o-ow, leisurely Southern watch."

"Besides," Ingle managed to put in, "Mr. Harrison here signed to me to enter."

"Yes," Copeland countered again, "but Mr. Harrison is a ge-e-nial Southern gentleman. And" — crossing his arms over his chest and shaking himself vigorously — "*I* am a co-o-ld fro-o-zen Northerner. Don't ever again enter this classroom later than five minutes past the hour! Take your seat, sir." "I slunk into the nearest vacant seat," writes Mr. Ingle, "amid the thunder of my fellow-classmen's stomping feet."

Another very brief tale concerns three late arrivals who were stopped in their tracks by being informed from the lecture platform that "All Gaul is divided in three parts." And the last has for its setting a class in Radcliffe College, where Copeland gave duplicate courses in his later career. This was one other time that the exchange ended in the student's favor. One of the girls came in late, and fetchingly dressed. Copeland removed his spectacles, looked at her benignantly, and asked, "And how will you have your tea, Miss Blank?" "With one lump, and no *lemon*, please, Mr. Copeland."

In these days he was a frequent visitor at the home in Highland Street of his sister, Mrs. William Dunbar. One afternoon, finding the front door open, he entered unobserved, and in the hall encountered a new maid, who, flabbergasted by this strange and sudden apparition, exclaimed "Jesus!" and turned to run. "No, no, my girl," purred Copeland, "only Mrs. Dunbar's brother."

CHAPTER EIGHT

The Young Iconoclast

MRS. DUNBAR's brother was really digging in. By the turn
of the century he had assessed himself; he knew what some
of us never learn: what he could and could not do. Although
never a truly happy man, because of the areas in which his
life remained unfulfilled, he had absorbed and accepted his
limitations. He would make the most of what he had, and
what there was in him to give he would spend to the utmost
of his capacity. He would capitalize insistently on his gifts,
which were by no means meager. If he could not tread the
boards in the fashion of his hero Edwin Booth or his beloved
Mrs. Fiske, he would read better than any other living American; if he could not himself match in creative energy such literary idols of his as Scott and Dickens, he would, with his almost unerring taste and his uncanny perceptiveness, foster and
feed the talents of those who came to him for instruction.
With his deep human sympathies, he would divine the true
direction of these talents and bring them into effective func-
tioning. He would, as one of his favorite pupils, John Reed,
was to write, stimulate generations of men "to find color and
strength and beauty in books and in the world, and to express
it again."

His great opportunity came in 1905, when he took over the
writing course with which his name was to be so long associated — English 12; it had been launched in 1884 by Barrett
Wendell. This, in his hands, together with Briggs's English

5 and Baker's 47 Workshop, was to be the most productive source of creative writing at Harvard — or, for that matter, in any American college, until the establishment of such seminars as Hudson Strode's writing course at the University of Alabama, Wallace Stegner's at Stanford, Theodore Roethke's at the University of Washington, and the current occupation of the historic Boylston chair (warmed briefly by the uncorrect Copeland bottom), by Archibald MacLeish, who, incidentally, is the first non-Harvard man ever to hold that post.

Copeland began his teaching as an assistant in English A, the composition course ordinarily required of freshmen. Its distinguishing feature was the writing of a daily theme, which, for the less articulate members of any entering class, was always one of the year's most trying ordeals. In 1901, Copeland and his friend and former pupil, Henry Milner Rideout, prepared a brief text on freshman composition which created wide and enthusiastic comment, both in academic circles and in the press. It is interesting to note, at a time when there is concern over the capacity of college students to express themselves in simple and grammatical English, that there was a similar shaking of heads sixty years ago. The Copeland-Rideout volume brought forth a column and a half of editorial comment in the *New York Sun*, which at that time had the reputation of being the best-written newspaper in the country.

"A college boy," said the *Sun*, "who can write of a woman's 'noze' and 'cheaks,' of a man's 'whit and humer,' is unfortunately not a freak in any freshman class in any American university. It is incredible how such spellers can squeeze their way through the entrance examinations. That they are not remanded back to study their spelling book shows a weakness on the part of college examiners as well as a curious complacence on the part of the teachers of secondary schools." (All of which might have been written yesterday.)

The *Sun* writer went on to remark that "the daily themes

which the Harvard freshman is required to write and to present to his instructor reveal also, in general, a painful and monumental habit of inaccuracy in telling things.

Inaccuracy of expression is here the sure mark of careless seeing and sleepy thinking. A boy who had passed the high school course in English and then is able in a theme to make sentences which by their structure tell strange if involuntary untruths may charge his mendacity to his former teacher. For it is the first business of a teacher of English composition to teach a pupil to observe correctly and to record his impressions truthfully.

To go back another step, it is the leading duty of a teacher of grammar to make a pupil comprehend that the aim of grammar is to enable us to tell the truth. We suspect that the difficulty is that very few elementary and secondary teachers comprehend that themselves. If they did see this ethical side of language study, the daily grammar lessons might stride along with animated interest, and our American youth might have a bit of reverence for the words that proceed from their mouths as the responsible signs of the inner things.

The editorial closed on an optimistic note.

In contrast with the mournful childishness of a large proportion of these freshman efforts, there is a goodly number of delightful surprises. There are themes that are thoroughly creditable not only in execution, but in literary spirit; themes that show a sense of literary reality in their substance, in their concrete directness, and in their avoidance of the trite and bombastic. In these particulars every freshman of twenty-five years ago was a cheerful sinner. It is evident that good instruction is going on somewhere in our secondary schools. It is also clear that with the rising volume of universal reading, the true literary standards have become so conspicuous that the elect of our youth can now discern them very early.

In only two or three respects did such criticism of English instruction differ from our own current dissatisfaction. There was no mention of the baneful influence of officialese, that contorted and flatulent simulacrum of good writing which the so-called social scientists and the bureaucrats have foisted upon us; there was no reference to the abuse of English by frenzied writers of advertising copy and there was no need to attack the crackpots who are now shouting about the importance of social adjustment over the skill in use of mental tools, because, happily, these betrayers of our educational process had not yet come to the fore.

Praise which greatly pleased Copeland came from his elder colleagues, Briggs and Wendell, even if there were no congratulatory messages from the President's office in University Hall. "I wholly approve the way in which the work has been done," wrote Dean Briggs, who thought "it cannot fail to be suggestive to every intelligent teacher of English composition" (the concern of college teachers of English not being limited, in those days, to "creative writing"). And Wendell wrote:

My dear Copeland,

I cannot too warmly express the pleasure I have had in reading the manuscript, prepared by Rideout and you concerning the teaching of English to Freshmen at Harvard. Perhaps the simplest way for me to define this pleasure is to state the effect which your chapters, with their documentary evidence, have had on my mind.

For ten years my work at Harvard has been confined to

the upper classes. The last time I taught Freshmen, I think, was in 1888-9. Meanwhile the Freshman class has so increased, and the methods of conducting English A have so developed, that I found myself unwittingly unaware of just how the problems in question were now faced. And I may as well confess that I had a vague impression that the instructors were rather fumbling in the dark — as I was in '88.

In the first place, your book completely removes this impression, replacing it by one of admiration for the broad and sensible system which has emerged from what was once confusion. But, after all, this by itself would merely be a question of "methods" — i.e., of devices by which modern teachers so often indicate on paper plans which have the fault in practice of never coming to fruition. The real question is how the method works. This question, the second and more important, seems to me conclusively and satisfactorily answered by your documentary evidence. No one can study this without conviction that the plan you have so excellently expounded is a plan which actually succeeds in practice. . . .

It seems needless to add that, in my opinion, this work of yours would be incalculably valuable to any professional teacher whose work is with young pupils. Should you desire to use this letter as evidence of how your manuscript affects one expert, it is quite at your service.

Sincerely yours,
BARRETT WENDELL

From Professor Adams Sherman Hill, who had been Copeland's own teacher, and the founder, really, of instruction in composition at Harvard, came another accolade. "I wish," he wrote, "that every teacher of English in the country was obliged to buy and to study the pages of a work so practical and so sane."

In these years Copeland had begun to attract attention also by his informal lectures and his readings. The lectures were given chiefly in Cambridge, but occasionally in Boston also; the readings were reaching a constantly larger segment of New England, and in a few years they would extend to New York. One of his lectures had for its subject "The Art of Reading." He spoke of it as a neglected art — which it still is, although the efforts in recent years of such able practitioners as Charles Laughton and Emlyn Williams have done something to revive it, as have also the recordings by Caedmon and other record companies. "It is no credit to a person to speak well," Copeland would say, "but it is a disgrace not to." The most serious difficulty, he thought:

in the way of our reading, or speaking really well, is the fact that we are Anglo-Saxons, or rather, perhaps, Americans. In England there is a standard to which almost every one subscribes. In Scotland and Ireland this is less so, while in America there is almost an entire absence of such a standard, while France, through her Academies, is ahead of all other nations in this particular. If we are so behind, what better place is there to perfect our language and to set a standard than here at our University, where so many opportunities are offered by the English departments.

In spoken as in written English, clearness, force and elegance [Wendell's trinity] must be striven for. Breathing has much to do with clear speech and also conduces much to its forcibleness. Mechanical exercises in teaching are to be avoided. Surely reading Shakespeare's works gives abundant opportunity for the practising of all sounds, and the reading of novels helps much in giving a resonant and delicate modulation of tone. Artificiality must be strictly avoided, though it is admissible in painting, sculpture and other arts. No man reads without its having an effect on his voice; he cannot speak well without a book education, namely, reading at large.

How refreshing his own approach on the lecture platform was to prove may be gathered from a report published in the Bryn Mawr paper, *The Philistine:*

> Notwithstanding the fact that there was a sudden dullness in the air and a universal frown of disapproval, when Mr. Copeland prefaced his address with the remark that "of course he would not give at all a university lecture, but merely make a few desultory remarks," he had so charmed us all before the end of the evening that we were quite willing to believe that he had intended no slight to our scholastic pretensions, and had quite forgotten our old grievances — that another Harvard dignitary some years ago expressed the sentiment that college education for women was still a doubtful good, and hinted rather broadly that we of this nineteenth century should rather "bear those ills we have/ Than fly to those we know not of."
>
> It was very delightful, and I am sure quite a revelation to more than one to learn of what importance actors consider seemingly minute details; as, whether in *Hamlet* the pipe should be broken at a certain point, whether there should be one picture, a picture and a miniature or two miniatures. Most interestingly did Mr. Copeland show by these small technicalities in the acting of the various actors, Booth, Irving, Mounet-Sully and Beerbohm Tree, their different interpretations of the play.

When Copeland lectured on Kipling in Boston, in 1899, the *Transcript* observed that, although his addresses were announced as "lectures," "they lack the cold and polished formalism of a stated lecture, and are really delightful 'talks,' in which the audience is taken into the confidence of the speaker, and where there is apparently no more restraint than if the audience numbered a round dozen instead of between three and four hundred. The feeling of *cameraderie* adds greatly to the charm of these 'talks.' "

2

Copeland had not been content to accept his university status as merely an instructor; he had asked and received permission during his first year as a Harvard teacher, to give informal lectures on literary subjects in Sever Hall, and from the first they were crowded. Ordinarily the public was not admitted, a fact on which the *Cambridge Witness* regretfully commented in May of 1894. It further noted in sorrow that

the native modesty of the lecturer will not permit him to have any report taken or given to the public press, so that a kind of "uncut leaves" sort of mystery pervades the whole affair. Although the talks are informal, they are certainly very bright, and it would seem that an old newspaper man like Mr. Copeland should recognize the fact that there are certain inalienable rights that the public has, among them "life, liberty, and the pursuit of happiness," and to bestow the brilliancy upon a favored few Harvard men, which might illuminate and cheer the whole arid mental horizon, seems, to say the least, to be a waste of raw material. Why cannot a larger hall be secured, or, if the college authorities are implacable, why cannot the Crimson give a full and accurate report?"

Looking back today, the Cambridge paper's concern had its unconsciously humorous aspects. Young Mr. Copeland was already growing pretty sure of what he had to give, and although he was never to lack humility, he was not overburdened by an "innate sense of modesty." One can be sure that the lack of adequate reporting on his university appearances had an official and not a personal origin; as for the *Crimson*'s shortcomings as a reflector of the university scene, they were to be the subject of acidulous remarks for many college generations to come.

Copeland was attracting a good deal of attention in the Boston press, with occasional references to him elsewhere in the country. One of the Boston papers had a columnist who signed himself "Ben Quill." One day he wrote:

I dropped in at the Colonial Club, on Quincy Street, out in Cambridge, the other night. That is where the members of the Harvard faculty do congregate, and several are always to be found there in the evening. As I was sitting reading, in came "Charley" Copeland, the university lecturer, to write a note. He looked about for a pen, and found a rusty old affair, that broke about as soon as he had touched it to the paper. He threw it away and tried another, which also snapped to pieces. Then he captured a third, which was about as bad, and went on with his writing, as this pen managed, in some way unusual with Colonial Club pens, to keep together. Writing with it, though, was not easy, and good chirography was out of the question.

"It does look pretty bad," said Copeland, looking up from his note, "but it will have to do, as I can't find a better pen. In fact," he continued, musingly, "I've had trouble all my life, about pens. Do you know, I think I could have become a great writer if I could only have found a pen!"

Pens were not the only contrivances with which Copeland had trouble all his life. He always had difficulty in doing anything with his hands. He could never shave himself, and habitually went to a barber. The use of a dial telephone baffled him, and besides, he abominated the telephone itself; if he could possibly avoid speaking over it, he did so. He had none in his Harvard quarters, and sometimes he would be called by students in his entry to the wall telephone in the hall outside his rooms in Hollis. One day the call was from the president of a women's club in a Boston suburb, demanding to speak to Professor Copeland. Ben Clough, '11, who was rooming opposite Copey, answered it, knocked on his door, and was greeted with a stare. Clough delivered the message, and Copey began to close the door, looking grim. "What shall I say to her, Mr. Copeland?" asked Clough. This query appeared to astound Copey, who answered, "Why, Clough, I don't care what you say to her." A pause. Then, "Oh, tell her I'm dead. Can't you do that for an aged friend?" Clough was stricken dumb. Then, he tells, "a crafty-confidential smile crossed Copey's face. 'I know,' he said, 'you just tell her that Mr. Copeland *never* answers the telephone, because there are *germs* in the receiver.'" With that, Copey shut his door and withdrew. "I suppose," writes Mr. Clough, "I told the lady something. Whatever it was, it must have seemed exceptionally banal."

Copey never learned to use a typewriter, and writing with pen or pencil was almost an ordeal; because he held it so tightly clutched, his hand quickly became cramped, and this physical incapacity, which grew upon him, no doubt had something to do with his increasing disinclination to write, for while he dictated his correspondence to a succession of student secretaries — and his correspondence was enormous — he was so self-exacting about what he wrote, that he could never have brought himself to dictate a book.

C. H. Burgess, '31, who lived his senior year in Hollis, remembers that the locks on the doors were of the Yale type;

"when one inserted the key and turned it, he could then push the door open with the hand holding the key; it was not necessary to turn a latch in addition. Late one afternoon I had been visiting a friend, and walked past someone in a hat and coat who was standing before a door. Shortly a sound came from the figure, but I was too engrossed in my own thoughts to give heed until I heard clearly, 'Young man, will you please help me open this door?' I looked more closely; the man was Copey. In his left hand he held a half-dozen letter-size envelopes; with the right he had turned the key in the lock. I was a bit baffled by just what was expected of me, and simply pushed the door with a few ounces of force, whereupon the door swung open, and left me wondering why Copey had not given the slight push required. He then turned to me and said, 'You are a benefactor, young man, but your mind works slowly.' "

3

The Browning cult was at its height in the nineties, and flourished nowhere more devotedly than in Boston and Cambridge. The meetings of the Browning Society must have been formidable and pretty solemn occasions, if one may judge from the rebuke administered to young Mr. Copeland in the spring of 1894. In company with J. H. Hayes and A. H. Pickering, he had taken part in the reading of "Colombe's Birthday," in commemoration of Browning's own birth. The reading of these three, while receiving the thanks of the Society, apparently made a much more favorable impression upon the members than did the behavior of two of them, which produced a tempest in a very small teapot. At the next meeting of the Society, its president, the Rev. Mr. Hornbrooke, offered a formal resolution which conveyed appre-

ciation of the reading, but expressed annoyance and deep regret that any of the readers should so far forget what was
due to the other readers, the society and the occasion as to indulge in an unbecoming levity during the reading and in full
view of the audience.

According to one newspaper story:

a member who is conversant with the whole affair says of
it: "While Mr. Hayes was reading the other two, who were
not busy, talked behind their books and whispered and
commented so loudly and so palpably as to annoy the club
very distinctly. There has been a great deal of talk about
the affair about town. . . . The members of the club have
talked it all over, and you may be sure that a high pitch of
feeling was reached when Mr. Hornbrooke proposed this
definite rebuke. I doubt very much if either Mr. Pickering
or Mr. Copeland will be asked to read again."

(All this might come verbatim out of the pages of *The
Late George Apley*.)

Such displeasure was not, however, universal. In Copeland's scrapbooks another clipping was included, which read:

The Browning Society seems to be very unhappy about
something. Reprimanding gentlemen in print, or otherwise,
for what was a most natural proceeding on their parts under the circumstances, is microscopic business for followers
of a poet to be about. People not belonging to the Browning cult saw nothing strange or unseemly in the conduct of
the two readers on that memorable birthday. But perhaps
the two sinners should have had their eyes blinded by the
electric lights and refrained from considering the occasion
something brighter than a funeral. Mr. Browning is dead,
it is true, but the meetings of the society, though solemn

enough, are not wholly intended for memorial services. A word or a smile is not inconsistent even during a Browning poem. [The source of this spirited defense is not obtainable, and there are those who may reach the conclusion that its sentiments and the phrasing of them are not unlike what Mr. Copeland could have written himself.]

The subjects of the lectures given by Copeland at this time included "The Friendships of Young Men in Literature"; in this Sever Hall talk he dwelt first on the relationship between David and Jonathan, followed by a reading of the Psalmist's lament, "How are the mighty fallen." Copeland then went on to discuss the self-sacrificing affection for one another of Antonio and Bassanio in *The Merchant of Venice;* for his third instance he chose the friendship between Arthur Hallam and Tennyson. The lecture closed with some remarks about the nature of friendship in general, and the lack of it in college life — a lack which Copeland was to do his best to supply, not only by offering his own to the undergraduates, but also by unremitting efforts to bring together boys who he thought might profit from one another's companionship. He had a sharp eye for the lonely and the ill at ease, and having himself experienced their suffering, he set tirelessly and effectively about its alleviation.

His great love, the theater, was not forgotten in his choice of themes; he talked at Harvard, and elsewhere, on Edwin Booth, Mounet-Sully, Henry Irving and other eminent players in the role of Hamlet; he talked on Rostand and the French drama, and on "Recent Dramatic Productions." Also, he lectured on Dickens, and gave readings from his work, and so with the new luminary, Rudyard Kipling. The Sever Hall appearances included a series of lectures on the English novelists. Occasionally, he ventured into the historical field, but in this he confined himself to New England;

a favorite topic was the history of Concord, which gave him an opportunity to talk about Emerson, Hawthorne and Thoreau.

When, many years later, he published *The Copeland Reader*, an anthology drawn from the books from which he had publicly read, he was here and there criticized for his omission of Emerson. This was not because he undervalued him, but because, as even Emersonians must admit, the Concord seer scarcely lends himself to dramatic interpretation. Some hint of his feeling about Emerson can be had from a letter he wrote to his friend Mark Howe in November of 1898; he was then living in Stoughton 7.

Dear Mark,

These eyes saw Emerson — old and very thin, a yellow silhouette against the blackness of a stormy afternoon — at the funeral services preached over Longfellow in the College Chapel. It is much to be hoped that the poet was dead, as they buried him the same day. At the service in Longfellow's house, intercalated between sermon and commitment to that earth from which it is the Pity of Pities that any of our sad race were ever raised, Emerson — whose memory had long been crumbling — looked into the dead man's coffin and sweetly spoke these words, or words to this effect: "That gentleman was a most lovely soul, but I have entirely forgotten his name."

I first read the anecdote in Holmes's life of Emerson, in the American Men of Letters series; and, if that is not the original, I cannot help you to it. Memory is my only prompter, for your letter came but this morning, and the weary, current minute is the first I have had to myself after a day of unusually dusty and choking struggles.

If your town contains a file of the Boston Post you will find the quotation in query in a review of Holmes's book,

— toward the end of 1886, or not far beyond the beginning of 1887. As all the journals of that time dealt with it,
and as it has made the usual biennial swing round the newspaper circle, a lack of bloom would to my thought make
more against the tale than the lack of truth which you need
no longer fear.

Since this hasty sacrifice of mine, although it is ill composed and yet has into the bargain a nauseating faux air of
literature, is probably the last long letter you will ever have
from me unless your Mother dies before you do — which
may the distant gods of pity forbid! — I should think
gratitude would move you to write me at length and in
the detail that is easy to you in the writing, dear to me in
the reading. — Bassanio had once a friend, and so has Mark
Howe.

How are your eyes, and when will they look upon our
bleak Boston? Whensoever that may be, I am afraid I cannot go thither to seek you; but if you will come to the still
precints of Santayana, you will find here the sad and dull
residium of,

Sir,

Your friend and faithful servant,

C. T. Copeland

Could we but know now the result of the Election! An
ordinary majority will do us little good.

Nota Bene. It may serve you to know that Emerson —
after ghoulish age had eaten his memory — could no longer
call a spade a spade (as he had been particularly fond of
doing), but had to fall weakly back on paraphrase and talk
about "the implement with which we dig." *Horresco pro-
spiciens!* That may not be Latin, but it's me. *Scit genius,
natale comes qui temperet astrum.* That's Latin, and it's
also me.

C.T.C.

4

One of the most persistent of the legends which grew up about Copeland was that he was one of the laziest of men. It is a charge that needs examination. Throughout his life he was a procrastinator in the matter of authorship; every editor who engaged his services came to the point of desperation; always Copeland was pleading for more time, whether the manuscript was a book or an article. Indeed, the book which he talked so much of writing in his later years, and which he had promised to do for Maxwell Perkins of Scribner's, was never committed to paper. The only trace of it among his papers was part of an introduction amounting to two hundred words. The story told of him by Kenneth Macgowan, who was one of his student secretaries, is typical of his failing in this respect. Two former students had found several unpublished stories by Kipling in an Indian periodical, and asked Copeland to do an introduction. He consented, and wrote half of it, then went to New York for the Christmas holidays. There he received a wire which Macgowan had forwarded to him: "We go to press. Where is the rest of your copy?" The answer was definite and laconic: "Go to press. C.T.C."

Yet during his newspaper years Copeland turned out hundreds of thousands of well-chosen and well-ordered words, in his reviews and editorials. There were among his papers the manuscripts of seventy-four lectures. He was indefatigable in his personal correspondence; he gave generously of his time and energy in writing letters of introduction and recommendation for his boys; these became famous as his "To Whom It May Concern Letters." He was tireless in writing letters of praise whenever one of his former students published an article or a book which he thought good. In 1930, when for two years he had been retired from the Harvard faculty ("emeritus," he liked to say, "means on the shelf"), he wrote to Mark Howe: "It was no joke the other night when I said I always read as soon as I can any book that the writer has been kind enough to dedicate to me; I might have said that I try hard to buy the first book of any pupil, whether I have eyes or time to read it or not. After the first book things have to be as they may."

The records are silent as to whether his editors had their patience tried when he wrote the book on English composition with Henry Rideout, or when, in 1899, Houghton Mifflin published his *Letters of Thomas Carlyle to His Younger Sister* — a volume whose editing and introduction brought him many welcoming reviews throughout the country; but Mark Howe was to sit on the anxious seat after he had asked Copeland to contribute a volume to his *Beacon Biographies,* a series of very brief lives which Howe edited for Small, Maynard & Co. Copeland had accepted his invitation to write the life of Edwin Booth, and there were soon to be complications. In a letter marked "Confidential" and dated "14th Sunday after Trinity, 1899," he wrote to Howe from Calais:

Dear Mark,

I couldn't sleep. I had shocking trouble with my teeth — my telegram was sent just after a trip up river to the dentist and 10 hours of continuous agony — and, before I agreed with you about the Booth book, I had promised to edit "The Princess" for a Chicago house. That is why I was forced to back out of writing about Booth. I regretted the default not only out of consideration for my word, for you, and for Small; but because the loss of the money obliges me now to test your benevolence by asking you very earnestly — to lend me a hundred dollars from the first of October to the first of January, when I shall have a great deal of money from one source and another. I will of course pay interest, and you must send me an I O U to sign, so that in the event of my release from all bonds you will have an evidence of my gratitude to present to your poor but honest parents. If you love me you will let me have a consenting answer by return of post.

To go back to Booth, — the choice seemed largely to be between doing the book and going back to Cambridge with strength enough to get through another year. I feel more strongly than ever a modest confidence in being able to write the first good book that has ever been printed about an actor. Do you want it for Oct. 1, 1900, sharp? That is the earliest date for which I can promise it, but you can be pretty sure of it for then, or of learning next June that I cannot safely undertake the job. I know I can do it, however, because I have determined to get through next year with less waste of strength; because the subject will have been long a-simmering in what I please to call my mind; and because I shall have no new course in College ahead of me and no other summer task on my hands.

No one is more conscious than I of my having no rights in the matter. All that I have just been saying is by way of statement, not of unfair pleading against your judgment, or — possibly — your already matured decision. Yet candor compels me to advise you to leave the work with me, and impatience cries out to know whether you will take the advice.

I am sure you have not been hawking my dewy Hawthorne about among persons who are used to buying only literary cresses or chickweed. But please just where is it, and please just at what place might it be cut off and used (as you suggest) in that slightly abbreviated form? I cannot find any place where the lopping could be successfully done. Small should know that I have never offered my work for sale, or caused any of it to be offered. It has always been bespoke, and Page urged me from time to time for a year, to finish this very piece. Surely H. & M. couldn't have been stupid enough to put him out? Do you know Perry? I don't see how he can be either artist or critic and go on writing those stories. [The reference is to Bliss Perry, later one of Copeland's colleagues, and at this time editor of the *Atlantic*.]

I have long been meaning to write my acknowledgments to Small. You must make them for me, telling him of my pleasure and gratitude at his accepting my candidate for the Gray enterprise. Rideout is a very stellar boy indeed. — Do you think Small would like to pamphlet my Stevenson paper — H. & M. consenting — and float it on the great Stevenson wave this fall and winter? I think it would go. Sound (but do not urge) him.

Whatever you do about the Beacon Booth, be sure not to let my defect appear in whatever form of advertisement you may adopt.

I cannot hurry to the conclusion of this long and presumptuous letter — written all in bewildered haste — without expressing the grateful affection of

Your friend and servent ever,

C. T. COPELAND

On October 12th, having been urged by Howe to go on with the book on Booth, Copeland wrote to him from Stoughton Hall:

Dear Mark,

I am not a woman in these matters: midwifery will not avail. I am rather a she-ass; and, when the physiologic pang and moment come, I drop my ass's colt without a prayer to Lucina, and without her aid.

To leave this asininity, I have been ill for a week with influenza and horrible peristaltic revolutions. This is one of the unexpected things. Another, far more important, is that a box containing all my marked books and other preparations for my new course — lectures twice a week — has not turned up, though it left Calais on the 19th of last month. Thus I live frenziedly from hand to mouth, and from Tuesday to Thursday [the days of his lectures].

It looks, nevertheless, as if I might give you the rest of the Ms. by next Tuesday. *But don't set* the day of my arrival until you have it in your hand. I gave you this identical warning two weeks ago today, and I told you last June that I would gladly say — as you well suggested — "the first of September or *never*."

You did a wrong as well as a foolish thing (forgetting your knowledge of me and of Thackeray's experience *in re* Mrs. Gaskell and the Cornhill Magazine) — an unkind as well as a wrong and foolish thing, in allowing the publishers to announce the Life of Booth as "out," when it is still bubbling under my lid like the Cratchits' potatoes on Christmas Day. You owe it to me to set me right with Small & Maynard.

If I seem procacious, it is only because I would not write as I feel. I am sorry for you and sorry for myself. Sick and sad, and egg-full of worry. "My operant powers their functions leave to do." If only my bowels would take such leave! Do yours feel no compassion?

Orderly to end as I began, I invite you to re-read my first paragraph, and to send me a thistle but no more forceps. A thistle send, or a letter, or a prickly pair of them, or any pot-herb calculated to promote delivery, or a special-delivery stamp.

Dear Mark, let this experience turn you from an orthodox churchman into a probalist; and believe nothing of me except that — in spite of phenomena — I am

Your faithful friend
C. T. COPELAND

By November 12th, when Copeland wrote again, the book was in proof:

Dear Mark,

I am helpless, but if it were ever to happen again I should contract against these atrocious methods.

Please look with especial care to the German episode and to the place about seeing Booth in Park Street. I marked out the word *young* with great determination.

I telegraphed to you an hour ago to take out the word *interesting* in the first line or two of the preface.

Although I had not intended the copy of the fragment for print — indeed I still marvel that they didn't use the original in facsimile — I probably transcribed it with the accuracy which is one of my many tiresome and irritating traits. But here, to make sure, is the fragment itself. Fail not to return it as soon as you have corrected the proof.

I bewail my inhospitality at each of your visits. When you come again you shall have something to drink if not something to eat. I forgot each time until you were gone.

C. T. C.

Nota bene. There must, I suppose, be introductory words to the fragment. If you write them they will be fit, but I am not so sure they will be few. All such formalities should be brief, and melodious brevity means an agony of labor. Whatever you do, don't let Maynard write it. I seem to see him writing it.

The thought of the whole dreary little mosaic makes me stomach-sick, even if each piece is set right. And when I think of what your printers have done, my heart beats a two-step in fear of what they may do.

Adsit Lucina!
Vale!
C. T. C.

If I didn't leave out that fool phrase about Booth's house having the only garden in Chestnut Street, *it must be left out.* Call it simply a house in Chestnut Street. It is toward the end — about A.D. 1884.

Copeland's *Edwin Booth* received an excellent press; and the little book, which ran to about 25,000 words in pocket-size format, was indeed, a model of brief and understanding biography, and still remains one of the best accounts of the great actor's life. Based on the already published sources, it made no claim to original research, but it was informed by insight and illuminated by Copeland's passion for the theater and his sharp critical sense. It brought him, in addition to admiring reviews, some letters which he greatly prized. William James wrote to him,

Dear Copeland,
Such has been my press of reading this winter that it has taken till now for me to 'get round' to your Edwin Booth. I am perfectly charmed by it. I don't know what could be more agreeable in tone — you love the hero, yet you are such a veracious discriminator and describer, that there is no impression whatever of the book being sympathetic. Then such humor, and such capital characterization. You ought to write more. I have only read 2 vols. in that series, the other one being Wister's Grant — a good mate for yours. If others are as distinguished in the same way, it will be a wonderful set of booklets. Thank you for it! Yours always truly,

W. M. JAMES

Except for the Copeland *Reader*, and the Copeland *Translations*, it was, unfortunately, to be his last book. Yet it is evident from the *Booth*, and from many of the lectures, that he had the equipment to become an outstanding biographer. That he did not was the result of several causes. His procrastination was one; his manual difficulty in writing was another; a third was his habitual lack of excess energy; and the last was his growing absorption in the art of teaching. When, finally, his dwindling physical resources forced him into retirement at sixty-eight, although Harvard would gladly have had him continue, mental deterioration gradually set in, and during his eighties, took on a swifter pace. Those who met him only as a very old man were sometimes disappointed in that feeble and dim materialization of the legend they had heard; and this, no doubt, was the case when Ernest Hemingway, whose genius Copeland was one of the first to recognize, was brought to see him by Waldo Pierce and Archibald MacLeish, for Hemingway was later unable even to recall the incident. Whether the fact that the trio, before mounting the stairs of Hollis, had been watching a Harvard-Dartmouth football game with the aid of a bottle of bourbon had anything to do with the absence of the anticipated mental fireworks is matter for serious doubt in the case of three such musketeers. It is far more likely that either the old gentleman was in an ornery mood or that he and Hemingway circled each other like two dogs who find one another mutually unsatisfactory.

By the time his *Edwin Booth* was published, the Copeland legend was firmly established; he was the outstanding personality of the Harvard teaching staff. Though he had discontinued his voluntary lectures in 1896, he was now giving official courses in the fields of his special interest — such subjects as the lives and times of English men of letters, Dr. Johnson and his circle, and the English letter writers; his readings were by now a Harvard institution, and he had begun the famous "evenings," when, if on a Monday or Wednesday (the day was changed from time to time) the lights shone from his study in Hollis Hall, undergraduates were welcome to come and warm themselves by his cannel-coal fire, listen to Copey talk or read, or be themselves prodded into general conversation. Often there was a celebrity from the theater or from the writing world to add luster to the warmth. Many a boy was to treasure those evenings as among the most profitable he had spent as an undergraduate.

CHAPTER NINE

Copeland the Catalyst, I

IT IS difficult to determine wherein Copeland made his greatest contribution to the needs of youth. The ways were various, and they were, especially at the time he began to make them, almost unique. At Harvard he had one peer when his influence was first felt; this was Dean Briggs, perhaps the most universally loved officer of instruction and government that Harvard has ever had; later these two were reinforced by the arrival of Bliss Perry, who after a term at Princeton and another as editor of the *Atlantic*, made himself admired and loved by generations of Harvard men; his addresses to a long succession of freshmen will never be forgotten by those who heard them, for he was one of the best speakers, in college or out, of his time, and as warm in his human sympathies as Copeland and Briggs.

Beyond the bounds of Cambridge, Copeland's foremost rival was William Lyon Phelps, "Billy" Phelps of Yale. He was five years Copeland's junior. Certain qualities they had in common: a great capacity for friendship, keen understanding of the young, the capacity to awaken enthusiasm for books and what they have to give. Both men left their mark upon many lives. But their differences were as marked as their similarities. Phelps had abounding health and energy; he was a complete extrovert; he loved traveling about, and was a prodigious "mixer" — a sort of academic Rotarian. His literary enthusiasms far outran his critical discrimination, and in this he differed much from Copeland, who seldom fell for the shoddy and the second-rate. But Phelps too, in New Haven, like Copeland in Cambridge, rapidly became a legend, and both men could count their friends, among young and old, in thousands — true friends, not the magnified acquaintances of back-slapping politicians. Both were well-read men, yet neither was a great scholar; their contribution to the life of the mind was primarily a human one — a kind increasingly infrequent in the academic world of today. There are two stories worth telling about them in their relations toward one another.

When, in 1939, Phelps published his *Autobiography with Letters*, I reviewed it in the *New York Times*. In that article Phelps was linked with Copeland, as they have been here. Both men wrote to me, and their letters reflect their personalities. Phelps wrote: "I do not think you can realize what you have done for me in your review. The book — like its author — is such an easy mark for satire or irony, that your deeply sympathetic and completely *understanding* review of the man & book will give me pleasure every day for the rest of my life, and I need it right now. I shall never forget you or your article."

Copeland's letter was no less revealing. It read in part:

I thank you heartily and from my heart for the splendid paragraph you gave me in the admirable Phelps review. . . . As to me — and this is a private line — I didn't make my customary revival after the terrible summer, and went along fairly well until February, which was very bad for me, March still worse, and April is now helping me to recover. When I told Dr. Breed that my legs felt weak, he said that I must force myself to walk, and that has turned out well enough.

Let me have a line from you, and tell me what you thought of my prophecy concerning the Brandeis and Frankfurter appointments. No more now, but thanks again from

Your oldest friend,
C. T. C.

But it is the handwritten postscript which says most: "I can't possibly vie with Phelps. Why do I try?" He was thinking, no doubt, Why can't I get on with my autobiography, which I have promised to write? His life had been more vicariously lived than Phelps's, but could he see, one wonders, that its impact had been even greater? It was one of those moments of self-distrust which come even to men who have accomplished much.

Beside these letters must be placed a story told by a former student, Alfred Putnam: "I knew Billy Phelps very well during the last ten years of his life. He was everything that the most enthusiastic Eli ever said about him. Once at dinner party of about eighteen, at the house of my parents-in-law, perhaps a little flushed with wine, I was moved to make a little speech about Billy. The guests had not expected anybody to make a speech, and they were rather startled when I arose. But I loved Billy and I said so, and I laid it on with a trowel. I concluded by saying that he was the Copeland of Yale. Billy cried. He said it was the greatest compliment he had ever had."

As a public reader, and as a lecturer on literary subjects, Copeland awoke in thousands of undergraduates their first appreciation of good writing; he was for many of these, and others too, a guide, a counselor and friend during their years in college and afterward — one who determined the course of many a career. In these ways he fed the needs of youth in a measure given to few men. This chapter, however, is concerned chiefly with his remarkable success as a teacher of writing. The phrase is an unfortunate one, since the art of writing cannot truly be taught; the words serve merely as a rough designation of the function performed by him in his writing course, the celebrated English 12. Writing can be taught only up to a certain point, beyond which the pupil must be able to carry himself — a limitation which holds for instruction in any art. The teacher can, as Copeland tirelessly did, inculcate certain basic principles and help his pupil in the avoidance of various pitfalls; he can, as Copeland often did, discern the type of writing which his pupil is best equipped by natural endowment to do; he can help him also to develop more strongly those qualities in which he is weak. Yet essentially every writer must in the end seek his own salvation, precisely as there is a point beyond which the psychiatrist cannot carry his patient; when he has made clear to him wherein his difficulty lies, the patient must take over and remold himself in the light which the psychiatrist has provided for him. Copeland was fully aware of this limitation upon the measure of his assistance, great though his help sometimes was. Thus he was once moved to disclaim all credit for Edward Sheldon's success as a playwright. The story is told in the biography of Sheldon by Eric W. Barnes, who wrote in *The Man Who Lived Twice:*

What Ned did possess were unusual powers of observation and a deeply intuitive nature. The combination produced something which to both his teachers and his fellow students seemed very like wisdom. Years after he had left Harvard, this was still remembered. In the late thirties, someone spoke to Copeland of Ned's enduring affection for his old professor. The dim eyes grew misty and Copey murmured, "Dear Ned! I never taught him anything — he knew better than any of us."

Before describing in more detail Copeland's methods as a teacher of writing, something should be said about that aspect of his teaching (aside from the public readings) by which he was known to most undergraduates. His writing course was, as such courses must be, strictly limited in its enrollment. There were never more than thirty students who gained admittance in any one year to English 12. Any larger number, because of Copeland's reliance upon private conferences in addition to class meetings, would have been impracticable — indeed, impossible. But the enrollment in his lecture courses on English literature was unlimited, and frequently there were as many as 250 men taking such courses as Dr. Johnson and His Circle, Scott, The English Letter Writers, or that very popular course which he abandoned in later years, covering the Romantic period and dealing especially with Wordsworth, Byron, Scott, Shelley and Keats. These were the chief figures to which he gave his attention during the first half year; the second was concerned largely with Tennyson and Browning.

The lectures for these courses were very carefully prepared. The manuscripts for scores of them were found among his papers; they were dictated to his numerous student secretaries, and while rather informal in style, reveal wide knowledge of the social backgrounds of these writers, as well as an acute appreciation of their several qualities. Above all, they were presented to his audiences as human personalities, not, like the writers dissected in our contemporary esoteric quarterlies — and, I fear, in too many college classes — as inanimate writing machines who somehow wrote novels or poems which provide a happy hunting ground for amateur psychoanalysts and myth and symbol hunters.

Naturally, Copeland was pleased at the mounting popularity of these lecture courses, and he was zealous in guarding against any falling off of the esteem in which they were held. Once he entrusted the preparation of an examination paper to one of his assistants, who put together such a tough one that the casualties struck terror to Copeland's heart. "My God," he exclaimed when he examined the results, "what have you done? Nobody will ever take one of my courses again."

Though he courted popularity, he was unwilling to do so at the expense of gaining the reputation of being a dispenser of "snap courses." This concern caused him, in the academic year 1905-6, to go on a flunking spree which became known among the student body as "the year of slaughter." It is vividly remembered by Aubrey Bowser, '07, who in his junior year was enrolled in the first half of the course on the Romantic period. "Copey," he recalls, "had become disgusted with mark-hounds. There is nothing unethical in a man wanting good marks, but when he chooses his courses primarily with regard to the instructor's severity or leniency in marking, it smacks of shysterism. . . . At the beginning of 'the year of slaughter' I heard that some fellows had told Copey they'd like to take his course, but first wanted to know how he was marking that year. He replied witheringly, 'Hard! damned hard!' He told us all in the course that his examination would be 'just but searching.' And it was. . . .

"Before I knew of the holocaust, I innocently went to to see Copey with my C+ blue book and asked him if he didn't think I should have a B. He stared at me as if I were someone just escaped from an insane asylum. 'What?' he rasped. 'You ask for a B, when the three highest marks were B minus, given to graduate men who need them for the master's degree? Suppose you leave your blue book with me, to be re-examined and given whatever mark I *then* think it is worth. If not,' and he waved his arms — 'go and breathe the fresh air!' "

The course was numbered English 8A, and that year Copey flunked more than half the men out of an enrollment of 162. Too many degrees were endangered, and pressure was brought to bear from University Hall. Copey revised his markings, and the official count stood at three B's, 59 C's, and 14 E's. Eight men were absent, and received no mark.

2

To call the roll of those who studied — and practiced writing — under Copeland is to name a remarkable number of men who later achieved distinction of one kind or another. It would be difficult, if not impossible, to verify the statement unimpeachably, but it is much to be doubted that any comparable list could be compiled from the class rosters of any other teacher of writing, either at Harvard or elsewhere. A possible exception would be in the case of Dean Briggs, and even that would be hard to substantiate, because many students who took Briggs's English 5 took Copeland's English 12 as well.

Copeland's students in his writing course included, in roughly chronological order, the following: Henry Milner Rideout, Father John La Farge, Earl Derr Biggers, Van Wyck Brooks, Henry Goddard Leach, Maxwell Evarts Perkins, Hans Kaltenborn, Edward Sheldon, Lee Simonson, Conrad Aiken, Norman Foerster, Wilson Follett, Edward Eyre Hunt, Joseph B. Husband, Haniel Long, Waldo Peirce, Heywood Broun, Edward M. Dodd, Jr., T. S. Eliot, William Maxwell Evarts, Kenneth Macgowan, Harford Powel, Jr., John Reed, Wheeler Sammons, Frederick L. Allen, Alan Gregg, Gardner Harding, Walter Lippmann, Hoffman Nickerson, Robert Benchley, Herbert J. Seligmann, Harold Edmond Stearns, Roger Burlingame, J. Donald Adams, Charles P. Curtis, Cyril Beverly Harris, Nicholas Roosevelt, Alanson B. Skinner, Kermit Roosevelt, Sydney Geoffrey Biddle, Grover Cleveland Loud, Irving Pichel, George Seldes, Gilbert Seldes, Laurance B. Siegfried, Richard Dana Skinner, Winslow Wilson, S. N.

Behrman, John Dos Passos, Herman Riddle Page, John Gallishaw, Robert Littell, Archibald Roosevelt, Samuel T. Williamson, Brooks Atkinson, Joseph Auslander, Malcolm Cowley, Bernard DeVoto, Gustav Eckstein, Stanley M. Rinehart, Lawrence E. Spivak, Stanley Kunitz, B. A. Botkin, Granville Hicks, Thomas S. Lamont, Oliver La Farge, Garrett Mattingly, W. L. White, Edmund Gilligan, Corliss Lamont, Frederick R. Rinehart, Robert Sherwood, and Walter D. Edmonds.

Some of these names will be recognized as having achieved eminence in other fields than writing. Several of these men became publishers: Maxwell Perkins (who was to publish Copeland's *Reader* and *Translations*, and hope, despairingly, to publish his memoirs), Wilson Follett, Edward M. Dodd, Jr., Wheeler Sammons, Stanley M. Rinehart, Frederick R. Rinehart and Lawrence E. Spivak. Two became painters, Waldo Peirce and Winslow Wilson. Edward Eyre Hunt abandoned a promising literary career for administrative work, Kenneth Macgowan and Irving Pichel became identified with the theater and with motion pictures; Charles P. Curtis distinguished himself in the law, and also as co-editor with Ferris Greenslet of that unique and stimulating anthology, *The Practical Cogitator*. Some became known as editors: Harford Powel, Frederick L. Allen, and Robert Littell. Sydney Biddle found himself as a psychiatrist, Laurance B. Siegfried as an authority on printing; Herman Riddle Page became a bishop.

There were students at Harvard during the years of Copeland's teaching who later distinguished themselves in literature, but who did not take his writing course, and some of these did not take Dean Briggs's either. One of them was James Gould Cozzens, whose first novel was published while he was still an undergraduate. "When I was at college," writes the author of *By Love Possessed*, "I had the much mistaken idea that I already knew how to write and did not need Professor Copeland's course, so I never took it." Neither did John Mason Brown, though he attended one of Copeland's lecture courses. John Marquand had intended to study writing under Copeland, but in the year he was admitted to English 12 (1913-14), Copeland was given leave of absence, and the course was conducted by Professor Woodbridge. It was difficult for Copey to believe that a writer as famous as Marquand had gone through college without benefit of his instruction; indeed, he refused to admit the omission publicly, and whenever the author of *The Late George Apley* was a guest at one of his evenings, Copey would proudly claim him as a former pupil — an assertion which Marquand never would contradict.

On the other hand, Copeland might confound you by an unexpected compliment implying that you had been in no need of instruction from him. William E. Spaulding, now President of Houghton Mifflin Company, several years after his graduation from Harvard was walking up Brattle Street in Cambridge with his wife, a former Radcliffe student, when they met Copeland, who had set forth on one of his afternoon rambles to Fresh Pond. Mrs. Spaulding introduced her husband, who in answer to a question said, "I think not" — an expression which Copey always insisted on instead of "I don't think so." Typically, Copey then assumed that he was talking to one of his former pupils, but when Spaulding denied having studied with him, Copey magnanimously observed, "You didn't need to," and continued on his walk.

Copeland's demands upon his writing students varied over the years. When I took English 12, in my junior year, 1911-12, we were free to write about anything we pleased. At other times there was a definite routine: one week a short story was called for, another an essay, another a book review, and so on. But there was one standing requirement; a brief piece of translation, from whatever language the student might choose, was expected to accompany each piece of original work. He used to say of French, "that language without which no man can be said to be truly educated." Incidentally, I have ever afterward been baffled by the fact that during the year I took the course I never once submitted for Copey's criticism a poem or a short story, although I was contributing both to *The Harvard Monthly*. What I gave him were essays, chiefly, I think, pieces of literary criticism. And I definitely recall that he allowed me to submit, for the final weeks of the course, a long essay I had written in competition for the Bowdoin Prize (which it did not receive) on Whitman's indebtedness to Emerson.

It may also be noted that during his first years of teaching, when he was an instructor in the freshman writing course, English A, he made it clear to those enrolled in his section that two subjects were tabu in the daily themes — the squirrels in the Yard, which were one of his pet aversions — and what he described as "the female element." This latter ruling led some of his students to set him down mistakenly as a woman-hater. As Mr. Bowser observes, "I actually thought he lived a womanless life, and it puzzled me. I could understand such an attitude in a scientist, economist, philosopher or mathematician, but not in a man who taught the humanities. How could a man love poetry and not love women?"

The most famous of Copeland's students is T. S. Eliot, who took English 12 in his junior year (1908-09), signing his themes "Thomas Eliot." He was one of the minority who were not *simpatico* with their instructor.

I did indeed [writes the Nobel Prize winner] take the famous course called English 12 under Copeland's direction, but alas I was not one of his real following and I never really hit it off with him. I don't really think, to be quite candid, that the course was very profitable to me. I say this with regret because I know that so many men have found it of very great value. He was certainly a strange and interesting figure, but I have racked my brains in vain to think of anything that I could offer of value. I think the difficulty was that I could not learn to write English according to the methods by which Copeland taught it.

A similar incompatibility is spoken of by other men whose names have figured prominently in the world of letters — among them Conrad Aiken, Van Wyck Brooks, Gilbert Seldes, and John Dos Passos.

I'm very glad to hear [wrote Mr. Aiken] that Copey is to be as it were put on record. But I'm afraid I haven't much to offer. By a mistake, due to my own ignorance of the rules, I took English 12 in my freshman year — handed in a poem, and was passed into the class before Copey knew that I wasn't eligible: he decided to say nothing to the authorities, and allowed me to stay. I found him stimulating, but to be candid I never could really take to him; the vanity, and the insistence on adulation, was too much for me. I tried: on one occasion when, years after college, I had come back to Cambridge and met him in the Yard, I asked him if I mightn't call one evening when he was NOT surrounded by the usual chorus of sycophants, i.e., alone, and he named a day; but sure enough when I reported that evening it was to find his room jammed with people, and my books laid out to be read from. I refused to read and never went to see him again.

In my opinion, Dean Briggs was a far greater teacher — I took his English 5 for two years; it was wonderful — and he was of course a greater man. But as a performer, mime, entertainer, self-projecting *character*, Copey was in-

COPELAND THE CATALYST, I

imitable. And his wit could be deadly. At the end of the year, at our final conference, he asked me if I considered I had benefited by his course. Partly out of an excessive shyness, but also partly because I resented his fishing for a compliment, I replied that it had had the virtue of compelling me to "write regularly." To which his rejoinder was, "Aiken, you're a very dry young man." It was some years before I understood what he meant!

John Dos Passos has testified that "our attitude was one of armed neutrality. We were very polite to each other but we didn't agree very well. He was certainly an influence on a great many generations of Harvard men." A similar antipathy has been expressed by Gilbert Seldes. Van Wyck Brooks has recorded his reactions to Copeland's teaching in his *Scenes and Portraits: Memories of Childhood and Youth:*

Years later, it seems to me that of all my Harvard teachers I had probably learned most from Irving Babbitt, much as he repelled me and little as I liked his curiously inhuman brand of humanism. With everyone else who aspired to write I had my course with "Copey" but somehow never hit it off with him, unlike Max Perkins, his publisher later and his favourite at the time who was to bring him a wide audience with *The Copeland Reader.* I was "wilful and stubborn," Copey said, and the reason for this was that I did not wish to write in the manner that pleased him, although I could not have said just why, and possibly did not learn why, until I fell in with J. B. Yeats. This true-bred artist and man of letters scarcely saw a line I wrote, but he constantly talked of the writers of the so-called Irish Renaissance so many of whom had grown up in his studio and presence. He had educated some of these in his informal fashion, and he liked least the traits that Copey praised. Not emphasis, or the striking phrase, or Kipling's kind of vividness but the opposite of these, for him, betokened good writing — Anatole France's *pas d'emphase,* vividness without effect and the phrase that is not striking but that haunts the mind. With these went the virtue of staying at home in one's imagination instead of going out and "seeing life," for he cared for the inner eye as he despised reporting; while Copey, who was an old newspaperman and Boston theatre critic, prepared his pupils of journalism by admiring just this. "I would never have seen what I did had it not been for your teaching me," said John Reed, dedicating *Insurgent Mexico* to him, and one saw in *The Copeland Reader,* by his omissions and choices alike, what most appealed to Copey in American writing. He included selections from Heywood Broun, Richard Harding Davis, Alexander Woollcott, O. Henry and R. C. Benchley — entirely omitting Emerson, as he omitted Howells — and his idols were the great journalist writers, especially Defoe. A lover of histrionic effects as well as good reporting, he had written a life of Edwin Booth, and, an actor himself as a public reader, he liked young men who were actors too, particularly when they were very good-looking. Copey, in fact, loved every kind of gallantry, the kind above all that is visible in the figure and the face, the most understandable of all tastes but one that tends to create a bond with the extrovert rather than the introvert mind of the writer.

It is true that Copeland greatly admired good journalism, that he was insistent in his teaching on the selection of the telling detail, and on the placing of emphasis, but surely good journalism can be good writing, and surely the qualities he strove to implant in his students are components of it. And, curiously, Mr. Brooks overlooks the fact that one of Copeland's criteria for choosing the selections for his *Reader* was their suitability for reading aloud; he included, indeed, nothing which had not met this test.

What we have here, of course, is a conflict of attitudes. It is possible, as Sean O'Faolain once demonstrated, to make out a case for the contention that Defoe's long-run influence upon English fiction was a baneful one, and one might do the same for French fiction in the case of Balzac, as Willa Cather, in her plea for the novel *démeublé*, once argued. One can contend, as the present writer often has, that American fiction has suffered by reason of too great reliance merely on the national skill in reporting; yet one can find, even in so great an artist as Tolstoy, elements contributing to his effectiveness which have their counterparts in good reporting. Creative literature is a house of many mansions, and can it not be said that in the greatest representations of human life, there are employed both the outer and the inner qualities to which Mr. Brooks refers? Surely Copeland was aware of the necessity for this ambivalence, or he could not have been as good a critic as he was. By natural inclination, however, he was attracted to the concrete and to the dramatic — and always by the spell which is cast by skilled narration.

The poet Stanley Kunitz recalls that when he took English 12, "I was much involved then in a world of private fantasy, and my stories were written in a high-flown style with which Copey could have had little sympathy. As I look back now, I see how patient he was with me when I resisted his efforts to pull me down to earth. My pride was hurt by his criticism; but just when I was prepared to yield to utter dejection, he would permit himself to cluck approvingly at the appropriate places in my manuscript. 'Write out of what you know,' is the admonition that sticks in my mind. We were not easy with each other in these intimate conferences — some of my classmates were much closer to him — but in the end he gave me an 'A' with his blessing and with a gift to boot, *The Art of Thought,* by Graham Wallas. The volume, in which he inscribed an unexpected compliment, is still in my possession. Perhaps I owe a greater debt to a less famous teacher, Robert Gay, of Simmons College, who (if memory serves me right) substituted for Copey the following year, with the title of visiting professor. It was he who returned a manuscript of mine one day with the written comment, 'You are a poet — why don't you write poems?' I did thereafter." It would seem, on the whole, from the available evidence, that Copey's teaching was likely to be more effective in the case of the natural prose writers than with those students whose true bent was poetry.

We have seen that there were some of Copeland's students, and among them men who were to become writers of great distinction, who were put off by him, and who felt that they derived little or nothing of value from his instruction. It is not improbable that some of them, at least, got more than they realized, or were willing to admit. I think this was true even in the case of his most renowned pupil.

3

The future winner of the Nobel Prize for Literature was twenty when he was admitted to Copeland's writing course, in September 1908. Then a junior, he had come to Harvard in the fall of 1906, after a year at Milton Academy. His earlier schooling had been at Smith Academy in St. Louis, where he was born. It would seem profitable to examine in some detail one of the pieces of writing submitted by Eliot in Copeland's course, together with the criticism it drew from his instructor. The essay available for this purpose was one written by Eliot in March, 1909, and its subject was "The Defects of Kipling." Interesting though the essay is in the light of Eliot's subsequent development into the most influential literary critic of his period, one regrets that it did not concern itself with Kipling as a poet as well as a writer of fiction, in view of Eliot's espousal, many years later, of Kipling's mastery in the field of verse writing — for Eliot was careful to distinguish that field from the adjacent one of poetry.

> As the novelty of certain innovations dies away [wrote Eliot], as the school of literature of which Mr. Kipling is the most illustrious representative, the exotic school, passes with all its blemishes exaggerated more and more into the hands of less able practitioners, so Kipling's fame is fading, and his unique charm is diminished. [Opposite these words Copeland had the young Eliot write, "A mouth-filling sentence."] He himself has made little effort to increase his reputation in his own special province of literature, the Anglo-Indian Orient, and in his late writings has turned to other subjects. This may well be the part of wisdom. For the popularity of his work was due not more to his emphatic and vigorous style, his unquestioned technical merits, than to the unfamiliarity and picturesqueness of his background. Now that a score of writers can boast of an acquaintance with the Equator, we are no longer so entranced by the Kiplingesque as we were when cobras had first learned to talk, and bears to bring up small boys "by hand." We are at ease with the Oogly; the China Sea, even with the Khyber Pass. [Alongside this entire first paragraph and page, Eliot was instructed to write down: "A harsh statement with some elements of truth."]

Eliot's essay proceeded to point out that local color, particularly when applied to exotic places, is "a dangerous literary tool," likely to cause the writer to emphasize background at the expense of characterization and narrative power. But he did not deny that truth and strangeness of locale are a possible combination and pointed to Stevenson's "Ebb-Tide" as a successful example.

After all [wrote Eliot], there is one fatal weakness penetrating and marring almost everything to which Kipling sets his hand; accounting for several of the minor blemishes; it is his restless and straining immaturity. Nothing is so pathetic in literature as the immaturity which the practiced brain cannot shake off, nor the practiced hand conceal. Always more anxious for the appearance of life than for life itself, the appearance of truth more than truth, Mr. Kipling has maintained the pose of a man of the world, a pose of the young and egotistic. He has seen everything and done everything. The discursive observer of life, the cosmopolitan like Kipling, often misconsiders that intimacy with sailors, barmen, whores, stokers, thieves, all people of squalid and strange professions — he thinks that such acquaintance gives one a knowledge of life. To the properly equipped it will. Most men will gain from such observation only delight in superficial phenomena, the bizarre and the brutal. In the "Light that Failed" and in "Kim," as in many of the shorter stories, there are characters and events which are bizarre and brutal. *Mr. Kipling was always more anxious to be striking than to be convincing.* [Here Copeland interrupted with, "Don't you suppose that he expects to convince by being striking?"]

So, even in the earlier work, the middle-class society tales of which I spoke one cannot feel perfect confidence, and *nowhere am I sure that Kipling is solicitous for accuracy.* And if these cynical Simla stories are not trustworthy, their only excuse is that they are always interesting, and always effective. [Here Copeland directed Eliot to write, "Youthful rashness is not likely to be one of your attributes, at least till you are middle-aged."]

Some critics [continued Eliot] have said that the giving interest to the commonplace constitutes Kipling's greatest merit. But to make the commonplace interesting in a legitimate way, needs insight. When Kipling tries, he distorts it. I have often heard that the British soldier of Kipling is not in the least like reality, and I have heard from the lips of Gloucester longshoremen that *Captains Courageous* is quite incorrect, the product of three weeks lounging about the wharves. The true masters of realism conquer it by grasping the vital fact, searching the soul of it for truth and beauty. There Kipling fails.

Mr. Kipling can do much; his bellbuoys and artillery discourse eloquently, and his animals are up to almost anything. He roams from Greenland to the South Seas in search of effects — always finding them, moreover. One of his most effective tools is the supernatural. The lurid horror and grimy setting of "The End of the Passage" make one of the most striking tales of fear that I have ever read; the hideousness of tropical heat has never been more vividly expressed. Yet when one halts after reading, to analyze the causes of the vivid emotions which one has felt, it is found that the whole effect is due to certain nightmares, the impression of which is adroitly intensified by vague allusions. The story is a masterpiece of workmanship. Still, it no longer affects me as at first.

In conclusion, Eliot observed:

Perhaps the best thing which Kipling has done, least marred by the faults upon which I have insisted is that Indian idyll called "Without Benefit of Clergy." More sincere, I think, more restrained and tender, less ambitious than most of his tales, it does not expose that lack of taste, the result of immaturity, which has always been a fatal defect. No tremendous impression is intended; yet there *exists in any language no more touching* idyll of illicit love with such ingenuous simplicity. ["Don't write so!" barked Copeland at this point.] The characters are natural; the background is not overdone. The story of an Englishman drawn more and more out of his normal life by a liaison entered into thoughtlessly and lightly, then broken by death as if it had not been, and all the delight and all the desolation of it to be concealed from the world in which he moved and worked — it is very poignant and very true, and will live, I think, when the rest is forgotten, or preserved chiefly for curiosity and technical instruction.

In looking back over what I have just written, I feel that I have (probably) overestimated the faults of Kipling's work, in the effort to bring them clearly forward; that is because I consider them vital defects, which have never been sufficiently emphasized. Hidden among Kipling's many volumes there are unpretentious stories which do not show these faults; *Muhammed Din*, for example, a charming picture of childhood. But, in the general impression of Kipling, do not the faults outweigh the virtues?

Copeland's general comment on the theme was as follows:

As usual you lean to the unduly harsh. Your opinion of Kipling's faults would carry more weight if you could appreciate without any niggling qualifications such masterpieces as the "End of the Passage," the "Incarnation of Krishna Mulvaney" and best of all perhaps, "The Man Who Would Be King."

Kipling is no favorite of mine — I am a pianola that often resents the music it plays — [and this statement will surprise, as it has Mr. Eliot, encountering it so many years later, all those who listened spellbound to Copeland's repeated readings of Kipling's stories and verse] — but we should all be heartily grateful for the mere vital energy of this immature middle-aged man in a feeble era of literature.

Although it is a great pleasure to see that you can at last swing a long sentence, swing several, each growing out of the one before, you must now be on your guard against becoming pompous, orotund, and voluminous.

Incidentally, it is interesting to note that the piece of translation students were required to submit with each original theme was in Eliot's case a rendering into English of a poem by Mallarmé, by whom his own writing of poetry was to be much influenced.

Two things must be at once readily apparent to the reader of Eliot's youthful essay and the comments made by his instructor: first, that in this young man the faculty of critical perception was already highly developed, and that in spite of Copeland's strictures, there was no little sound sense in some of his observations. As a piece of undergraduate writing — especially in the field of criticism — it was much above the average level; secondly, that very little escaped the listener who issued his cautions and his objections from the depths of his armchair in Hollis. They were specific and they were broad, and they were penetrating in their psychological appraisal. Of this episode Mr. Eliot has written me: "I am not very much impressed by my own essay which is, as Copeland remarked, unduly harsh. But, of course, it must be said that a large part of the work for which I admire Kipling was still unwritten at the date of this essay. My own handwriting at that age seems to me surprisingly good, indeed very much better than my ideas. It is also rather odd to find that my handwriting at that period looks so similar to that of Mr.

Copeland himself." (It had slipped Mr. Eliot's mind, evidently, that Copey's criticisms were always dictated and written down in his presence by the student.)

Nevertheless, the essay itself and the criticism of it do much to point up underlying differences between Eliot as he then was and the older man who was trying to guide him. The one underestimated, perhaps, the value of raw experience to the writer, just as the other — in the case of some of his students — placed too great an emphasis upon it. And this divergence, one suspects, had more than a little to do with Eliot's feeling that Copeland was not the teacher for him; the same would hold true, probably, for Van Wyck Brooks and others whose developing attitudes and capacities ran counter to those of their instructor.

CHAPTER TEN

Copeland the Catalyst, II

IN CONTRAST to the reactions of these men, one must record a majority vote of indebtedness by other writers who took the training provided by English 12, nor were they all, or even most of them, men whose writing mark was made in journalism. Their tributes to Copeland were fervent, even though, in some instances, their gratitude was tempered with hot resentment at the process to which they had to submit themselves. This was true, for example, of Bernard DeVoto. The boy who was to write with love and passion of the American West often left his conferences with Copey seething with anger. He gave a detailed account of his reactions in the Copey 75th Birthday Issue of the *Harvard Crimson:*

A good many of the qualities that shaped Copey's teaching can be named. But when I try naming them I realize that the axioms of an alien science can betray one and that Copey is much more than the sum of his parts. One quality struck you at once, the moment you presented yourself for the first ordeal. I write "ordeal," and yet that does him an injury. It was an ordeal to me from the first time I sat facing a pair of baleful, even demonic spectacles and began to read, or stumble through, twenty pages of a young cub's fiction. I knew that it was dreadful stuff and yet, as young cubs must, I hotly believed in it and just

as hotly desired to engage his belief. And every two weeks
I addressed a man whose morose discomfort was silent and
even courteous for a while but soon began to find expression in sighs and finally in groans from which all courtesy
was gone. I do not know whether Copey ever actually
wept over those stories; I do know that when I finished
reading them he contrived to look as if they had bored him
beyond the solace of tears. He would drift for a moment
in that depression and then, rousing himself, would dictate
a comment on the theme which was acute and lethal —
and all the more insulting because one must write it on the
back of one's own work. Then he would be enchanting,
bowing me out with paternal tenderness as if to imply that
he bore me no grudge for writing like a fool. It goes without saying that I left with murder in my heart. But there
was more than murder: there was a seething resolution to
write, before I murdered him, just one set of twenty pages
which would show the beggar that he was wrong. . . .
Some years later I realized that this was the purpose behind
those embellished groans — that, at his first glimpse of me,
Copey had divined the best way to make me write.

I put this divination first of all his qualities. It was part
histrionism, part intuition and part black magic. Somehow, by way of his nerve-ends or his pores, he knew at
once the way to make a student do his best. If these conferences, with my voice creaking through sceptical silence
or more awful sighing, were ordeals for me, there were
others who emerged from interviews with my oppressor
heartened and led on. The timid man who distrusted the
faint stirrings of his talent, the man who shrank from un-
kindness and would have withered under brutality, met a
Copey altogether different from the one who had just committed mayhem on my stories. The roars were, when that
way was best, the roars of any sucking dove. A smile at

the right place, a chuckle, a wave of an eloquent and singularly graceful hand — and Copey had suggested that, though certainly this particular theme fell short of genius, it had its moments and those moments might be a lead to something better, and more carefully written, next time. I cannot without a shudder think of the millions of words he listened to, with an interest and a hope that never flagged. Hundreds of students: I doubt that he ever used the same approach with any two of them.

Next there was a fine honesty. He had too deep a reverence for the art of writing to encourage the dull and the hopeless, to praise bad work however well-intentioned, or to tolerate the mischievous superficiality and mere cleverness that are the worst vices of college writers. Praise came rarely to his lips: it was a rare thing and it meant that for a moment the young writer had found some beauty of phrase or had fixed some vivid realization of life. Life was what he wanted — the thing seen or heard, the thing felt, the experience of living men. He would rail at us from his desk in Emerson with the rhapsodic speech of Amos or Ezekiel. Look, the world was all around us and we ourselves were tumultuous with emotions begotten in it — why, then, did we persist in turning in to him pallid little violets from our reading?

The same honesty withheld him from promising us success. Few of us would ever write well, and those who did must serve an apprenticeship much longer and more painful than he could make clear. He prophesied achievement for none of us — he never told a man, I believe, that he would be a writer. Men frantic with the ambitions and terrors of the young besought that comforting, too easy assurance. He did not give it. The way was hard, the promise deceitful, the flesh weak, and the issue uncertain. Copey shook his head and was silent. That refusal was a hard fact and a bitter tonic. It suggested something of the sternness, the discipline and the labor of the task to which, it might be, one was too lightly dedicated.

Again there was his insistence on the highest possible standard of self-criticism. You could not fool him: he forbade you to fool yourself. Whatever was shoddy or pretentious, whatever emotion was faked, whatever phrasing came from a devout appreciation of purple — he came down on like a hawk. His richest periods were provoked by the merely literary, and for the poses and affectations of precious talents uncontaminated by good sense he had a corrosive malice that ate away insincerity by handfuls.

There was, too, his love of literature. The English masterpieces were his Church: he has gathered his Scripture in *The Copeland Reader*. He tirelessly read them to us, and tirelessly discussed their power, magic and beauty. Out of that love he gave us something intangible that could show itself only as it altered or confirmed one's whole attitude toward writing. He kept us in the presence of masterpieces and commanded us to walk humbly there.

But it is idle to analyze Copey. He is, I have said, much greater than the sum of his parts. He taught the art of writing: he did so by a unique mastery of the art of teaching. We hear a good deal these days about "personal" teaching. I doubt that Copey ever used the phrase. There was no tutorial system in those days, no rationale of bringing the students in touch with presumably inspiring minds, and now that we have both there are no more Copeys. He had no thought of method and statistics when he came, with a feigned reluctance, up the path to Emerson Hall, or when, at 10 P.M. on Monday evenings, Hollis 15 opened to a rush of youngsters in no way ignorant of their privileges. He was merely a man born with a genius for making himself felt — for translating into terms young men could understand the wisdom and expectation that were himself. That is great teaching and a fine art.

The experience of Oliver La Farge as a student under Copey closely paralleled that of DeVoto. "You can't teach a man to write," he has said, "any more than you can teach him to paint."

He has to have it in himself and teach himself. Writing is an art, as lawless and as completely subject to laws as any other; most academicians approach it as a craft, and thereby waste the time and money of innumerable young men, most of whom will never be writers. Copey is the great exception; he ran, not so much a class as an *atelier*, where aspirants worked along their own lines and offered the results to him for the same criticism, made coherent and intelligible, which later they must take from their audience, from the grotesque combination of editors, publishers, copy readers and public which, whether they like it or not, will judge their work.

To call it the same criticism is hardly adequate. He used the same hardness, absoluteness, lack of sympathy, which the writer must later encounter, and which no writer can, no friends or relatives will, give him in judgment. But beyond that he brought the gifts which are his own, and which I, for one, am not going to describe.

My year of Copey was one long feud, the causes of which I do not yet understand fully, though some of it has become clear since. How to reconcile almost daily battle with steadily increasing affection? I was a Sophomore. A Sophomore is a juvenile delinquent who thinks he's half Robin Hood, half Kosciuzko and wholly mature. Jejune opinion mistrusted the irregularity of a class conducted by a man who realized that the lecture as such was grotesquely out of place in teaching an art, and who turned the fixed hour into a session of conversational fireworks, letting the work be carried on where it should be done, the privacy of one's desk and the criticisms up next to heaven.

Because fame drew to the class, yearly, a certain number of masochists who waggled their tails every time Copey excoriated them, one mistook him to be susceptible to bootlicking. By the end of the year one saw that this was not so.

But a Sophomore irreconcilable could get off on the wrong foot. For good and sufficient reason Copey put me alone in the middle of the front row, so I developed a set of small, nervous habits calculated to be irritating, interrupting in effect. I walked out of his class, with Bill Fitzgerald and another whose name I forget, to signify disapproval of his behavior. I was thrown out of his room at one conference, for telling him he hadn't acted like a gentleman. We sent him lilacs, with intent to annoy, and were thanked in class in such manner that we squirmed. But he always fought fair, and by and by it dawned upon whatever set of infantile reactions we used then instead of minds, that this amazing man enjoyed the fighting, liked us for it, and despised the masochists.

Like the sense of richness when one has just won twenty dollars on the Yale game, long college years stretched out ahead of us, to be spent. And in the same manner, were gone before even our plans for using them were perfected. Perspective was just beginning. In another four years I might have got the full of what Harvard was good for. But it was all over then, and with it, Copey out of reach became apparent as a much desired friend, a more than fortunate experience.

But I am trying to sort out in my mind, to write down, what my Copey was. I say "my Copey," because like any major phenomenon of life, each individual must see him

subjectively. Out of the symposium of many such perceptions may evolve the absolute; I believe that this qualifica-
tion is true even for his expression of himself. As far as I
am concerned, I have since then talked about him often,
for in the strangest and remotest places people will question
me, even by campfires and behind mountains. I could extract from memory detail upon detail, sift the perceptions
of a former state of being through my present self, and
still fail. There has been a great deal written about him,
there will be much more. Harvard today handles him,
self-consciously, as a legend in the flesh. Perhaps the Boswell he desires and should have will appear to do the job —
perhaps. But as for the rest of us, if we have any sense we'll
realize that it's a bit too big for us, too complex, too inti-
mately tied in to the processes of our growth and transition.

2

In that same 75th Birthday Issue of the *Crimson* (April 27,
1935), Walter Lippmann wrote:

Nearly thirty years ago when I first came to college, the
cult of Copey was already firmly established. It is more
vigorous today than it ever was, and to the devotees now
scattered throughout all the communities of Harvard men,
his seventy-fifth birthday provides a most convenient excuse for a celebration.

What the uproar will seem like to those who have never
come within the circle I do not know. To convey to them
the quality of the devotion which his pupils feel is like trying to explain to one who never heard him the spell which
Garrick cast upon his audience. For the Copey of his pupils is not to be found in works of art, in books that anyone
may read, in contributions to knowledge which all can

share. He is a teacher who has drawn out of a long succession of pupils whatever native gifts they had for writing in
the English language and of appreciating what has been
written in English. That is his magic. The conviction that
but for their luck in having known him, they would be
more deaf and more dumb than they are, that in truth he
has helped them to live, is the reason why he is the object of
a cult in which there is such fervor, such affection and such
gratitude.

The method of his teaching, as it lives in my own memory, seems to me to have been more like a catch-as-catch-
can wrestling match than like ordinary instruction. What
happened was that you were summoned to his chambers
in Hollis and told to bring with you your manuscript.
You were told how to read what you had written. Soon
you began to feel that out of the darkness all around you
long fingers were searching through the layers of fat and
fluff to find your bones and muscles underneath. You could
fight back but eventually he stripped you to your essential
self. Then he cuffed the battered remains and challenged
them into their own authentic activity.

If this description of Copey's teaching sounds a little
mad, all I can say is that by the conventional rules it was
mad, as genius is so often mad. But in these personal bouts,
which were his substitute for pedagogy, miracles were occasionally performed that have placed him among the
very great teachers of our time.

He is inimitable. And yet, if I understand the new system which has revolutionized the method of instruction
since I was at Harvard, Copey was one of its pioneers.
Thirty years ago he was already acting on the assumption
that teaching is not the handing down of knowledge from a
platform to an anonymous mass of note-takers, but that it
is the personal encounter of two individuals. Those appall-

ing clinches in Hollis, those dreaded exposures in the classroom, the searching intimacy from which all protection was removed, were in fact a continuing demonstration against mass instruction and the regimentation of learning. Copey was not a professor teaching a crowd in a classroom. He was a very distinct person in a unique relationship with each individual who interested him.

And so his reputation grows continually greater, nourished by the gratitude of his pupils and the admiring recognition of his peers. He was already a legendary figure when he was young. He will be a legendary figure when he is old. For the legend expresses a realization by Harvard men that they have among them an incomparable teacher.

Heywood Broun was one of the Copeland idolaters; it was through his enthusiasm that Alexander Woollcott was introduced to Copey, became himself a disciple, and an honorary member (as a Hamilton graduate) of the Charles Townsend Copeland Alumni Association. In *Collier's* of May 10, 1924, Broun wrote:

But there was another man at Harvard in my time, and he's there now and ever will be, I rather imagine, who did most of all to fire the imaginations of the youngsters. Hart [Professor Albert Bushnell Hart] had just one good performance, but C. T. Copeland played repertoire. He lectured on Doctor Johnson and he taught English composition, and you could go to his room and sit in front of a fire and listen a good deal and talk a little. Copeland has said fifty things that I remember, but more important than that, I carried away the feeling and touch of an enthusiastic personality.

He made us know that writing is honorable and alive. Hundreds of men left Cambridge and Harvard eager to sit down and write the great American novel. None of them has done it yet, but they feel, after knowing him, that about the most important thing anybody could do in the world would be to create something fine in words. After fifteen years of newspaper work, I still think it would be.

In his "It Seems to Me" column in *The World* for February 25, 1922, writing of Copeland's reactions when listening to his students' themes, he observed that "American literature would be much more sentimental than it is if it were not for the persuasive quality of Copeland's moaning."

Back in 1909 the members of the class invariably wrote sad poems about the ocean and things like that. They said that it was going to go on and on and they would not, and Copeland had to grumble like a heavy swell on a rockbound coast to get them out of it. All the stories ended with suicide and sudden madness and grisly, mocking laughter, but nobody could make it strong enough to stand up against the mocking noises of Copeland. By the end of the year several persons in each class would be writing readily about things which they knew, and many a jaded junior decided to give life another trial before firmly committing himself to an attitude.

Broun stood in awe of Copeland long after he became famous as a newspaper columnist, and Alexander Woollcott remembered how Broun would shift uneasily from foot to foot in Copeland's presence, if by chance his former teacher took him to task about something he had written. One day, on a visit to Boston, he made an unexpected call on his old professor. He was met at the door of Hollis 15 with "Go away, Heywood, I can't see you now. Come back at seven punct." And Broun, that lumbering, genial bear of a man, stumbled down the stairs of Hollis, having muttered, "All right, Copey," forgetting that he had to make the five o'clock train to New York. But when he did remember, he knew he'd have to climb those stairs again at "seven punct." And did.

Walter D. Edmonds, another writer in whose accomplishment Copey took great pride, and his last star pupil, said this:

What makes Copey a great reader, but an even greater teacher, is his understanding of language as a living force. The purpose of writing is to set down truthfully one's meaning; and style, therefore, is not a manufactured process, the manipulation of words for their own sake, but the organization of ideas. A writer cannot "create a style" any more than he can create himself, but he can train himself to think, and if he hopes to succeed, he must.

That is not only the key to writing, but the key to all phases of civilized living. Moreover to make the student aware of the fact is the purpose of all teaching, not merely that this word derives from middle Gothic, or that those two chemicals if married will produce explosion. If Copey had lived in the days of Elisha, he would have been set down in the Bible as a prophet.

But if that had been so, we should not now have Copey to read the Bible to us as no minister I have ever sat beneath knows how to read it.

Perhaps this seems a simple point to make so much of. But there are certain simplicities that are worth remembering. That so many of Copey's pupils each year in April will cross half a continent (or whole continent for all I know) to attend his birthday dinner in New York, would seem to be proof that they have remembered this with profit and affection.

You might ask what this has to do with Copey's reading. It has everything to do with it. For his prime purpose is always to get at exactly what the author had in his mind. I have often thought that all his apparent nonsense of eliminating draughts and hushing coughs and stilling creaks was for the purpose of bringing his audience's attention inside the room and so to what he had read. Certainly when three or four are gathered in his room, these preliminaries have no place; and he reads directly, eliminating himself, letting the English flow. I have always had a clearer consciousness of the writer, from hearing Copey read a page from his work, than from a year's course with any other man. It is significant that his finest reading is from great literature. He brings no artificial graces to the work; when none are needed, his reading is an experience which is unforgettable.

I wonder how many persons have noticed his hands upon the book after he has begun to read. They treat it almost contemptuously. The center of his consciousness is so completely fixed upon the writer's utterance of thought that he has no awareness of paper, thread, and cloth. The small, erect figure seems to fade; there is only his voice and what it says.

3

Dean Briggs once wrote of Copeland's manner of teaching that it

would wreck a man without his peculiar gifts. Much of his criticism is delivered orally in his own room to students who go to him, one by one, and read their themes aloud. So far the method, except for the hours which a single student consumes, looks easy, but to read a theme for the first time under these conditions, to give it criticism, both offhand and searching, phrased with consummate literary finish, and unforgettable — to do this, theme after theme and year after year, implies a power and a training that are acquired by few. Combined with this critical skill and constantly ministering to its success, are skill in dispensing a hospitality generous, well regulated, and as characteristic as the teaching itself, or rather, a characteristic part of the teaching. He has hundreds of disciples who, as long as they live, will look back with affection to the spacious yet cosy rooms at the top of Hollis Hall and to their presiding genius. I doubt whether a single one of these pupils could succeed with his method. It is, rather:

> . . . . the brand
> which none but he can wield.

How well all his students remember those hours they spent alone with him — the silences on Copey's part, the sudden cries of anguish, the writhings in his chair, the snorts of disgust, sometimes even, the feigned snoring — and rarely, oh how rarely, the sudden and delighted smile! And the interruptions while you read: "Write, 'What a swag-bellied sentence!'" or, "Write, 'March of the elephants!'" Write, 'What a jaw-breaker!'" Or, perhaps, a single word — 'Pish!'"

It was difficult, sometimes, because of Copey's highly individual methods, for a student to determine just where he stood with him. Listen to Roger Burlingame:

One afternoon during a January thaw I wandered away from the Yard toward the river, doubting whether there was much left to live for. It was already dark and there was mud everywhere, most of all in my mind. I was more bewildered and desperate, I think, than I ever was before or since, for that is the time of life when despair, even over small matters, seizes you the hardest. When I got to the river, I thought how pleasant it would be to drift away until I drowned; and I took some comfort in brooding over the effort they would make, come morning, to drag the Charles for my body.

It was my junior year. The year before I had switched from engineering to literature — a considerable switch. My father, who was an editor, had persuaded me to try not to be a writer. He had seen enough of writers' troubles. Well, it hadn't worked; the engineering professor had invented a mark for me — F — in calculus. Father had conceded and this third year I had plunged into reading and writing with all my heart. Now writing had licked me too. Just this afternoon it had licked me. What now? The river? It looked very cold.

I was startled out of the ecstasy of my misery by a voice.

"For God's sake, Roger, what's the matter with you?"

It was my closest friend. We all had "closest friends" in college — people you confessed to, borrowed money from or lent it to; they usually disappeared later and you forgot who they were.

"Oh hell, nothing," I answered, but I knew that wouldn't do. "O.K., if you've got to know. Copey just kicked me out of his course."

"Kicked you?"

"Yes. Never mind what he said. Well, what he said was, 'Come to see me, if you like, as a friend. But never again as a pupil.' That is precisely what he said."

I was shocked at the sudden delight in my friend's face.

"So you think it's funny," I said.

"Funny! It's terrific! It's wonderful! I wish it had happened to me! Copey is polite to me. Very polite! He al-

ways calls me 'Mister.' My God, man, you ought to cele-
brate! You should have a drink! Come somewhere where
it's warm and drink to your great future career!"

In the warm place he took me to, he talked — a mono-
logue, for I was paralyzed out of speech.

"You haven't been kicked out, you poor fool. You've
been paid the greatest compliment Copey ever gave. It's
because he thinks you've got something. I'll bet he doesn't
call you 'Mister' or say 'Please' and 'Thank you' as he does
to some of us. Go back and pretend you didn't hear him.
That's what he expects — what he wants. Do what I say!
My God! what a chance!"

In unbelief I went back. But Copey said nothing about
the devastating incident. Copey's course was an intimate
one. In his study you read your themes aloud to him. He
would pretend to sleep — he even snored — through the
dull passages. But suddenly he would jump out of his chair
and swear at you. "You'll never be a writer," he would
shout at me. "Never! Unless — which is unlikely . . ."
and so forth. Again, he fired me, but, as I thought I remembered afterward, with something vaguely like a twin-
kle, and again I came back. And all this time, he was telling my friend how 'pleasant' his themes were.

Well, he gave me an A at the end — scolding me and
warning me as he told me. It took me years to figure it
out, years of knowing Copey as a beloved friend and
knowing the pain of writing. And then I was certain that
the really valuable thing his course had given me — for
no writing course ever teaches writing — was discipline.
And discipline is the thing writers need most. The capacity for taking criticism — the most pitiless attack on his
precious words — is the quality that most sharply dis-
tinguishes the professional from the amateur.

That dark January afternoon was forty-five years ago.

But I still remember it as giving me the most useful hours in all my four years at Harvard.

Once when Malcolm Cowley was reading Copey a piece he had written about his boyhood in Pennsylvania, and had described the swirling dust in a downtown Pittsburgh street, Cowley remembers how "he dictated slowly, without unfolding his hands, 'Don't you remember the smell of dried horse dung? Why didn't you put that in?' And once when I read him a sententious article written for the Advocate, in which one wondered how the country knew who . . . he shook his head and groaned, 'Malcolm, when are you going to stop using those knew-whoings and one-wonderings?' I stopped that afternoon. He may have been referring to the same theme when, in a scathing voice, he said, 'It's good enough for a New Republic editorial. B-minus.' Did he guess where I was going to wind up?"

The playwright S. N. Behrman, another Copeland alumnus, recalls how "Some years after I left Harvard, in Hollywood I met, at Montague Glass's, Earl Derr Biggers. He was an alumnus of English 12 too; I asked him whether reading themes to Copey had been the ordeal for him that it had been for me. 'Ordeal!' he exclaimed, and even then mopped his brow. 'I brought Copey a story once,' he told me, 'a triangle story; I thought I had invented the surprising situation in which a man is in love with the wife of his friend. In the first few sentences Copey fell elaborately asleep, and those great whistling snores filled the room. I struggled on until I reached my great and unprecedented climax: the wife was in the lover's arms, and her husband made a tactless entrance. "Immediately," I read, "he understood." This flash of percipience on the part of the husband was so dazzling that it woke Copey up. "What a brain!" he said.'

"The reading ended right there, and so, Biggers felt, his

Silhouette of
Reuben Lowell, grandfather of
Charles Townsend Copeland

Sarah Lowell, grandmother of Charles Townsend Copeland

Henry Clay Copeland,
father of
Charles Townsend Copeland

Sarah Lowell Copeland,
mother of Charles Townsend Copeland

Charles Townsend Copeland,
aged four

Charles Townsend
Copeland
at twenty-two

Caricature of Copeland in *Harvard Celebrities*.
Drawn by Edward Revere Little. *Harvard Alumni Bulletin*

Charles Townsend Copeland,
after an unfinished portrait by William James

Copeland's Study in Hollis 15

Hollis Hall. *Harvard University News Office*

Charles Townsend Copeland at seventy, from a photograph
by Richard Carver Wood. *Courtesy of Charles F. Dunbar*

career as a writer of fiction. He turned then to philosophy, and next time brought in an abstruse essay on aesthetics. At the end of the first paragraph Copey said: 'Biggers, where do you get your hair cut?' Earl was so startled that he answered literally, 'Brattle Street.' 'You should try the one on Harvard Square,' said Copey. 'Much better there.' This experience drove Biggers back to fiction."

4

Brooks Atkinson, dramatic critic of the *New York Times*, and now the dean of that particular writing fraternity, was not only one of Copeland's students, but also served a term as one of his student secretaries.

Copey [he writes] was certainly the most effective teacher of English composition in my experience, and the only one who took an exacting interest in details. He had the most profound influence on me. To this day — forty years after I studied with him — I imagine that I adhere to some of his maxims. For instance, the use of the periodic sentence: he explained its value and also cautioned me against over-using it. He explained to me the value of carrying over one thought into a new paragraph, and thus pulling together the whole structure of an article. 'Good old A,' he used to say acidly, or 'Good old The,' when I began several sentences with those colorless words. He was death on over-use of the definite or indefinite article. He was also alert to the exact meaning of words.

In 1916-17 his ideal of journalistic writing was the Frank Cobb editorial page in The World. He admired it for its terseness, clarity and force. I naturally accepted his judgment, and I think his judgment was sound. Although

I was interested in writing long before I joined Copey's course, he was the only man I ever knew who made the use of words an exciting adventure.

W. L. White, the son of William Allen White, who not only continues to publish and edit the paper made famous by his father but has in addition, beginning with his war book *They Were Expendable*, made a literary reputation of his own, has told how he applied for admission to English 12 through the urgings of Robert Benchley and Frederick L. Allen. He was one of the men who took Copey's course for two years. "Of the myriads who hold classes and write books purporting to teach writing," said Mr. White, "he was the only one who taught me anything."

I remember the course as a routine of two weeks of brilliant classroom vaudeville — for he was a lovely ham actor — punctuated by two hours of sweating hell: these being the periods when by appointment you went to his rooms in the evening and read aloud to him your offering.

I remember when, in the middle of a windy, descriptive passage I had written, stopping completely whatever narrative I had contrived for the occasion — he said: "Come to Hecuba!"

There was then the excruciatingly painful disclosure that I didn't know what Hecuba was: had to have it beaten into my skull that this was a quotation from *Hamlet* in which the Prince was railing at the players to get on with their little show — and out of it all I learned not only *Hamlet*, but also something of the art of literary contrivance; learned that you cannot stop the story to fiddle about with some descriptive conceit at the point where you have built the reader up to wanting to get on with the tale.

His great force as a teacher lay in his ability to give you, as a groping writer, the irritation of the average reader when he is bored, puzzled, or confused by what you do. Suddenly as a writer you were face to face with your audience as an actor is at every performance. The actor on the stage knows that he has lost the attention of the theater when they begin to cough and shuffle their feet. The writer, lacking this guide, spins words endlessly. What Copey did was to supply "audience-reaction" without which the young writer can whirl in a vacuum, never knowing why his stuff is neither bought nor read. . . . Of all the men under whom I studied at Harvard he is the only one that I ever would have cared to meet again.

Ben Lucien Burman was one of the many to whom Copey showed his many-faceted and sometimes deeply contradictory nature. He writes in recollection:

To me he was always a great contradiction. He could be either extremely kind or caustic and sardonic. My first meeting with him showed his kindly side. I came to Harvard very anxious to enter his course, and met him at his rooms in the Yard. At this meeting I did something I never did in my life before or afterward. I became hysterical. I suppose it was one of those silly things that we do in our adolescence, probably caused by my over-anxiety to be admitted into his course. I started a sort of hysterical laughing and couldn't stop. He might have been extremely cruel, but on the contrary he was very tactful and understanding, and after I eventually quieted down and apologized, said that it didn't matter at all. I was certain that as a result my chances of becoming one of his students were finished. I was overjoyed a few days later, when the class list was posted and I saw my name there and knew that he had not allowed my silly action to prejudice him against me. I can't remember any other occasion when he showed anything like the same kindliness toward me, though on several occasions he told me that I was one of his favorite pupils.

I saw the evidence of his sardonic side in one of my early conferences with him. I had just written a story of which I was very proud, and began reading it aloud to him, certain that it would move him greatly. In the midst of what I considered a tense emotional scene, he took out an old shoe and began studying it intently. My story reached its climax. I paused, greatly moved by the power of my own writing, and looked up at Copey, certain that he would be similarly stirred.

He pried at the sole of the shoe with a screwdriver. "Do you think this shoe is worth taking to the cobbler?" he asked. "Or would it be better if I threw it away?"

I think that one of the proudest times of my life was on the occasion when he was good enough to be enthusiastic about a Southern story I had written and asked me to read it before the class, praising it publicly. My reverence for his critical ability was such that I don't believe any experience I've had ever surpassed that hour.

I think his great contribution, so far as I was concerned, was in making me write so that my characters became visible, tangible people. He kept saying to me constantly, "I can't see this man. Let me see him — let me see him." If I have achieved any of this quality in my work I owe Copey an enormous debt.

In the estimation of Nicholas Roosevelt, who was to distinguish himself in writing on public affairs (and currently, in his retirement, on cookery), part of Copeland's greatness as a teacher came from the fact that "he made each of us feel that he had a very special interest and confidence in each of us; there was enough of the feminine in him for him to want each individual to feel that Copey valued him just a little more than anyone else."

After these forty-seven years, which have brought me in contact with all manner of people, I still look back on

Copey as the only really great teacher that I have known. Other men with whom I have been thrown had as good an intellect, or better. Many made a greater mark in a worldly sense. But Copey was what 999 out of a thousand professors are not — a teacher of rare skill and sensitivity. The French distinguish between the two words (I am using them in their French sense) *éducation* and *instruction.* The latter may be translated as the process of pumping facts and theories into the individual. The former, translated, means the drawing out, the development, the fertilizing of the mental processes. This was Copey's greatest gift. He was relatively indifferent to what interested his pupils, but whatever this was, he sought to encourage and to foster the interest, to appraise its value, and to induce the student to pursue it to its conclusion. I don't think I learned much from Copey about composition. But I was spurred by him to read, to appraise, to weigh, and to enjoy, good writing by others. Furthermore, he encouraged me to place things in perspective, and to detect interrelationships. I was probably rather more intolerant, prejudiced, narrow, snobbish and ignorant than most of my fellow-pupils in English 12. It was largely thanks to him that I began early to get over these sophomoric attitudes. Furthermore, his own example as a teacher gave me a standard by which to judge not only other teachers, but other sources of intellectual guidance.

5

Although, as Nicholas Roosevelt observed, Copey could practice, when he wished, the art of making each individual feel that he was of particular interest, he did have his favorites. One of them, in whom he was to take special pride when the young man began his meteoric rise in journalism, but whose political affiliations he was soon to deplore, was John Reed, one of the heroes of the Bolshevik revolution. Reed was a complex personality. He came to Harvard in 1906 from Portland, Oregon, where his father was a United States Marshal. As a boy, and through his brief manhood — he died in Russia of typhus at thirty-three — he was marked by great vitality, great love of life, and of experience for experience's sake. As an undergraduate, his interests spilled over in various directions. He was an athlete, a poet, a cheerleader, an organizer, something of a roisterer, and somewhat oddly, in view of his subsequent career as a radical, a socially ambitious boy who zealously, but with little success, stormed the citadels of social preferment. As ardent in his discipleship to Copey as in everything to which he attached himself, he not only won the affection of his admiring teacher; he pleased him enormously by his writing. It was good, and became better; the articles he wrote from Mexico when he rode with Pancho Villa were notably vivid reporting; so too, was his firsthand account of the Bolshevik revolution, in *Ten Days That Shook the World*.

Copey followed his career with delighted interest. Partly this came from satisfaction in seeing a youngster put so fervently into practice his teacher's precepts about seeing and living things for oneself; he was the more fascinated because Reed's headlong and passionate activity was alien to Copeland's own temperament, much as he admired it in others. Reed was almost a pure romantic; his teacher, although, as Van Wyck Brooks remarked, he "loved every form of gallantry," was basically *l'homme rationale*, after the fashion of those eighteenth century figures in whom he delighted. At times, one imagines, he fancied himself as a kind of twentieth century Samuel Johnson.

During his senior year, writing in the *Lampoon*, Reed addressed the following verses to Copeland:

Chamber'd Nautilus of Hollis,
　　When you'd play the lover's part,
Do you find sufficient solace
　　For your heart?

Don't your acolytes distress you,
　　In their circle Johnsonese?
Vying which shall cry "God bless you!"
　　When you sneeze?

Does your fancy scorn the Present
　　When your chorus leaves at last?
Do you flirt with ladies pleasant
　　From the Past?

In your chamber, dim and lonely,
　　Swept by each November gale,
Is there none to love you, only
　　Mrs. Thrale?

Does the shade of Fanny Kemble
　　Share your waking dreams tonight?
Copey — prithee don't dissemble —
　　Is it right?

Show some living maid your pity,
　　Make her happy past her hope;
Here's her health — the lovely, witty
　　Mrs. Cope!

For several years after Reed's graduation in 1910 they carried on an animated correspondence, and whenever Reed
came to Cambridge, with tales to tell of his newest adventures, whether he had been crossing to Europe on a cattle
boat, observing the strike in the Paterson silk mills, or watching trouble brew in the Balkans, Copeland was sure to corral
him as the guest of honor at one of his evenings, for the edifi-

cation of the undergraduates who crowded into Hollis 15 and squatted on the floor. Shortly after graduation, Reed had joined the staff of the *American Magazine* in New York, where, naturally, he was showered with unsolicited contributions from hopeful students who had taken, or were enrolled in English 12. And Reed, ever eager to spread the fame of his teacher, planned to include him in the magazine's Department of Interesting People (forerunner of the *New Yorker* profiles and *The Reader's Digest*'s "Unforgettable Characters").

Copeland wired him in July 1911 from the Algonquin Hotel in St. Andrews: "Much pleased you think me worthy article in Department of Interesting People stress doubtless on function as teacher not on so-called wit and humor stop Don't use snapshot stop where shall I send recent Tupper [Cambridge photographer] cabinet stop. October far more to my advantage stop No friend of mine would use snapshot." And a week later:

"Why haven't you acknowledged photo sent Harvard Club special delivery stop never man so benevolent and so churlish stop you have put a bankrupt to the expense of two night letters stop now assure him you have the cabinet to be enlarged if you like and that you have destroyed snapshot and negative."

In February, 1912, he wrote to Reed from Hollis a typically urgent Copeland letter of invitation; always these were precise and insistent:

I shall be sadly disappointed if you cannot come here on Sunday March 3, for the hour from five to six. There will be nothing to eat or drink but a glass of yellow chartreuse (one of my favorite drinks) and a biscuit, and perhaps a glass of sherry. But there will be, I trust, Henry Rideout and his charming young wife, Langdon Warner and his charming young wife, and Nat Simpkins and his charming young wife. Pray let me know immediately that you will come. . . .

If you cannot come then, when are you coming to dine with me? We could dine that evening at the dreary old Union and talk of several things that concern us both. Don't let anybody put the idea of the sailing ship and the Horn out of your mind. Think of Conrad! Think also and often of

Your faithful, ancient friend,

C. T. Cope

N.B. You know, I trust, that Hollis 11, the subsidiary chamber and solarium, is always at your disposal, if I can know ahead.

The following month he wrote again:

Dear Jack:

I shall be very glad indeed to dine with you on Sunday the 24th. It is probably because things move so much faster in New York that you call it the 25th; even the calendar has to give way. I shall expect you here at 7 punct.

Can't you address English 12 on Tuesday the 26th at half-past two, on how to get started as a writer, and what experiences are valuable as material, and how regular work under a competent master — you couldn't possibly be meaning me by such a one — is of the highest possible importance?

Please let me know immediately if the Sunday engagement will do, and if you will address English 12.

Yours ever truly, C.T.C.

In April, 1914, Reed, now back from Mexico, wrote to him from the New York Harvard Club:

Dear Cope:

I'm having them send you my Metropolitan Magazine

war articles on Mexico. If there's anything of good in them, it is due entirely to you and English 12. I feel that perhaps they are the first piece of reporting I have done. If they're bad, it's your fault too. Much love from

Jack Reed.

To this note, Copeland replied two weeks later:

Dear Jack,

Here is a paragraph about Waldo [Peirce]. Can't the facts — especially the fact of the Salon — be given wide circulation? If you see your way to it, here is a statement in regard to his training, made by a friend.

The card with which you heralded two copies of the Metropolitan Magazine overwhelmed me. Whatever you owe to me, you owe a great deal more to yourself, and to the World. Nevertheless, as I said to you once before, it is better for a man's happiness to be over-proud than not to be proud at all. I had bought the April number of the magazine long ago, had read portions of the article, more than my eyes should have allowed, had the magazine on my table and bragged of it unceasingly. I have been doing the same with the May number, which I have read completely. It is all good, and more than good. As you know, I like to have writing march, and so I took my chief personal pleasure from the beginning of the skirmish to the end.

Of course you will give me good notice of your coming here. When are you coming? My lamps don't get well, and I proceed with difficulty. But I proceed.

Affectionately, and truly yours,

C. T. COPELAND

You are a born writer — I discovered long ago. But I think you don't work hard enough at writing.

Let me briefly interrupt Reed's story to record my own experience in addressing English 12 when I was three years out of college. I had been reporting on the New Bedford *Evening Standard*, where another tough-minded Yankee, George A. Hough, ran a little training school of his own as the *Standard*'s managing editor. He would put in a call to the Harvard employment bureau when in need of a new recruit, and if the lad showed any gift for journalism, Hough, after having ridden herd on him for six months or so, would have the city editor fire him with some lame excuse, and the boy would move on to Providence or New York. Anyhow, I was to tell English 12, out of the wealth of my seven months' experience, why newspaper work was worth doing, even for fifteen dollars a week. I was not, and never have been, a fluent speaker, and besides, there was Copey, sitting in the back row, calling for more. After I had finished with the help of a long question period, Copey took me aside and said, quite gently, "Donald, why didn't you tell me it is difficult for you to make a speech?" At least, I learned years later, I had gathered one recruit, S. T. Williamson.

When *Insurgent Mexico* was published, Reed's dedication was one that Copeland highly prized. It read: "To listen to you is to learn how to see the hidden beauty of the visible world; to be your friend is to try to be intellectually honest." But the relations between the proud teacher and the devoted pupil were to be sorely tried. For a time, all went well, until Reed's increasing involvement in the Communist cause became evident. On his first visit to Russia, Reed sent Copeland a postcard from Moscow, telling him that a Copeland club was being formed there, and adding, "You are read on the banks of the Moskva." On his return he sent him a Russian present, which Copeland thus acknowledged: "I value the ancient brasses for their own sake, but much more because you took the trouble to bring them from Moscow to me. Good-bye, *batushka*, when are you coming to Cambridge?"

As Reed became progressively *persona non grata* with the government of his own country, Copeland grew more and more distressed and angered by his involvement in the Bolshevik cause. It is to Reed's credit that as his position became steadily more serious, he wrote to Copeland insisting that it would be wiser, for Copeland's sake, if they ceased to correspond. In 1935, when Granville Hicks was preparing his biography of Reed, Copeland wrote to him: "I spoke to English 12 about Reed after his death and urged upon them the need of respecting and praising an honest man who made great sacrifices for a cause, no matter how strong our own feeling might be against it. None of us knew what incredible sacrifices he was making in Russia until after it was all over."

6

Waldo Peirce, in whose career as a painter Copeland took great interest, and aided in any way he could, was another prime favorite, and when Peirce wrote him letters from the Western Front in World War I, Copeland delighted in reading their vividly bawdy or scatological pages aloud to his classes. He delighted, too, in the adventurous spirit of these two classmates, and no doubt gave them his blessing when, shortly after Commencement in 1910, they sailed from Boston for England as cattle hands aboard the *Bostonian*. The *Bostonian* carried a thousand head of cows, sheep and pigs, and about a dozen college boys in search of a free passage to Europe, who customarily signed the ship's articles on these voyages, under contract to work their way over by watering and feeding the beasts and cleaning out their stalls.

On this trip, the *Bostonian* was still in Boston Harbor when Peirce began to regret his agreement to join Reed on the expedition, for the *Bostonian* was no bed of roses. Over Reed's protests, he decided to swim ashore. Leaving his money, his watch and his letter of credit where Reed would be sure to find them, he went out on the after well deck, and clad in a pair of pants, dived overboard. Peirce was a strong swimmer, and though there were several fishing boats within sight, he decided to avoid them, lest on picking him up they turn him over to the *Bostonian*'s captain. He swam about until the *Bostonian* was well away, and then hailed a lobsterman who took him aboard his dory and put him ashore on one of the harbor islands where there was a military post. There Peirce got himself some dry clothes, crossed to Boston on the military ferry, and thence out to Cambridge for a visit to the bank. The next day he went to New York and boarded the *Mauretania*. He arrived in England to learn that an admiralty hearing was in progress, and that Reed was being held in connection with his disappearance. He hired a lawyer, and attended the hearing, where, when the ship's roll was called, Peirce answered to his name. The captain of the *Bostonian* questioned him angrily. "Don't you realize that you signed the ship's articles, that you broke your contract, and that you are liable?" Prompted by his lawyer, Peirce had his rejoinder ready. "Yes," said he, "and you are guilty of criminal negligence. The stink on your ship made me sick. I went to the rail to throw up. I saw you on the bridge. I threw up, but I lost my hold and fell overboard — and you made no effort to save my life." The fact was then established that the captain had been on the bridge at the time, and that no effort had been made to pick Peirce up. The case against Reed was dismissed, and no charge was brought against Peirce.

7

When Corliss Lamont was an assiduous fellow traveler, Copeland wrote to him in February, 1935:

Dear Corliss, —
Instead of trying any longer to understand Soviet Russia,
do try to extricate yourself as soon as you can from the
toils of that cruel and sadistically bloody oligarchy.
                    No more now from
                    Your old true friend, COPELAND

Lamont defended his position, and a few weeks later, Copeland wrote again:

Dear Corliss,
I take back the violent letter I wrote to you, because I
had too little information to go on, and the tone of it to a
benevolent young friend would have been bad under any
circumstances. Please tell me that the note is already destroyed, and send me one of your expositional pamphlets.
                    Yours sincerely,
                    C. T. COPELAND

Of this incident Lamont has noted: "I did not obey Copey's
instructions and destroy his little blast of February 13, 1935,
on Soviet Russia. Either I forgot about the matter or I felt
that any communication from Copey was too precious to destroy." Concerning his relations with Copeland he has written:

I took English 12 and learned a great deal from it about
writing. I also enjoyed enormously the evenings in Hollis.
And I sat with Copey on the Library Committee of the
Harvard Union. His conversation was always very stimulating and full of fascinating literary allusions. . . .
Yet my devotion to Copey was always qualified, primarily because I reacted against his colossal egotism. Perhaps I should have regarded this trait as a trivial and even

endearing quality in a great teacher. But I was spiritually repelled by that egotism. As I grew older, I discovered that many of the great had this same quality; and I guess that I always held it against them.

As we have already noted, it was difficult for Copeland to accept that any Harvard graduate of his time who had achieved success either in journalism or in literature had done so without benefit of English 12. Neal O'Hara, who became well known as a newspaper columnist, recalls that he was denied admission to the course, though he had, while an undergraduate, already spent a summer as a reporter on the New Bedford *Evening Standard*. Forty years later O'Hara was walking through the lobby of the Hotel Commander in Cambridge, with Mayor Corcoran. They encountered Copey, then eighty-five, who lived across the street and came frequently to the Commander either for lunch or to be shaved. "The Mayor," O'Hara recalls, "grasped Copey's hand in the manner of a politico and caused the enfeebled but physically Spartan scholar to wince. 'Please, not so warmly, Mr. Mayor,' said Copey, as he waved his hand and wrist.

"Here's a fellow you wouldn't let into English 12," chided the Mayor, and pointed at me.

"Copey had remembered me, by name at least, because one can't be a columnist on a metropolitan newspaper without attaining some restricted celebrity.

" 'True,' said Copey, with reference to my rejection. Still nursing his infallibility, he countered, 'But it was not my misjudgment, Mr. Mayor.' Then he continued, addressing me, 'O'Hara, you fooled yourself, or bludgeoned yourself, into becoming a better writer than you were to me!'

"Then, with a brevity and what I thought was a wisp of affection, he said he had enjoyed a few things of mine that had come to his attention; he was happy that I had done well in the newspaper and speechifying crafts; and that he still considered me 'one of my old boys.' That was the last time I saw him, but it was a pleasant meeting."

8

A little now about Copeland's teaching on the distaff side — for he gave his writing course at Radcliffe also. There his most distinguished pupil was Helen Keller. She entered Radcliffe in 1900, and in *The Story of My Life*, written for *The Ladies' Home Journal* while still in college, she made special mention of one teacher:

This last year, my second year at Radcliffe, I studied English Composition, the English Bible from a literary rather than a religious point of view, the Governments of America and Europe, the Odes of Horace, and Latin Comedy. The class in Composition, I think, has been the pleasantest. It met in the afternoon and was very lively. The lectures in that course are always interesting, vivacious, witty; for the instructor, Mr. Copeland, more than any one I know, brings before you literature in all its original freshness and power. For one short hour you are permitted to drink in the all-time beauty of the old masters without definition, needless interpretation or exposition. You revel in their fine thoughts. You enjoy with all your soul the sweet thunder of the Old Testament, forgetting the existence of Jahveh and Elohim; and you go home feeling that you have had "a glimpse of that perfection in which spirit and form dwell in immortal harmony; truth and beauty bearing a new growth on the ancient stem of time."

There is testimony to the effect that though Copeland's readings were as much admired at Radcliffe and at other

feminine gatherings as they were at Harvard and elsewhere, he was not — and this is understandable — quite the
same catalytic force among women students that he was
among the men. One of his Radcliffe students, Constance
Bridges (Mrs. David Fitzgibbon) writes of him:

I think in fairness I should give you my *impression* that
Copey did not influence girls quite as much or as deeply as
he did men, because he wasn't influenced by them. I really
believe he was rather frightened of them, although they
did not escape his caustic tongue. (Although too frequently I panted into class late, I was *not* the heroine of the
classic "And how will you have your tea, Miss Blank?")

Copey stimulated, instructed and entertained me, but he
never mesmerized. On the other hand, as "choirboy" in a
47 Workshop production, I had fallen in love, that is to say
I contracted an acute case of Bakeritis. I took every course
that George Pierce Baker gave, including English 47, and
hung on every word that fell from the spell-binding lips.
To this day I can, and will, at the drop of a hat, quote him
on every aspect of dramaturgy. Unlike Copey, Baker was
neither unaware of nor displeased by youthful feminine admiration from the front row. There was a touch of the
frustrated matinee idol about him that helped him give the
bits of personal encouragement that brought out strenu-
ous efforts from his students. If you shared his passionate
interest in the theatre, he liked you and showed it. It always seemed to me that Copey could not get out of the
Radcliffe Yard fast enough. If he felt more than impatient
toleration for his girl students, he concealed it well.

Against these observations we may place those of Katharine Barbey, who became Copeland's niece by marriage to
Charles F. Dunbar, some years after she had taken English 12,
not once, but twice. She recalls that

It was brazenly advertised in the course that no reading was required, except a chapter of the Old Testament read aloud every day, including Sundays, and *Lavengro*, since women never read it otherwise. However, there was a crafty device agreed upon, or rather, enforced, that the monitor should take down the name of any book mentioned in class by Teacher, and that the book should instantly go on the reserved shelf for English 5 (Radcliffe's English 12). About a week after such mention, someone in the class would find herself exchanging ideas with Teacher, this time very, very uncomfortable if she had not run like mad and read the book in the intervening week. A cheap but effective method, never acknowledged by Teacher. By the end of the season, I think I am right in saying that there were more or at least as many books on his reserved shelf (English Composition — no outside reading) as on that of any literature course. In addition to a thousand words of original writing and six hundred of translation every week, always signed by the author, "I have read this aloud."

Mrs. Dunbar vividly recalls the histrionic lengths to which Copeland would go in order to seize and hold the attention of a class or to drive home a point. Once, during Summer School, she was crossing the Yard when she encountered Copey, wearing now, in deference to the season, a stiff-brimmed straw hat instead of the customary iron-bound derby. He doffed it vertically with that oddly stiff-jointed motion characteristic of his arms and legs, and inquired sternly why she was not enrolled in one of his courses. "But I took your course last year, Mr. Copeland," she pleaded, "and just now there's other work I must do; besides, I can't spare the money for the extra fee." Copey appeared somewhat mollified, but, with an odd glint in his eye, issued a peremptory order: "Be in Emerson D at 1:45 this afternoon."

"Yes sir." At the appointed hour Miss Barbey arrived at Copeland's class in Emerson Hall, having meantime persuaded a friend to accompany her. They took seats in a rear row. It was the first meeting of the course. Presently, having called attention to the movements of a fly on one of the windowpanes, Copeland inquired, "Is there anyone present who can tell me who my Uncle Toby was — in what book he appears?" He pointed a finger at a youth in the front row. "Can you tell me?" His luckless victim ventured, "Wasn't he a character in *Twelfth Night*, sir?" "Oh, my God," groaned Copeland, "does no one here read? What do they teach you where you come from?" "You, sir" (pointing again), "perhaps you can tell us who my Uncle Toby was." "I — I'm afraid I don't know, sir." A moment of silence, and then Copey asked, "Is there no one in this room who can tell me who my Uncle Toby was?" Then up spoke Miss Barbey: "Wasn't he in *Tristram Shandy*, sir?" Copeland smote one palm against the other. "Right! Now where did *you* go to college?" "Radcliffe, sir." "Ah," said Copey, "Radcliffe. And were you one of my students?" "Yes, sir," said Miss Barbey. "Aha," exclaimed Copey, rubbing his hands delightedly, "one of my students knows who my Uncle Toby was." Miss Barbey and Mr. Copeland met again in the Yard that afternoon. Again the straw hat was stiffly lifted. "Hope you didn't mind the old man, Katharine," he muttered in passing.

Copeland's methods with his girl students (they included also Katharine Fullerton Gerould and Rachel Field), differed in some respects from those he employed with the boys. He did not see as many of them in an unofficial capacity; only a few were invited to his evenings, and this practice did not come about until after World War I; up to that time these gatherings were strictly limited to the male sex. Perhaps it should be added that, prior to that time, there was little con-

tact, physical or otherwise, between Harvard and Radcliffe
students. Harvard snooted Radcliffe, and all classes were
separate; for the most part, when Harvard undergraduates
sought female company, they went, aside from the Brattle
Hall dances in Cambridge, to Boston or out to Wellesley.
Today, of course, Harvard is in fact, if not in theory, a co-
educational college.

There were other differences. At Harvard, a boy in Copeland's writing course read everything he had written to the
great man himself; at Radcliffe, the girls' compositions were
screened by Copeland's young assistants; these changed from
year to year. It was part of their job to read everything submitted in the course, and to reserve for the master's criticism only what they judged to be the more promising material.

Though many of the girls, like Constance Bridges, were
more attracted by Professor Baker's air of the matinee idol,
his manner of flourishing his black-ribboned eyeglasses, and
his casual references to "my good friend, Sir Arthur Pinero,"
there were others who were more charmed by Copeland's
wit, and his own variety of stage presence. As much as the
boys who, though they did not study writing under Copeland, took his lecture courses on Dr. Johnson and His Circle,
or Scott, or The English Letter Writers, they were fascinated
by his incisive characterizations of these literary figures and
of their work, as they were also by his aphorisms on life and
manners. More than most teachers of his period, he was always at pains to present the man against the background of
his time, and it is the truth to say that he was better read in
history than most of the men who were then teaching
English literature.

Copeland was a shrewd judge of character as well as a
deeply perceptive literary critic; how few other professors of
his time would have said, as he was fond of saying, "A man

is always better than a book." Harvard and Radcliffe alike
relished such remarks by Copeland as this of Dr. Johnson:
"He would ask a blessing on a meal he would presently pronounce uneatable"; or how when Mrs. Siddons, the greatest
actress of her period, went to see Johnson while he was ill, he
told her, lacking a chair, that now she knew how people had
to stand to see her act. They were delighted when he mentioned, apropos of Johnson's definition of oatmeal (food for
men in Scotland and for horses in England), a Scot's unper-
turbed comment, "Weel, whaur can ye find such men as in
Scotland or such horses as in England?" He liked to quote
Lord Chesterfield's penetrating comment on Dr. Johnson's
books — that in them "we have Johnson all alone, and Johnson did not like to be alone," adding that there is always sad-
ness in Johnson's writing, gaiety in his talk. Of Johnson's
melancholy and fear of death, he used to say that if Johnson
had entered the ministry, and had thus been forced constantly to meditate on life and death, he would have gone
insane. And had Copeland's students known what the distant
future held for their professor, they would have been not
only interested, but moved as well, when he quoted Dean
Swift's prediction, "I shall die like that tree; I shall die at the
top," for to Copeland, as to Swift, came the heavy burden,
in his declining years, of a failing mind.

CHAPTER ELEVEN

The Recruiting Sergeant

THE MOST PASSIONATE involvement of Copeland's life was his dedication to the cause of the Allies in World War I. So great was his zeal that he made himself one of the most effective recruiting sergeants the country ever had. This ardor of his had diverse roots. He might be called an Anglophile by literary osmosis, but not to the lengths of his slightly older colleague, Barrett Wendell, whose attitude was one of condescension toward the literature of his native land. It was not merely Copeland's admiration for the glories of English letters that made him so intense a partisan; there was, among other influences, the imprint of that close identification with the British which, before the days of Canada's nationalist urge, left its mark upon the citizens of Calais. There was, too, a deep devotion to the democratic principles which he believed were at stake. To these factors must be added his worship of gallantry, and a devout patriotism which was without the blemish of chauvinism.

Its quality is best illustrated by a habit of Copeland's which is remembered by the Rev. C. Leslie Glenn, who from 1930 to 1940 was the rector of Christ Church in Cambridge. "He did not belong to my church" writes Mr. Glenn [Copeland was a Unitarian], but we had many mutual friends and I thought I should call and pay my respects when I first arrived in Cambridge. . . . I had on a gray suit which I am not sure he approved of in the clergy. In any case, when he opened the door and I told him who I was, he said, 'Come in. I like the cloth even if it is gray.'

"My office in Christ Church overlooked the Old Burying Ground and I became aware that from time to time Copey would go into the burying ground and stand in front of a small tombstone, take off his hat, pause a minute and then walk away. I asked him about this one time and he told me that every Monday morning he would stand in front of a certain stone, take off his hat, read the inscription, and go on."

This was the inscription:

"Here lies ye body of Mr. John Stearns son of the late Mr. David Stearns of Lunenberg. He died in the service of His country Aug 22d 1775 and in ye 23d year of his age."

Many times in his classes, Copeland would gaze out the window, and then inquire, "Does anybody know who John Stearns was?"

From the years of the Revolution, Harvard College had been quick to respond to the exigencies of war; she has never been cloistered in times of crisis. Shortly after the Boston Massacre, the Reverend Andrew Eliot, a member of the Harvard Corporation, wrote to Thomas Hollis:

The young gentlemen are already taken up with politics. They have caught the spirit of the times. Their declamations and forensic disputes breathe the spirit of liberty. This has always been encouraged, but they have sometimes been wrought up to such a pitch of enthusiasm that it has been difficult for their Tutors to keep them within due bounds; but their Tutors are fearful of giving too great a check to a disposition, which may, hereafter, fill the country with patriots; and choose to leave it to age and experience to check their ardor.

Although Harvard had her share of Loyalists — they numbered, in 1776, 16 per cent of her living graduates — and though few undergraduates left college to serve in the Continental Army, she had her Revolutionary heroes in such men as Major Isaac Gardner, the first Harvard man to fall in the war, who was killed in the British retreat from Concord, Dr. Joseph Warren, who died on Bunker Hill, and Major General Artemas Ward, Washington's predecessor in the high command. But, as Samuel Eliot Morison has observed in his *Three Centuries of Harvard,* "The College rendered her proper service to the country in council, through the constructive labors of such men as John Adams and James Bowdoin, rather than in the field or at sea." Briefly, for eight months in 1775-76, the college was removed to Concord; during that period the college buildings had been taken over by the Provincial Congress, and nearly 2000 soldiers were quartered in Massachusetts, Hollis and Stoughton Halls, and in Holden Chapel.

In the War of 1812 Harvard men, with few exceptions, played little part, for in New England the war met with scant favor. Nevertheless, there was more fervor among the students than among their elders, and they organized the Washington Corps, in which a hundred or more undergraduates drilled twice a week, and paraded several times on Cambridge Common.

One is struck by the sharp contrast between the atmosphere at Harvard during the Civil War and that which prevailed during the two world wars. There were various causes. For a generation preceding the Civil War, Harvard had a large Southern enrollment; most Southern students left in the winter of 1860-61, and were never afterward to come in equal numbers, because of Harvard's undiscriminatory attitude toward Negro students. That winter a volunteer company of undergraduates and teachers began drilling — oddly enough, under a French officer, as they were to do on a much larger scale in Copeland's time.

A student company [writes Mr. Morison] volunteered to guard the Cambridge arsenal (a survival of the siege of Boston) with its piles of cannonballs and eighteenth-century ordnance, which were popularly supposed to be the destined objective of a dastardly attack by "rebel" sympathizers. . . . By the fall of 1861 students began to leave College to enlist; but not many did so, and the first undergraduate to lose his life was Lieutenant Horace S. Dunn '63, who died of typhoid as a result of the Peninsular campaign.

It is difficult for anyone who knew Harvard in the years 1916-18 to understand the cool attitude of the College toward the Civil War. College life went on much as usual, and with scarcely diminished attendance. Public opinion in the North did not require students to take up arms, as in the World War; there was no mass movement into the army or navy, and draftees who hired a substitute were not despised. President Lincoln kept his son at Harvard until he graduated in 1864, and then gave him a safe staff appointment. The Harvard-Yale boat race was rowed off Worcester, before a large and enthusiastic crowd, on July 29, 1864, at a time when the Union was desperately in need of men; but not one of the twelve oarsmen enlisted. Among the graduates and undergraduates who did join the Union forces, the fatalities were proportionally three times greater than those suffered by the Harvard contingent in the World War; and of the 257 Harvard men who fought for the Southern Confederacy, one-quarter were killed or died in service.

The history of Harvard shows a gradually mounting interest in public affairs among the student body. In the closing years of the nineteenth century it had not approached the intensity it was to assume, beginning with World War I, but President Cleveland's Venezuela Message in 1895, widening the bounds of the Monroe Doctrine and creating the possibility of war with Britain, set up a ferment in Cambridge, and many meetings were called to defend or attack the Administration. Three years later came the war with Spain, and, as Mr. Morison notes in his history of the university, three Harvard graduates had much to do with bringing it about; they were Henry Cabot Lodge, Theodore Roosevelt, and William Randolph Hearst. Another Harvard man, John D. Long, was Secretary of the Navy, and Leonard Wood, a graduate of the Medical School, commanded the Rough Riders. "Yet, as on other public occasions," writes Mr. Morison,

Harvard spoke with no single voice. Charles Eliot Norton, addressing the students shortly after the outbreak, declared that the war was needless, inglorious, and criminal, and advised them to consider carefully whether the best use they could make of themselves in their country's service was to enlist. For this he was abused by politicians, newspapers, and even clergymen, through the length and breadth of the land. His prompt dismissal was demanded, although his resignation had already been accepted, and certain local politicians went so far as to suggest that he be tarred and feathered, or even lynched. And his classmate, Senator George F. Hoar, who later struggled against the consequences of the war, wrote to Norton: "All lovers of Harvard, and all lovers of the country, have felt for a long time that your relation to the University made your influence bad for the college and bad for the youth of the country." William James, addressing his class at the Jefferson Laboratory, made a speech concluding with a sentence they never forgot: "Don't yelp with the pack!" President

Eliot, however, offered no discouragement to public service, and in the short four months' war about a hundred students enlisted, and ten made the supreme sacrifice.

2

World War I was to work a transformation such as Harvard had never known. When it broke, the present writer, like Mr. Morison, was teaching in a western university. Of its impact on the students there he remembers an impression identical with Mr. Morison's: "it seemed to the average student as unreal as the War of the Roses." But when Morison returned to Harvard early in 1915, "one was on the outskirts of battle." In Seattle, where I was until we entered the war in April 1917, this transformation did not occur.

The first ambulance and hospital units went over from the Harvard Medical and Dental Schools; undergraduates and recent graduates were volunteering for ambulance service, and enlisting in the Canadian and British forces, and the Lafayette flying squadron. Although prevailing sentiment, both in the student body and among the faculty, was overwhelmingly in favor of the Allied cause, there was a minority of undergraduates who were unconvinced of its righteousness. John Dos Passos, who, after his graduation in 1916, was to enlist in the ambulance service, writes that

we were quite exercised by the advance of militarism — the people I saw had a strong pacifist tinge — and some even viewed Plattsburg and the ROTC with alarm. Of course all the right thinkers were full of horror and atrocity stories about the Lusitania and Brave Little Belgium. So far as I can remember, as so often has happened in my life, I was on the fence. . . . My actual contact with politics came after I was graduated, though I can remember following Wilson's "kept us out of war" campaign with great enthusiasm, although I was too young to vote in that election. The right thinkers again were, as I remember, all for Hughes. There was an Intercollegiate Socialist Society rooting for Debs, but the superior young men — and my God, we were superior — I went around with, regarded its activities with derision. I can't speak for the others, but Wilson's switch to a war policy gave me my first great disillusionment with statesmen and politicians. By the way, I still think that if we had kept out of that war and insisted on a negotiated peace — T.R.'s attitude toward the Russo-Japanese war — the twentieth would have been a far easier century to live in for the tribes of men.

It was because Copeland's influence was individually exercised — as the teacher who maintained a closer contact with the members of the student body than any other — that he was so effective in adding to the number of early volunteers. President Lowell, from the time that "preparedness" had become a slogan, encouraged undergraduates to attend the Plattsburg training camps, and in 1916 a course in Military Science, given by General Wood and two other regular army officers, was offered at Harvard to Plattsburg graduates and members of the National Guard.

The Corporation [Mr. Morison records] was convinced, somewhat earlier than the War Department, that Harvard students were officer material, and should be given an officer's training; for that reason the course provided in the National Defense Act of 1916, including an unnecessary amount of drill with a modicum of theory, was too elementary. The War Department consented to modify the provisions of this Act for Harvard and other colleges; Captain

Constant Cordier, U.S.A., was detailed to Cambridge; and 864 students enrolled under him in "Military Science 1" during the fall of 1916. Most of the actual instruction was done by Harvard professors, such as Theodore Lyman, William B. Munro, and Julian L. Coolidge, who had had Plattsburg training. The course counted for a Harvard degree, and, in connection with work in the training camps, prepared students for commissions in the United States Army.

Then, several weeks before our declaration of war on Germany, President Lowell requested the French Government to send over a few disabled officers to train the Harvard R.O.T.C. in the new methods of warfare which had developed. A group of these officers arrived in April, 1917, and the R.O.T.C., now grown to 1227 men, began training under them. President Lowell urged the younger men not to "mistake excitement for duty," pointing out that they could serve their country more effectively by taking officers' training than by rushing into the ranks of the Army and Navy, or the Marines. In the fall of 1917 the Cadet School for the First Naval District was established in Holyoke House, and the University offered a special course preparing students for an ensign's commission. Altogether, in the course of the war, over 11,000 Harvard students and graduates enlisted in the armed forces, and of these 373 were killed or died in service.

During all this period, Copeland persistently asked the same question of every boy he encountered: "What are you doing for the country?" His evenings at home in Hollis Hall were adapted to a similar purpose, and whenever one of his former students got back to Cambridge after having seen something of the war, whether as a correspondent or as an active participant, he was sure to be commandeered by Copey to talk to the boys about what he had seen and done.

He carried this zeal into his classes also, and they were from time to time addressed by men who had observed the war at first hand.

These efforts were continued even after Copeland fell prey to the fear that the Germans would try to exterminate him. John Gallishaw, a Newfoundland boy whom Copeland had befriended, and who was one of the first Harvard undergraduates to enlist in the Canadian army, remembers that after he was invalided home and re-entered college in 1916, Copeland returned to Hollis one day and heard what he supposed to be an infernal machine loudly ticking away in his rooms. He sent for the Yard police; they came, and discovered that during his absence the authorities had installed a new steam radiator in Hollis 15. When the story reached President Lowell, it appealed to his lively sense of humor, and sometimes, with dramatic gestures, he would, before a small group, re-enact the scene. Copeland never knew this, but if he had, his own sense of the incongruous was so strong that he would no doubt have relished the story.

"I think the only time I saw him really angry," recalls Edmund Kiernan, "was when I read to him a free-verse poem about a visit of King George V to the munition makers. I was a pacifist and CTC had been pretty tolerant of it until then. He ordered me in a great voice to tear up the poem if I wanted to continue in the course. Rather spinelessly, I think now, I did so. I joined the ROTC under his proddings, and am not sorry that I did so. And I did see the war in a new light. But I was mixed up and was finally drafted a few months before the end."

3

As each man left college to enter the service, he was asked by Copey to write to him. Nearly all did, and the hundreds of letters they sent him were his most precious possession. Many of those he thought of particular interest were published in the *Harvard Crimson*, the *Alumni Weekly*, and the Boston newspapers. At the war's end he had six volumes of them handsomely bound. The letters came from camp, from the trenches, from ships at sea, and they told him everything. Those who had studied writing under him and knew his hunger for the vivid detail tried as hard as they could to make him see what they had seen. And there was nothing they held back — their fears, their hopes, their disappointments, their griefs, their pride or their shame for what they had done. They wrote as they could not write even to their fathers and mothers, or to friends of their own age.

They wrote, "Dear Copey, I'm in love. I wouldn't tell most people I know such a secret, but with you it's different. You've been entrusted with so many such secrets, that I know you have learned how to keep them. So bless me." They wrote, "I'd walk forty miles to look at an ankle." They wrote, as they wouldn't write home, "Dear Copey, I'm blue, and it's all so cruelly useless. And hopeless. And lonely. I get sick thinking of what my friends are facing — those who are really doing the work." They said the things they couldn't say to the men they fought beside: "Dear Copey — Poor old Bill — one doesn't say it aloud — among fellows — but I swear I loved him. He was so — well, just absolutely all right. A big man if ever there was one — and everything ahead. Aren't there a million others could have gone in his place and not mattered? Why did it have to be him? He counted so much."

Many of the letters must deeply have satisfied Copeland's hunger for vicarious experience. By temperament, by lack of physical energy, by the iron bonds of habit, he was cut off from firsthand acquaintance with adventures for which, with his avid interest in human beings and his deep concern with the forces which were shaping the world he lived in, he found a substitute in the more freely moving lives of the boys he cherished. Always, he urged them to live as fully as they could, to forsake the safe and conventional avenues to achievement which, for many of them, could so easily be followed. At Harvard in the years immediately preceding World War I, and again in the early twenties, there was a reasonably secure and well-trodden path which beckoned invitingly to youngsters with the requisite social connections — they could leave college and sell bonds for the best investment houses — and Copey never tired of trying to deflect them from this accepted but unchallenging objective.

It is not hard to imagine his delighted interest in a letter he received from Jack Reed in Bucharest, dated August 8, 1915:

Dear Cope:

Circumstances of mailing — convenience, neutrality, and so forth, force me always to return to Roumania, and to the "Paris of the Balkans," though I detest the country and the people.

Imagine a small Paris in every essential respect, — cafés, kiosks, *pissoirs*, an Academy occupied with producing a dictionary, Futurist painters and poets who are pederasts in all but name, politicians who are known by the mistresses they keep, craven newspapers, bawdy weeklies and *poires* eternally *cocus*.

They claim to be descendants of Rome's Dacian legions, who came from hereabouts, and from old Roman soldiers of Italy colonized north of the Danube. My private opinion is that they derive from a tribe of gypsies become respectable, — and there is nothing more awful than that. Their language I believe to have been made up by a retired Professor at the Sorbonne, or a superannuated associate of the Comédie Française, while suffering a nervous breakdown. It is largely composed of words with Latin roots ending in *-u, -ul,* and *-urilor;* a more unsonorous tongue it would be impossible to invent. Roumanian literature, when not written in French and then translated into the local dialect, is modeled upon Hugo, Voltaire, Octave Mirabeau and Baudelaire. And Roumanian civilization is so Frenchified that the people dress like caricatures of French fashion plates. The women are too fantastic, high-heeled and modern to be believed. And there are millions. Your true Roumanian boasts that there are more *cocottes* in Bucharest in proportion to the population than in any other two cities of the world. No one does anything but screw, drink and gabble. I refer you to Borrow's "Romany Rye," my acquaintance with which, as with most other good books, I owe to you, — Chapter 39, where the Hungarian speaks of the "mad Wallacks," for an earlier description of them. Read it to English 12, if they want to know anything about the Roumanians.

It is a comic opera country; officers in salmon-pink and baby-blue uniforms stolen out of "Rupert of Hentzau" sit at the cafés sipping ices and eating tartlets all day, or drive up and down the Calea Victoriei in cabs, winking at the throngs of women who parade there. They have bloated white faces. There is a dinky Hohenzollern king here, a dinky throne and court, a dinky aristocracy of fake Byzantine Emperor's spawn. Everybody is crooked. Everyone is disobliging, — shopkeepers prefer to rob you than to make a legitimate sale, — I mean that they will refuse to sell at a handsome profit when you refuse to be robbed. It is the most expensive place to live in the world. It reeks with millionaires, grown rich by hogging the oil-wells, or by the absentee ownership of vast lands, where the peasants sweat out their lives for a franc a day. Whenever they can, the rich here go to Paris or the Riviera to spend their money.

In conclusion, their politics is as mean as anything about

them. They persecute the Jews with petty police tyranny; they sell the military secrets and the Cabinet to Germans and Entente, turn about; in the second Balkan war the Roumanians fell on the back of the defenseless Bulgarians, and took away their richest province without risking a battle; and now, they are trying to sell the lives of their peasant-soldiers to whichever side will pay the most cash to the capitalist class.

If ever I saw a place ripe for a revolution, this country is ripe. The peasants are a very fine and poetic people, but they are cowed.

I hate old Europe more every day. America's the place. . . .

Love
REED

Reading Reed's letter today — a letter written obviously in all sincerity to a man he honored and loved, it is easy to see by what forces Rumania has now been impelled to stand on the other side of the Iron Curtain.

4

In May 1916, Copeland received a letter from Waldo Peirce, which, like Reed's, was undoubtedly read aloud to the students in English 12, and to the Monday evening guests in Hollis Hall, for it had the vivid quality Copeland so insistently demanded from his writing apprentices:

Dear Cope:
I spent the winter at Haute Alsace, around a certain old nubbin — "a protuberance of terra firma," as la Doctor Johnson called Hartmansweilerkopf. I wish to God I were

still there. When I was there I usually wished I were anywhere else in the world — the bottom of a sewer to the
armpits and over in liquid manure would have seemed a
wholesome and savory situation — provided the sewer
were profound enough, and manure resistant enough to
defy obus and all their kind. To see the old nubbin itself —
spur of the Vosges — concealed between two parallel
spurs — one must grind up the old mule paths — since
broadened into fair woods roads — quite close.

Leave the main artery, go out toward a battery of
observation posts, crawl into an old shell hole, and where
the trees have snapped like straws to the obus, take a good
look through. Before you are still trees, but as the ground
rises "en face" they dwindle and disappear as disappears all
vegetation in great altitudes, or diminish toward the north,
quietly, quietly, toward the ice fields. Here, however, no
great altitude, nor any ice fields. First come the maimed
trees, then the skeletons of those dead with their boots on,
then a bare stump or two, a few ankle bones, then nothing.
Before the war all was forest, and a damned thick one at
that; then all our goodly timber grown to its prime, lulled
into a false security, sun basking *en beau temps*, buffeting
and jostling their neighbors in the wind. Crash, one fine
day — out of a clear sky they all get unmercifully shat on
— the nubbin, the old ridge, the spur, the razor back,
whatever you call it, loses its pelt, after its pelt its hide,
after that its whole scorched anatomy is drubbed, hammered, ploughed, furrowed, ripped, scoured, torn, shat-
tered (consult dictionary of synonyms) and beplastered
with every caliber of obus that whines — for they whine,
the bastards, they whine to tell you of their coming, and
give the flesh a moment to goose itself in, and a damned
pagan, like some of us, to find a religion. No Moslem
ever cased his vertebrae into a quicker parabola at the sight

of Mecca, or the antics of the sun; no armadillo or ant-
eater ever entrenched his proboscis in the ground with the
dispatch of our hero at the whine of an obus to all in-
tents and purposes about to land between the eyes. . . .
Sometimes the whining becomes a drone. Feebler and
feebler, perhaps she isn't going to make the grade — you
help her on her way with every muscle in your prostrate
form. Once I dove into an abri side of the road and stuck
at the entrance, a damned narrow passage not for maternity
girdles, leaving two friends outside alternately pushing and
pulling in vain. I was known as the human *bouchon* thereafter; another man the human "magnet" attracting always
tons of metal. . . .

I started out, I think, to give you a little description of
our mountain. I left you peering through the gap in the
trees, *n'est-ce-pas?* *Eh bien,* before you, the old scalped
nubbin, the most awful moment of war I have seen. It's
inhabited, this mass of *terra inferma, muy, muy inferma* —
as the Spaniard would say . . . There are small ants of
men who crawl amid its boils, ruptures and gaping sores
— some are French, some boches. The lines are about a
yard apart, at the top, for no one side can hold it against
the other, though taken and retaken many times; thus they
live together, only in the fear of killing one's own lies their
security. It's a sort of terrific altar of war against the sky,
drenched with a thousand sacrifices, rising grim and naked
and scarred above the valley and low lying slopes, tree covered. It was always a spectacle that chased every red
corpuscle in my veins down into my heels and brought
every white one to the surface. The last time I looked at
it — perhaps we were seen, we were three — the obus began whining at us from somewhere in Bocheland. I meas-
ured my length in mule shit, as I will measure it again.
Somewhere on that Vosgean steep, if the mules' exuvia or

spoor has weathered time and lies untampered, there must be a perfect mold, the life mask of one Peirce, *conducteur d'ambulance*. I have not seen the old nubbin since, nor tasted excrement. After a big attack for which we were held, we migrated, and are now in Lorraine, Alsace Lorraine. I've learned to know them both. War has become my livelihood. I shall stay to the end.

WALDO

Late in the summer of 1916, Copeland received a letter from Frederick Pope, giving him a picture of the Allied troops as they had marched to the station, on their way to the front, on the 15th of July:

The French were men of victory; it was in their faces; in their movements; in the very air about them. They were smiling but it was the serious confident smile of men about a great task, undertaken and to be carried through. They were flower laden, flowers stuck in the gun bands, in their belts and their hands. The wives and sweethearts of some marched along with them. Perhaps what impressed me most was the expression of their boots as they stepped out. The élan was magnificent, it choked my thought. I have never been so gripped before as when I saw them go by and on, not even when behind the battle line.

Later the Russians, huge men with great bodies and large legs. They sang as they marched, loudly — a wild chant that sounded like a combination of a football cheer and a hymn. What impressed me most about them was the bayonets, long, bright, and very sharp; one commended at once the bulk of the men and the very long, bright, sharp steel; it was terrible and grand.

The English were very fine too, — the Scotch the best

— the other Tommies seemed very casual on their way to kill a few Prussians — not much to do — just kill a few Prussians. . . .

There seems to be a curious feeling in France — wonderful France — about Americans. It seems to be a disillusionment — they must have given us credit for an idealism that we have not . . . They are not angry, hold no resentment, but seem a little disappointed. All France lauds Roosevelt and avoids the mention of Wilson.

Henry Beston, who then signed himself Henry Beston Sheahan, had early enlisted in the French army, and in the fall of 1916 he published his *Volunteer Poilu*. The dedication to Copeland read:

Dear Copey: At Verdun I thought of you and the friendly hearth of Hollis 15 seemed very far away from the deserted, snow-swept streets of the tragic city. Then suddenly I remembered how you had encouraged me and many others to go over and help in any way that we could: and I remembered your keen understanding of the epic and the deep sympathy with human beings which you taught those whose privilege it was to be your pupils. And so you did not seem far away, but closer to the heart of the war than any other friend I had.

When diplomatic relations between the United States and Germany were broken off, Copeland turned one of his large lecture courses into a preparedness meeting; John Gallishaw told the assembled students about the fighting at Gallipoli, in which he had taken part; Walter H. Wheeler, who had served as an ambulance driver and was slated to be next season's football captain, urged the class of 200 youngsters to sign up for the R.O.T.C.

At the Monday evenings men like Gallishaw and Reed and Peirce, or Edward Eyre Hunt, who had been one of Herbert Hoover's aides in the relief work at Antwerp, or J. B. Millet, who discovered and introduced submarine signaling, came to tell what they had seen and done. The Boston papers reported that standing room at these gatherings was at a premium; week after week the boys struggled for admittance and a spot somewhere on the floor where they could listen. "Probably no more complete idea of war conditions," ventured a writer in the *Boston Post*, "has been laid before a single group of people in the country. The 'Monday evenings' have been a virtual melting pot of war information, and their influence upon undergraduates tremendous."

5

There was a special group of Copeland's "To Whom It May Concern" letters which were written during the war years. Always indefatigable in trying to secure openings for his young friends when they left college, he now set about helping them gain admission to the Plattsburg camps, recommending them as promising officer material. Scores of such letters were couched in terms like these: "This letter introduces my friend and house-mate, Daniel O'Keefe. His strength of body and mind, and the ardor of his purpose will make O'Keefe a valuable officer in the army of the United States."

Somehow, too, he found time to write to many of the men in the services; their letters contain many pleas for a word from him, and grateful acknowledgments of his response. In September 1917, Richard C. Evarts, an English 12 alumnus who had been one of the Harvard *Lampoon*'s most amusing writers, wrote to him, "I was very glad to receive from you a clipping containing an extract from your address on Jane Austen. I read it with approval as I am very fond of Jane Austen, though I scarcely knew why, till you told me." Evarts was one of the relatively few nonconformists who spurned the easier road to a commission open to men with a college background, and enlisted as a private in the regular army, shortly after his graduation from law school. His letters to Copeland have a particular interest because at a time when there was a more snobbish attitude on the part of the elect toward the enlisted man than we witnessed in World War II, Evarts wrote glowingly to his former teacher about the virtues he had discovered in the regular army private, and urged Copeland to help in correcting the condescension and, often, the contempt, with which these men were regarded in the circles where Evarts himself had moved.

Evarts was getting an education in human values, the worth of which he was sure Copeland would appreciate — one which would have been less readily come by had he chosen to follow the customary pattern.

I am still glad [he wrote] that I enlisted, although promotion is slow. I have become a first class private and was on the way to be a corporal when they put me up in Headquarters doing clerical work. That's what comes of having a college education. Ever since our first sergeant discovered I was a lawyer and a college graduate, he has been trying to get me to help in the orderly room as a clerk. Now apparently he has seen that I got this job and considers he has done me a good turn, as he told me I would become a sergeant-major very shortly if I picked up the work quickly, as there is a vacancy. Sergeant-major sounds fine, but it is a clerk's job and not a soldier's in my opinion. However, I shall stay on the job for a while (I have only been at it a little over a week) and then try to

get relieved. To be an officer you must learn the red tape
as well as the rest of the stuff. I associate in business hours
with a very refined and cultured set of men compared with
my comrades in arms. They are to me less interesting.
. . . Copey, I have made some friends here that I hope
will be my friends the rest of my life. They have ceased to
be interesting as human phenomena, but are just friends of
the best kind. There are others, amusing, interesting, or
pathetic, but mostly pathetic, — fellows who have had no
schooling since they were twelve and yet have made fine
men of themselves by struggles which must have been quite
severe compared to the struggles men have had picking
snap courses at Harvard, or any other college. Our ranking duty sergeant, for instance, has had practically no education and yet he can handle our company about five
times as well as some new officers we have fresh from
Plattsburg. I know I would follow him with confidence
where I would be filled with doubt under the leadership of
many officers I have seen here. But I have no kick coming
about the Plattsburg officers, as they have enough intelligence and training to catch on to new stuff quickly. But
they are taking up the hardest part of their training here.
By the time we go to the front we couldn't want a better
set of officers, as I think they will develop to be better than
the regular old-timer. The regular army is too much imbued with the spirit of precedent, and is slow to take up
new ideas. . . . It's perfectly ridiculous for people to pa-
tronize the enlisted man. They average up about the same
as any other crowd of men. They are not all bums nor are
they all angels. Whenever you hear anybody saying anything derogatory of the enlisted men in our regular army,
take issue with them at once and don't stop until you have
absolutely squashed them. I have heard people call them the
scum of the earth, but I think I ought to know by this

time, and I do know that some of them are scum, but most of them are not, and many are true gentlemen.

It was not only about their new lives in the army or navy that his boys wrote to Copey. They told him about their domestic troubles, "because I know you will understand." One of them thinks that he may have seen in the papers that a brother-in-law has shot himself, and Copey must be assured that he was suffering a mental disturbance: "He was one of the finest, and had he been as he was but four years ago, he would have 'gone over the top' on the fields of Flanders. I want you to know this — the sort of man he was, worth a hundred of most men." And of his wife he writes: "If you could see her you would undoubtedly wonder how she ever came to marry me . . . The lad is five years old — which I don't believe for one moment. Do you? But you believe in many things and you made me believe in them, and that is why I am writing you now."

He was understanding, in spite of his zeal, of those among his young friends who felt that certain obligations precluded their entering the service. He wrote to one:

I trust that you didn't think for a moment that I wanted you to leave your family and business for either the Army or the Navy. Quite to the contrary, I feel and keep saying that married men, especially when they have children, do very wrong in going, unless some expert knowledge makes them highly important in the war. Such an expert is Frederick Pope of 1901, who has dropped everything to take a staff appointment with General Pershing in the Gas and Flame Division.

What I still hope, however, is that you will strongly and loyally support the Government in this most awful struggle. Even if you can't agree in your attitude towards it with the greatest and most thoughtful men of all parties, still you must agree with everybody in desiring the war to be over. The best possible way to prolong it is to be half-hearted, and to allow your half-heartedness to be known. The best way of shortening the war is for everybody to get behind and shove. Be the war long or short, we must win.

The conflict has brought me care, labor, bewilderment, and even some grief. Therefore, think often and kindly of

Your faithful old friend,

C. T. COPELAND

Now and then one of his young correspondents quoted back to him one of his remembered observations, and applied it to the circumstances in which he found himself, as in this letter from Fort Leavenworth:

Dear Copey:

I was glad to get your letter. I was homesick for Harvard, and all the men there who might have written to me from the Yard, are now away in the service except yourself. You used to refer to the Yard as Plato's cave, meaning that there is something unreal about academic life, and that it is removed from the rest of the world and sheltered from criticism by virtue of its elegance and learning. Now it seems to me that the Yard and its little enclosure of red brick buildings is as Sodom compared to a military post, and that the Fort here was in truth modeled after the classic cave. If any existence could be further removed from the ordinary phases of human experience, if any life could have less of the human touch, it must be something of which I have never dreamed and something that Dante never conceived in any portion of the Comedy.

Occasionally Copeland's alumni, hitherto unmet, and now thrown together by the circumstances of war, discovered that they had an unsuspected bond:

Dear Copey,

Said my new corporal and bunk-mate to me, as we talked about Boston, "I used to go to the old Bell-in-Hand at the Castle Square with Heywood Broun and Bob Middlemass and Copey." And I leapt up with a shout of joy and we talked of you for an hour! It was like a breath from Hollis 15. He is Alan Rogers, Williams and Harvard Law, who roomed with Broun. A hell of a fine fellow! You remember him, of course. I've no time for more just now — a real letter later. This is just to let you know that the Copey Club is in session!

Best regards,
GENE [Galligan]

In March 1918, from the Hotel Lutetia on the Boulevard Raspail, Paris, Copeland received this notice of a "Meeting of the Charles Townsend Copeland Alumni Association, Overseas Branch:

We, the undersigned, in consideration of the love and affection which we bear toward our distinguished founder, and recalling the many delightful hours spent in his company, send him our greetings, and wish him all prosperity.

Hugh Cabot, George Jones, William M. Chadbourne, Van Dwyer Burton, Beverley Duer, T. H. McKittrick, John R. Pratt, Robert W. Wood, J. A. Hodder, R. Withington, Edward Angell, John Weare, George R. Harding, Robert Woods Bliss, W. H. Roope, J. R. Hyde.

Let Bernard DeVoto speak for perhaps a majority of these young men about the task in which they were engaged and about what they believed Copeland had contributed toward the attitudes they held. In a long letter written in the midst of his infantry training, he said this:

There is no feeling of romance in the job, nor, on the contrary, any feeling of self-sacrifice. We are going into it with everything we have, sure of eventual victory and careless about the personal outcome. There is no attempt to evade the meaning of death, and no attempt at mock and sublimity in its presence. If we come back, all right. If we do not — well, we might have loved some woman and we could have done the work of our choosing, but to have died honorably were better than women and work, and above all else, the cause will triumph.

That is the end of the matter. The army does not consider other problems. For you see, we are living splendidly. If I may correctly interpret the life I am leading in the army, one thing has been abundantly, triumphantly, demonstrated. And that is this, the spirit triumphs over all else. There is a sureness and simplicity to life which make it a finer thing than ever it has been before. Never before was I so confident of myself. Never was I so completely at peace.

All this is a far cry from Hollis 15 and the Monday evenings around the fire. But I feel that those same Monday evenings were preparing us to be good soldiers. You showed us a good many aspects of truth, gave meaning to our aspirations, helped us to realize ourselves. Can you not take great comfort to yourself, knowing that the best part of each one of us bears your mark?

And so the essentially lonely little figure, seeing through the eyes of these men he had known, and in whom he had been so tirelessly interested, the world which was widening and deepening about them, a world from which he was cut off save through their part in it, must sometimes have assured himself that he had been something more than a zealous recruiting sergeant; that he had been for them, at least, a steadying and reassuring, well-remembered and deeply cherished molding force in their lives.

CHAPTER TWELVE

The Man Becomes an Institution

IN THE FALL of 1904 Copeland moved into the rooms on the top floor of Hollis Hall with which his name has ever since been identified. There he lived until the summer of 1932, when his departure was signalized by an editorial in the *Boston Herald* bearing the caption, "The Lights Go Out in Hollis." These were the years in which the Copeland tradition crystallized, the years in which he conducted the famous writing course (he took over English 12 in 1905), and began the long series of readings at the Harvard Club of New York (the first was in 1906); they were also the years of his long-deferred academic advancement; he was made an assistant professor in 1910, associate professor in 1917, and eight years later succeeded Dean Briggs in the historic Boylston Professorship of Rhetoric and Oratory. The celebrated *Copeland Reader* was published the following year. His fame was spreading; he had become copy for the New York papers as well as the Boston press, and with *Time* magazine's cover on January 17, 1927, he was established as a national figure.

Copeland had been deeply touched by the manner in which the news of his elevation to the Boylston Chair was conveyed to him. On the day of his appointment, he had returned to Hollis late in the afternoon, after one of his dogged walks out to Fresh Pond, and found President Lowell sitting on the steps of the south entry, where he had been waiting nearly an hour to congratulate Copeland on his promotion. That impulsiveness and warmth of personal interest, that disregard for what anybody might think at seeing the president of Harvard University sitting idly on the steps of a dormitory, were characteristic of Lowell. There is, unfortunately, no record of their conversation on that occasion; it must have been an odd blend of the old-school manners to which they both held and that unpredictable freedom of expression they had in common.

It had been a long wait for Copeland. First, there had been President Eliot's disapproval, and then the attitude held by most of the senior members of the English department, whose committee made recommendations for advancement to the Faculty, the President and the Corporation. In the light of professional academic standards, it is not hard to see why he had been passed over time and again. True, he had been an extremely popular and effective teacher, attracting year after year a growing number of students. But he had made no contributions to scholarship or to graduate teaching, and his publications were meager. There were other men who had worked harder as professional scholars; were they to be denied advancement in his favor? This was the point of view held by his classmate Kittredge and others. On the other hand, men like Briggs and Bliss Perry felt that Copeland had made a unique contribution to Harvard teaching, and finally, aided by pressure brought to bear by a group of influential alumni who were members of the Copeland Association, their point of view prevailed, and even Kittredge was won over.

At long last, Copeland was on an equal academic level with his old rival, who had outpaced him from the time when they were undergraduates together. The appointment did much to bolster his self-assurance, a quality Kittredge had never lacked. Once the great scholar had been asked why he had never taken a Ph.D., and had unblushingly replied, "Who

could have examined me?" Nor was the answer wholly unbecoming, for Kittredge had once been told, when in quest of
certain information at Oxford's Bodleian Library, "There is
only one man in the world who might be able to answer your
question, and that is Professor Kittredge of Harvard."

One of the perquisites of the Boylston Chair, which was
established in the eighteenth century, is the privilege of pastur-
ing a cow in the Yard. When Copeland succeeded to the post
this right had, understandably, not been exercised for generations, but its existence soon engaged the attention of the
Harvard *Lampoon*'s editors, and one morning an apathetic
Guernsey was found tethered to a tree in front of Sever Hall.
From her neck hung a red-lettered card reading, "Property of
Charles Townsend Copeland." She was soon discovered by
the Yard's caretakers, and led across Harvard Square for
temporary confinement in a garage, whence she was removed
in a truck to her home at the Brighton abattoir.

In 1928, the year of Copeland's retirement, the university,
much to his delight, offered continuance of his tenantry at
Hollis until the end of his life. Strongly as he wished to remain in the rooms which held so many memories for him and
for so many hundreds of friends, sentiment was forced to
yield to practicality. Dr. William Breed, his friend and physician, told him he must go, and Copeland himself realized the
time had come when he must bid farewell to Hollis 15. The
creaking stairs were steep, and there were three flights of
them; they were proving too much to be mounted several
times by a frail man of seventy-two. He was in need of con-
veniences that were lacking, chief among them someone to
prepare his meals — there were no kitchen facilities in Hollis
— and to provide the attention he required. And so an apartment was found for him, hard by the College Yard, at 5
Concord Avenue; there he spent the remaining twenty years.

Already a cherished figure and the subject of countless

stories both apocryphal and true when he moved from Stoughton 7 to Hollis 15, the iconoclastic young instructor, then forty-four, steadily assumed the character of a Harvard institution. Year after year, to the end of the century's first decade, through the deceptive calm of the years approaching 1914, the war and its aftermath, on through the twenties and into the Great Depression, a succession of students and distinguished visitors climbed the stairs of Hollis, to have fixed in their minds a picture of those low-ceilinged rooms under the roof that had been raised in 1764. They were rooms steeped in history long before they were occupied by Copeland, though never, perhaps, had they possessed so much the look of having been thoroughly lived in. Their tenants had been briefly transitory, but Copeland, in his long residence, deeply and pungently imbued them with the color and flavor of a distinctive personality.

Though he made them reflect his own present and past, he was intensely aware, historically minded as he was, of the many generations which had preceded him in Hollis. Its corridors had resounded to the thumping boots of more than six hundred Continental militia who had barracked there in 1775 and 1776. But besides the shadowy figures of his beloved eighteenth century and those of the Victorian period, to whom he was scarcely less attached, there had been predecessors far less shadowy. Emerson, whom he had seen at the funeral services for Longfellow in Appleton Chapel, lived in Hollis 15 during the academic year 1819-20, and Copeland was both interested and amused when Emerson's son, on a visit to Hollis, had shown him a drawing of the study made by his father during his occupancy. Copeland was struck by the Spartan character of the furnishings and, even more so, by the fact that Emerson, with what Copeland termed his "incurable idealism," had in his drawing given a window facing on the Yard an arch it never possessed. No Hollis windows were ever arched, though two in the pediment are circular; all the others are rectangular, and more nearly square, because of the lower height of the top story, than those on the floor below.

President Eliot too, scarcely a shadowy figure to the new tenant, had lived in these quarters as an undergraduate, and Copeland "shuddered" to think what might have happened had Emerson and Eliot shared the same year. Also there had been his father's first cousin, Morris Copeland, named for the signer of the Declaration, and writer of the first American book on landscape gardening. Two of the Quincy Adamses, John and Charles Francis, had shared these rooms in 1822-23, and in later years, Rockwood Hoar, who was to be Senator from Massachusetts, lived there. Copeland's immediate predecessor was Samuel A. Welldon. An influential alumnus and a devoted friend and admirer, he was one of the most active organizers of the Copeland Alumni Association.

2

The windows of sun-flooded Hollis 15, which includes a study and a bedroom, on one side look east across the Yard to University Hall; the other faces Harvard Hall immediately on the south, with the Old Burying Ground and Christ Church, where Washington worshiped during his Cambridge residence, to the west. Throughout Copeland's tenure the study was lit by two oil lamps and a green-shaded gas light by the fireplace. Although electricity was introduced before his departure, he would have none of it, nor would he have a telephone in his rooms until he moved to Concord Avenue. In the fireplace he burned cannel, or sea coal. Two of the walls held bookshelves crowded from floor to ceiling; the others were given over to such mementos as signed photographs of Joseph Jefferson, Madame Modjeska, Minnie Maddern Fiske, John Barrymore, and the water colors of the Calais countryside painted by his childhood teacher, Laura Burns, whom he steadfastly regarded as one of the most beautiful of women. Prominent on one of the tables was the first edition of Dr. Johnson's dictionary, presented to him by the Harvard Club of New York.

A small sofa, two armchairs on either side of the fireplace — one his own customary seat, the other, known as "the lion's chair," reserved for the guest of honor at teas and evenings, and two or three smaller chairs, comprised the furnishings of a small room into which twenty or more undergraduates often crowded, most of them content to occupy a square foot or two on the floor. One flight below, he soon acquired an additional room, Hollis 11. Though used for various purposes, it became best known, during World War I, as containing "the hero's couch." The bedroom above, occupied by Copeland himself, barely left room for him to turn about. Aside from bed, bureaus and chairs, most of the available space was filled by an enormous desk piled high with orderly stacks of papers, books and pamphlets. On one wall hung a portrait by Waldo Peirce of an ancient Spanish peasant. "I like to have him here," Copeland would say, "because no matter how old and ugly I may get, he'll always be older and uglier."

As the years in Hollis rolled on, and the Copeland legend steadily grew, there came into being certain events as much a part of the college calendar as midyears, the Christmas and Easter vacations, and Commencement itself. There was the annual reading to the freshmen in the Harvard Union, the Christmas Eve reading at the President's house, begun shortly after Lawrence Lowell's election to the presidency, and continued, as long as Copeland was able to give them, through

President Conant's term of office. These were open to those students, of whom there were always many, who could not go home for the Christmas holidays. In addition there were, of course, the traditional gatherings once a week in Hollis 15, when Copeland read to his visitors or had invited a distinguished alumnus to speak. Always, whether he read, or a visitor made an informal talk, Copeland was sure to prime the pump of conversation. He would have been widely sought today, had he overcome his dislike of radio, the talking films, and television, on the various conversation programs, both for his ready wit and because, like his eighteenth century friends, he regarded and practiced conversation as one of the fine arts.

As it was, he made several readings over the radio, and one short film, a brief lecture on Dickens. In December 1927, he went on the air for the first time, over a Boston station, reading from Dickens's *Christmas Carol* and from Kipling. A few years later David McCord got the idea that Copeland could be induced to read over a national network. After a first flat refusal, he consented, and McCord at once got in touch with Alexander Woollcott, one of the non-Harvard members of the Copeland Alumni Association, who had written in *Enchanted Aisles* that it was through his reading at a tender age of Flandrau's *Diary of a Freshman*, and his interest in the character of Fleetwood (for whom Copeland had been the model), that he decided to go to college. It was to be Hamilton rather than Harvard, but in the late twenties Woollcott was taken to one of the Harvard Club readings by Heywood Broun, and became, with his customary fervor, no less an *aficionado* than the habitués of Hollis.* Woollcott's infatuation with Copeland was further strengthened, no doubt, by

---

* In addition to Woollcott, the non-Harvard members of the Copeland Association included, at one time or another, Hervey Allen, John Barrymore, Stephen Vincent Benét, Henry Seidel Canby, Finley Peter Dunne, John Farrar, MacKenzie King, Walter de la Mare, Julian Street, Laurence Stallings, H. M. Tomlinson, Hendrik Willem Van Loon, E. B. White, and Thornton Wilder. There were, in 1937, more than five hundred members.

their mutual devotion to Mrs. Fiske. On hearing from Mc-
Cord, Woollcott at once brought his powers of browbeating
persuasion to bear on the executives of CBS, and arrangements were made for a broadcast over WNAC in Boston on
February 2, 1936. Though these recordings were highly successful, Copeland detested them; he chafed at the absence of
a visible audience and felt deprived, no doubt, of the opportunity to build up by his customary side play — his way of
fastening securely the attention of his hearers — to the moment when he would begin to read. He was annoyed too by
the precautions *he* must take against sounds which might in-
terfere with the reception. This was putting the shoe on the
other foot, and he was heard to mutter, when the need for
caution was urged, "They'll be damned lucky if they don't
hear me spit!"

The pre-Christmas broadcasts were frequently repeated, the
last of them, after a lapse of several years, being made in his
eighty-eighth year. Robert C. Seaver, then a sophomore, was
working at the university radio station, WHRB, and arranged
for the broadcast to be made from Copeland's Concord Avenue apartment. He still held to his aversion for being called
"Professor," and Seaver recalls that when he so addressed him,
the old man glowered and said, "Never call me Professor. I
am Mr. Copeland. But you may call me Copey if you like."
(This in spite of the fact that he had long since formed a dislike of the nickname by which he had for so many years asked
undergraduates to call him.) In his later life, with those who
had become his good friends, he was likely to ask that they
call him Charles, even though the difference in their ages
might be great. Edith Roelker Curtis remembers how, when
he asked her to call him by that name, and she answered that
she couldn't do that, but could manage "Copey," he exclaimed, "No! Not that hideous appellation by which I am
known among the undergraduates. You will call me Copeland." And so she did, from that time forward.

3

In 1906, the year in which the Charles Townsend Copeland
Alumni Association was formed, he made the first of his annual spring visits to the Harvard Club of New York, for a
dinner in his honor and a reading which was attended not only
by the graduates resident in New York, but many who came
down from Boston and other New England cities, up from
Philadelphia and Washington, and east from as far as Chicago.
The Association was a loosely organized body, brought into
being by a group of his former students who numbered among
them some of the most active and influential alumni in New
York. It included such men as Samuel A. Welldon, James F.
Curtis, Thomas W. Lamont, Thomas W. Slocum, Langdon P.
Marvin, John Price Jones, Arthur Train and Jerome D.
Greene, who, according to Copeland himself, was chiefly
responsible for having persuaded him, always a reluctant
traveler, to make the journey to New York. The visits, the
dinners and the readings were repeated with but few breaks
for more than thirty years. As he once observed, even the
first visit was made against the advice of two doctors. Nevertheless they were continued, with mixed feelings on his part
of anticipation and dread, until he was seventy-seven.

These visits were productions in more ways than one. On
their part, the officers of the Harvard Club and the members
of the Association spared no effort to make them memorable
occasions, both for the guest of honor and for those who assembled to see and hear him; and on his part, Copeland,
deeply appreciative as he was of the attention being shown
him, nevertheless adhered firmly to the peccadillos which, he
was well aware, were expected of him. The Association always saw to it that he was provided with a drawing room on
the train between Boston and New York; Frank Melia, for

most of the years of Copeland's visits the club's manager, was always on hand to shepherd his baggage, while in another cab, one or more members of the Association escorted him to the club. He would protest these attentions — especially the expense of the drawing room — but he would have been as disappointed as a small boy without presents at Christmas, had they not been forthcoming.

Few things, indeed, meant more to him than the interest which he knew these occasions aroused. They fed, like nothing else, the craving for attention which had been so marked for many years. Thus, in 1919, with the war just over, and many of his friends still scattered about the world, he was obviously troubled lest that year's visit be a dud. Writing to Samuel Welldon he asked, "Don't you think it a mistake for me to come at all in this terrible year?" and went on to say,

> I am afraid, my dear Major, that if there are to be any men there, and if everything is to be right, you and poor Langdon [Marvin] must speed things up. I am writing to him to that effect, and telling him that you have a long letter from me which you will impart to him. Jim [Curtis] mustn't be bothered about anything because he has been so ill, perhaps is not yet well. God knows I am sorry enough to trouble well men.

In a postscript he added:

> Is Cullinan still manager? He was very good and helpful last year. If he has gone, don't you think that you and Langdon will have to make the new manager, as well as the new secretary, understand that my yearly visit to that wonderful Club is not an ordinary happening like a visit from President Lowell, or from Emeritus, but that it is an extra-special event that has to be looked out for?

If you think that I'd better not come, just telegraph a wink, and I will regretfully withdraw. But if I am to come, you must plan to lunch with me on Saturday, the twelfth. We will go far down the forest path where no one will find us.

There was a fixed ritual — a favorite room, a favorite waiter to serve his breakfast, the stipulation that on the day of the reading he must not be disturbed after lunch until five minutes before — and with Copeland five minutes meant neither a minute more nor less — it was time for him to come down and begin the evening's entertainment. In 1933 he wrote to Frank Melia:

I shall be delighted to have the room once more, and if I might find in it a pint of good whiskey, I should enjoy the room still more. I prefer Scotch, but should rather have *good* Bourbon than indifferent Scotch, on account of my interior. But I must be allowed to pay for it, so don't tell any of my friends in the Club whom you are getting it for. Seek information generally or indirectly, as it were, and then act upon it.

Ordinarily, he would make the journey a day or two before the date set for his reading, customarily a Saturday. There was often a favorite excursion to the Metropolitan Museum, and a lunch with a few of his oldest and closest friends. On years when he was feeling in especially good fettle, he would, when encountering any of his old students in the rooms of the club, greet them with what was more a summons than an invitation, to join him at breakfast in the dining room the next morning. Ordinarily he breakfasted alone by preference, but these were occasions, when his health was good, which afforded him an opportunity to keep, like Dr.

Johnson — he was fond of saying — "his friendships in re-pair."

Curt Hansen, who served as chairman of the Copeland Alumni Association during the thirties, and upon whom de-volved most of the details which would insure Copeland's comfort and convenience, remembers that as he grew older, more and more persuasion was needed to bring him down to New York. This was partly because he enjoyed being coaxed and made to feel that his coming was still important, but it was true also that the journey had become increasingly an effort, and that he had become more than ever conscious of his physical shortcomings, beyond the matter of ebbing vitality itself. He fretted about the effect false teeth might have upon his diction, and was very self-conscious about his appearance. He thought of himself as frightening to children, and as he grew balder, would refer to his large but well-proportioned head as "monstrous." He was too much the actor ever to forget the impression he would make on his audience.

There were seldom any surprises at the Harvard Club read-ings; they followed a pattern which the audience preferred to have repeated. The members of the Copeland Association were not only paying tribute to their old friend; they were also, for the space of an evening, recapturing their youth. They wanted, time and again, to hear once more the pieces by which they had been stirred, moved, or delighted when they were undergraduates, and had first come under the spell of Copey's voice. Many of them maintained they had never heard the Bible read, in church or out, as he could read it, and few persons who had listened to his reading of the Book of Ruth, from Ecclesiastes or the Book of Revelation, would dis-pute their claim. The powerful rhythms and the grandeur of the great passages were conveyed by Copeland with an in-tensity and conviction which his hearers would remember all their lives. But there were many other favorite selections from English and American writers, humorous, tender, dramatic — for his range was wide — of which his audiences never tired. Almost always there was some Kipling, and if he did not read "Mandalay," "The Truce of the Bear," "The Bell Buoy," or, among the stories, "The Man Who Would Be King," "Bertran and Bimi," "The Man Who Was," or "The Taking of Lung-tung-pen," someone was certain to be disappointed. They looked forward also to his selections from Dickens, to Thackeray's "The Ballad of Bouillabaisse," and Burns's "John Anderson My Jo." He delighted in Finley Peter Dunne's "Mr. Dooley," and read him with an unimpeachable brogue. Nor did he neglect his young contemporaries, particularly if they had been his students; Benchley and Broun were often on his list. Never did he read a poem or a story which did not lend itself to oral delivery, and much writing that he prized was excluded from the *Copeland Reader* because, in his estimation, it failed to pass that test. No one, he liked to say, ever found him reading Kipling by himself.

No small part of the pattern were the Copeland preliminaries. When he had marched down the aisle, followed by a bookbearer, and seated himself, there were certain movements, comments and requests which had to be gone through before he gave his spectacles a final wipe, opened a book and began to read. They were his means of fastening attention upon himself, of closing a door on the outer world, and building up anticipation of what was to come. They seemed like idiosyncrasies, willfully indulged; actually, they were carefully planned maneuvers designed to set the stage. First he would stare at his audience, fixing with a reproving eye any latecomers whose efforts to find a seat broke the anticipatory hush. Then would come the fiddling with the lamp, the testing of the chair, the demand that the draft at the back of his neck be stopped, or he would say, "The wind is dallying with my shoestrings." There might be a complaint about the ventilation — "Must we all suffocate? Will some good mother's son" — or "some good Christian — open a window?" Presently he would toy with the books on the table, pick up one, set it down, take up another — knowing all the time precisely what he was going to read, and in what order.

When these preliminaries had been concluded and the reading was begun, Copeland appeared to have forgotten himself completely. He and the page before him were merged; he gave himself over entirely to identification with what he was reading. It was one of the qualities of his technique that he was able to bring out, with no relation to himself, whatever his chosen author had to give. He became an instrument, adjusted with the utmost sensitivity to what the words before him were intended to convey. His voice had extraordinary resonance, and in spite of a certain harshness, great flexibility and range. He could assume a childish treble, the quaver of weakness or age, the clarion call of a trumpet, or the profundity of drum-like tones. He had a perfect sense both of time and of timing; William James, son of the philosopher, who painted one of the two portraits of Copeland, remembered half a century afterward how, in his course on nineteenth century English literature, Copeland closed his lecture on Coleridge by reading "Kubla Khan," ending with the lines:

> Weave a circle round him thrice,
> And close your eyes with holy dread,
> For he on honey-dew hath fed,
> And drunk the milk of Paradise.

The last syllable had just left Copey's lips when the college bell clanged. "The class," said James, "rose and staggered out as if in a dream" — which of course, was where it had been.

Only once in the history of the Harvard Club readings did Copeland falter. It was an evening in the early thirties, and Tom Slocum, a former president of the club who was one of Copeland's staunchest friends, and who had not hesitated to let President Lowell know that fund-raising in New York might prove difficult if Copeland were not soon advanced to a full professorship, had come from a sickbed to attend the reading. A chair had been reserved for him in the front row; he had come feebly down the aisle, and many of those present had commented on how ill he looked. Copeland, on his own entrance, busy as he was with the usual setting of his stage, had apparently been unaware of Slocum's condition until, after the intermission, he had returned for the second half of his reading. At some moment then, his eyes fell upon Slocum; he read one brief selection, gathered up his books, and without a further word, marched down the aisle and took the elevator up to his room. It was the only time he failed to carry through his program.

4

The most memorable of these gatherings took place the evening before his seventieth birthday, on April 26, 1930. It was also the twenty-fifth anniversary of his first visit to the club. More than three hundred men were there to do him honor. Slocum, in the absence of Thomas W. Lamont, then the club's president, was toastmaster. Tributes in verse were read for M. A. DeWolfe Howe, who could not be there, and by Robert E. Sherwood. Howe's verses have appeared on an earlier page of this book. These were Sherwood's:

> Where'er we look, we see the storms
> Of bafflement, and disappointment,

We see that there are evil swarms
　Of flies for every drop of ointment.
And yet — although our lives be fraught
With care and pain — let's not be mopey,
But dwell on this consoling thought:
　There's always Copey!

A gruesome uproar fills the void
　Of Progress, deafening, frenetic,
Our sons and daughters take to Freud
　And gin, that's equally synthetic,
The world's a movietone, that yells
And curvets like a drunken Hopi —
And yet, despite ten thousand hells,
　There's always Copey!

So we, escaping from despair,
　Despatch our thoughts, in quest of solace,
To breathe again that calm, clean air
　Within th'eternal bricks of Hollis;
And tread those squeaking boards we trod
When we were sophomores, pure and soapy,
And tell this cock-eyed world: By God
　There's always Copey!

A large English eighteenth century silver tray, handsomely inscribed, was given him; it bore the coat-of-arms of the O'Grady Family, with the motto, "Vulneratus non victus," which W. G. Wendell, who, as the club's secretary, made the presentation, said might be freely translated as "Emeritus but not retired." Paul Hollister read a "Report of the Condition of the Charles Townsend Copeland–Manuel Garcia Cigar Co., Limited," a spoof which had its origin in Copeland's frequent observation that he hoped to live, like Manuel Garcia, to be a hundred, and then turn into a cigar. Special labels had been printed; one of them bore the notation, "Small Perfecto Size." Following a reminiscent speech by the guest of honor, the club was presented with an oil portrait of him by Charles Hopkinson; this had been commissioned by a fund-raising committee headed by James F. Curtis, who made the presentation. It hangs now in the club's grill room.

In accordance with a promise made to Copeland, Sherwood reported on these proceedings in a letter to Alexander Woollcott, who was unable to be present. He quoted from Copeland's speech, "When your invitation reached me, I was lying on the shelf, where I had been reverently placed some two years ago. My legs, as I lay, were crossed, but only at the ankles, to indicate that although I had been on the Crusades, I had never reached the Holy Land." Sherwood continued, "I love to hear his peroration when he speaks at these meetings. It is always the same: 'Mr. Chairman, members of the Harvard Club of New York city, and (with a prideful tremor suddenly evident in his voice) members of the Charles — Townsend — Copeland — Association.' "

Of the portrait, wrote Sherwood, Copeland had said: "There I shall hang, in the most beautiful room in America [it was hung first in the great hall which was one of Stanford White's handsomest designs], and fifty years from now some of you will be telling young men of that time highly untruthful stories of the curious little man who was the subject of that portrait, and so I will become a legend, which is as it should be."

The James and Hopkinson portraits were painted a decade apart, the first in 1920, the second late in 1929. Copeland would not have been amused had he known the whole story of how the earlier painting came to be made. John Singer Sargent, who had encountered Copeland several times at the Tavern Club in Boston, said one day to James, "Why don't you paint Copeland? He has a face like a spider." Just what suggested this comparison to Sargent is difficult to determine, unless it was the bulbous contours of Copeland's head, and a kind of patient, waiting quality that was often apparent in his face. The head shape is more pronounced in the Hopkinson portrait, painted when Copeland had become much balder. Both portraits convey the feeling of watchful waiting; in the James picture there is in addition a quality of wistfulness less often evident in later years. Sixty at the time it was executed, he looks no more than fifty, and it is still the face of a middle-aged man that more assuredly confronts us in the Hopkinson portrait, completed when he was on the verge of seventy. However much he might rage at the passing years, his heart had remained young, a fact of which no painter could be oblivious.

Both artists found him a difficult subject. He was self-conscious, restive, and apprehensive. After a few sittings to James, he broke off abruptly, came no more, and wrote asking that the canvas be destroyed. Although it was never finished, years later he asked James why he didn't exhibit it. In 1959 James presented the portrait to the Signet Club of Harvard, where it hangs today. While sitting for Hopkinson, Copeland was constantly concerned lest he be made to appear with "wattles and dewlaps," and asked a promise never to quote his protests or to make sport of him. The last time painter and subject met was in the hall of the Harvard Club in New York, several years after the portrait had been hung. "Hello," said Hopkinson. "Hello," said Copeland, "I thought you were dead." And there the conversation ended.

CHAPTER THIRTEEN

The Copeland Anthologies

IN JULY 1920, Copeland wrote to his former pupil, Maxwell Perkins, then editor of Charles Scribner's Sons:

Dear Max:

If a publisher had suggested to you to write your memoirs, if a well-known painter had asked to paint your portrait, and if the President of Bowdoin College had given you the degree of Doctor of Letters — Litt. D. [This was the only honorary degree Copeland received.] — if all these things had been done to you, what should you think they meant? It all sounds to me like twilight and evening bell, and one clear call for me. But I refuse to go. In five years I shall be sixty-five years old, the prescribed age for retirement on a pension. [Actually, this was not mandatory, and he did not retire until 1928, and then at his own request.] In about three years my friends will all kindly set up the loud cry, "How shall we persuade him to go on teaching?" Then, I think, the Powers will invite me to proceed. Will you add your voice to the call?

In all seriousness, I care more for my work, my teaching, than for anything else in the world. Without it, I should be little better than a stray cat.

No more now from

Your old friend
C. T. C.

I am sending this same letter to a few friends.

Perkins replied:

> Dear Mr. Copeland: I think the instances you cite in the
> beginning of your letter constitute one clear call for you to
> continue in 15 Hollis indefinitely. I have frequently given
> private testimony to the fact that so far as I am concerned,
> you did more good than all the rest of Harvard put together
> and if I ever had an opportunity to say this to the authori-
> ties, I should be glad to do it.
>
> As for the publisher's request that you write your mem-
> oirs, you know the only reason one publisher had not done
> it, is that he thought he could not persuade you. I should
> like to put this on record now as urging you to do it: if
> you do you must give us a chance to compete, at least.
>
> Yours as ever,
MAX

What publisher had asked for Copeland's memoirs at this
time his correspondence does not reveal. Perkins, who was
to do the *Copeland Reader* and the *Translations*, later hoped
in vain that the memoirs would be written. In 1922, Copeland
was approached by the *Boston Post* with the suggestion that
his reminiscences be prepared for that newspaper, with possible syndication in others. There were to be ten installments,
either written by him or prepared in the form of interviews.
The *Post* would pay $1500 for the ten installments, and in
addition allow him all profits from syndication. E. A. Gro-
zier, the *Post*'s publisher and editor, knew his man, for he suggested that "the pleasantest plan" from Copeland's viewpoint
would be for him to talk the articles rather than write them.
From that labor-saving arrangement, however, Copeland
backed away, and the memoirs, in whatever form, were to
be repeatedly postponed until, thirty years later, his voice was
stilled. He had been asking Perkins's advice about the offer,
and Perkins urged him to write the articles, in the hope that

they would hasten production of a book. But in May, 1922, Copeland wrote him:

> The more I think it all over, the more I am sure that all that memoirizing business had better wait until I retire from teaching. I thought two years ago that would be when I am seventy: now I am more inclined to think it will be when I am seventy-two. . . . It may amuse you to know that since I wrote I have had still another offer, not yet definitely shaped, from Braithwaite of the Transcript, who has gone into a new publishing firm without giving up his connection with the Transcript.

(This was William Stanley Braithwaite, who had founded the short-lived firm of B. J. Brimmer & Co., and was trying to interest Copeland in editing the anthology which Scribner's would eventually publish as *The Copeland Reader*.)

> What you are all afraid of [continued Copeland in his letter to Perkins] when you urge me to do the work now is that I shall die on you. But four very long-lived lines meet in me, and unless I am run over I shall not get away before the age of eighty-five — damn it. I have stated a good reason for postponing my writing until I am seventy or seventy-two. Another capital reason is that I shall not be less well known by that time, and that in the eight or ten years between now and then I shall in all probability be accumulating more interesting material. . . .
> When the time comes, shall I be blamed if I encourage all the people to bid against each other? One thing I am sure you know, that even if you hadn't been so very good to me in more ways than one, I should rather have you for my publisher than anybody else in the country. . . .

Scrupulous in all his dealings, Copeland would not forget that Braithwaite had proposed the anthology to him, and he gave the book, which proved highly profitable, to Scribner's only after the Brimmer Company found itself in irretrievable financial difficulties. The firm's collapse was not surprising, considering the fact that first volumes by young poets bulked so large on its list; one was by a Harvard undergraduate, lately of Yale, named Lucius Beebe, whom Braithwaite enlisted as an emissary to Copeland. Braithwaite had published also, under the title *Confusion*, the first novel of a Harvard student named James Gould Cozzens, and he was playing a constructive part in the revival of public interest in poetry through his annual *Anthology of Magazine Verse*, which he had begun to edit in 1913. Beebe, whose chief concerns are now the publishing of the *Virginia City Territorial Enterprise* in Nevada, and the celebration of American railroad history, undertook his assignment with pleasure that rapidly became distaste. Copeland was persuaded to undertake the book, and Beebe invested with a somewhat vague status as a kind of editorial assistant; he recalls now that his duties amounted to little more than fetching books from the Widener Library. He found Copeland far too exacting a taskmaster, and happily pursued his role as man-about-town when the house of Brimmer collapsed.

The preparations for *The Copeland Reader* had dragged on for nearly three years when early in June 1925, Copeland wrote to Perkins, informing him of Braithwaite's difficulties, and of the offer he had just received from another publisher, who had "scented disaster." He invited Perkins to come to see him, cannily adding, "I could easily excite the trade, and therefore feel that I must have a contract equal to the very liberal one with Braithwaite. I like him and am very sorry for him."

2

Thus began what became one of the most extraordinary relationships between author and publisher in the history of the trade. Perkins, in his eagerness to publish the work of a man he so highly regarded, was ready to meet any reasonable demands; he was to bear, too, with many that were difficult, although these were not of a financial kind. In matters of editorial co-operation Copeland would exact the last pound of flesh. His correspondence with the firm would mount to incredible proportions; the files relating to *The Copeland Reader* and *The Copeland Translations* are more voluminous than those concerning any other books in Scribner's history. His letters dealing with textual matters, with the choice of selections, with advertising and other promotion, were incessant; his inquiries as to when there would be another printing, and of what size, were repeated and insistent. Under this barrage, Perkins, and later Wallace Meyer, displayed remarkable patience and courtesy. No matter how querulous the communications, so often requesting a reply "by return of post," they were always answered with consideration and dispatch.

No anthologist was ever so pampered by his publisher as Copeland was by the house of Scribner. Not only did the firm assume the cost of all copyright permissions; it acquired for him all the texts he needed, and undertook all correspondence and negotiations necessary in obtaining the permissions. He made no visits to the Scribner offices, but there were frequent journeys from New York by Perkins or Meyer, summoned to confer with him in Cambridge or at the Walpole Inn in New Hampshire, where, during those years, he spent his vacations.

But nothing was more singular in their business relations than Copeland's attitude in the matter of advances on royalties. These he insisted upon regarding as what, in actuality, they are — a loan, secured, more or less, by the publisher's expectation of eventual profit. Copeland is probably the only author in publishing history who would accept an advance only with the stipulation that he be charged interest for this accommodation. As every publisher knows, a small minority of authors prefer not to receive advances, but one with Copeland's convictions was unique. On this point he was adamant; and, indeed, his attitude was consonant with the intense awareness he had of all obligations, and which he expected of his friends. There was one revealing exception; he made many loans (and many gifts of money which strained his small resources), but he never asked for their return. In other respects his code was rigid; he would not tolerate unpunctuality, or failure to respond to a letter which required answer. In his engagement books, whenever an entry appears recording lunch or dinner with one of his friends, there is always the notation, "I the host," or "Smith the host." He wanted always to be sure he was holding up his end.

There was strong affection between Perkins and Copeland, and a mutual admiration and sense of indebtedness, evident in all their letters. One aspect of their correspondence was unique in Copeland's relations with his younger friends. Early in their relationship he protested at being addressed as "Dear Mr. Copeland," and time and again he urged Perkins to be less formal, but Max, a shy man, of iron-clad reserve, could never take the step. Soon Copeland began to tease him about the inhibition, and would sometimes prefix the signature to his letters with a Mr., the whole enclosed in quotation marks. And occasionally, instead of beginning, "Dear Max," he would write "Dear Mr. Perkins." But Perkins never abandoned the formal mode of address, whether in writing or speech. It would have amused Copeland to hear, as perhaps he did, the story of Perkins's distress when he had to consult Charles Scribner about the presence of four-letter words in a Hemingway manuscript. "What are the words?" asked Scribner. Max couldn't bring himself to pronounce them; he scribbled hastily on a piece of paper, and shoved it across the desk.

The Copeland Reader (so titled by Braithwaite and retained by Perkins) was a huge anthology running to nearly
1700 pages. Containing both English and American poetry
and prose, it began with passages from the King James version
of the Bible, and came down to writers as contemporary as
Ring Lardner and Robert Benchley. The ordinary trade edition was in one volume, which demanded the most careful
planning. There was also a school edition, with notes provided by Thurman L. Hood of the Harvard English department, who was of great assistance to Copeland in the
book's preparation, and a five-volume subscription edition
which had a large sale among Harvard alumni. This, over
Copeland's angry protests, was called *Copeland's Treasury.*
Perkins had hoped for a long introduction from the editor,
but by this time Copeland's aversion for the labors of the
written word had become deep-seated and intense. Between
two scant pages at the beginning and two at the end, he inserted several brief pieces, most of which he had delivered
orally, bearing upon certain writers included in the book:
"Bacon as an Essayist," "Not 'Poor Charles Lamb,'" "Hawthorne's Inheritance and His Art," "Dickens: His Best Book?"
"Tennyson and Browning as Religious Poets," and a note on
Barrie's *Margaret Ogilvy.* Like whatever he forced himself
to write they showed a keen critical sense, a human awareness, and a power to evoke whatever was most interesting
about the writers he was discussing.

As Copeland explained in the Introduction: "The title of
this anthology to a great degree expresses its composition and
purpose. Wide as is its range, the selection includes only what
I have read aloud during thirty-four years of teaching, lec-
turing, and reading." He added that "although I do not always read the best literature — audiences are great choosers
— I almost never, for any audience, choose either verse or
prose that is not literature." It was a justifiable statement; the

anthology, within the limitations he had imposed, was deserving of the large audience it won. It was published late in 1926, and for months to come Copeland feasted on the reviews, which were without exception welcoming and warm. The sales, particularly of the subscription edition, were excellent; the book continued to sell for twenty years, and earned its compiler about $35,000 in royalties. Copeland probably could never have been induced to undertake the work had it not held out the prospect of adding substantially to his meager income, and from time to time, during its preparation, cries of anguish issued from Hollis Hall. In January 1926, on a postcard written to remind Perkins that the Table of Contents "must be liberally spaced," he added, "I have come to loathe this book and task, and to wish it had never been thought of."

3

By 1932, concerned more than ever about his financial future because of losses in the 1929 crash and the menace of the ensuing depression, he was turning over in his mind other publishing ventures which might help to cushion his declining years. Actually, this concern was always exaggerated, and was to become an obsession in his old age. Yet he had reason to be apprehensive. For years he had been wholly dependent upon a small teaching salary, supplemented by occasional paid readings; from 1892 through 1910, holding only the rank of instructor, his salary had never exceeded $2500 a year; even the Boylston Professorship, to which he was appointed in 1925, at that time carried a salary of only $6000, and after his retirement in 1928, this would be materially reduced to the retiring allowance provided by his pension.

Always he had lived frugally; he had no extravagances, nor

had he any dependents. His only financial indiscretion was a liberality toward those in need which, until his last years, had been habitually out of scale with his income. On the death of his mother in 1916, the few thousand dollars he received from her small estate provided him with the first opportunity he had for investment. In such matters he benefited by the advice and assistance of his brother-in-law, William H. Dunbar, and later, of James F. Curtis. These two men handled his investments for him, and by their sagacity and care saw to it that he would not be in want. After their deaths, his finances were administered for him by his nephew, Charles F. Dunbar, whom he made executor of his estate. Much of his capital was put into annuities by Curtis and the younger Dunbar to such good effect that although his estate did not exceed $60,000, he had for some years before he died an income, including his pension, of over $12,000 a year.

With the memoirs reserved for some distant date, Perkins had discussed with him the possibility of a small book based on his experience as a teacher of writing. It was to be called "One Way of Teaching," and in May 1932 Copeland tentatively returned to the idea. He wrote to Perkins, suggesting that he might proceed with this, "on your alluring recipe of one hour a day." Or what would his publisher say to an anthology of translations, "many of them the most effective things for my purpose that I have ever read aloud?" And did he think that within a few months it would be advisable to print "a minimum of five thousand copies of the Treasury?"

In English [Copeland's letter concluded] there are only two places for emphasizing, so I always taught, — the beginning and the end of a sentence, the beginning and end of a chapter, the beginning and the end of a letter, the last being always the best for emphasis. So let me say now that I liked Louise's story, and liked very much indeed all of it that came after the girl's waking up to the dismal life she was leading. I should write this, and more too, to Louise herself [Perkins's wife] except that writing a letter to her is like posting it in the well-known hollow tree in the opera *Don Giovanni.*

How do things go? No matter how they go, please answer one question without delay: When do we print?

Do you take August for your holiday?

The book on his teaching methods was put aside, and like the memoirs, never written. Soon many friends of Copeland were receiving letters from him, asking for suggestions as to pieces which might be included in the new anthology. He himself put in many hours of reading, Perkins and Meyer (who supplied the biographical notes) were indefatigably helpful, and in the fall of 1934 *The Copeland Translations* was ready for publication. The book, designed as a companion volume to the *Reader*, ran to a thousand pages, and the selections ranged through French, German, Italian and Russian literature. There were a few pages of rambling Introductory Notes by the editor, who remarked at one point:

Literature in translation is almost always sure to be literature at least once removed. And in the case of poetry the removes are always likely to be as those of Scotch cousins. The discussion of these principles must be left until I next have a lot of *traduttori* together between the covers of a book. That is until I make another anthology.

One suspects that he felt guilty over saying so little about the selections he had made, for he included a note of apology:

I have had to give up the intention of a reasoned, coherent, introduction to a superb thousand pages of selected translations from modern literature. Not all of it is by any means great literature, but it so attracted and held us that we gave too much time to making the book, and allowed far too little for an introduction.

He dedicated the book

To Maxwell Perkins
Great Publisher
and
Steadfast Friend

The *Reader* had been dedicated to a lifetime older friend, Mrs. Charles E. Swan of Calais, to whom he had written a weekly letter for something like forty years.

Although *The Copeland Translations* met with a cordial reception in the press, it failed, by a wide margin, to match the financial success of its predecessor. Scribner's lost money on the venture, which was an expensive one, and Copeland's royalties were less than $1500. Nevertheless, plans were soon in the making for a big volume of selections from the Greek and Latin classics. These were not far advanced when Copeland decided to make the book wholly a Greek anthology. The task, in which he had enlisted the help of Professor James B. Munn of the Harvard English department, was nearing completion when, in March 1937, he wrote to Perkins:

I must give up the Greek Anthology. By April twenty-fourth, when I hope to lunch with you at the quondam speakeasy, I can give you my excellent reasons. That is, I can do so if I am sleeping better, and if my ears don't hum louder. It is better to give you the cold fact now, so as to avoid making announcements. You will doubtless tell Wallace [Meyer] immediately, so that he won't set to work on the Notes, which he does so incomparably well.

The chief and determining impediment would seem to have been the thought of preparing an introduction, which preyed upon his mind. He was troubled, too, by his action in withdrawing from a project to which he had been committed, for he wrote to Perkins:

> Of course, if you and the House of Scribner, of which you are the most important member, lose by my having to back down, I know you will let me pay gradually, and perhaps be willing to wait for your due until I finish "One Way of Teaching," which you once said would sweep the country. I think it will, and I mean to get to work, deliberately and steadily, as soon after July fourth as may be.

4

But there were to be no more references to "One Way of Teaching." That once cherished project seemed to fade from his mind. Now and then, however, for several years to come, he or Perkins would blow a faint breath of hope on the idea of the memoirs. In October, 1938, Copeland wrote:

> Perhaps you have read a book once famous, entitled "Voyage Autour de ma Chambre" by Xavier de Maistre. I have an idea that my reminiscences might well begin with some such sketch, more lightly touched, of my own surroundings here in this flat. You know there are a good many books and prints and objects that interest people, and would interest them mentioned as I speed along. What do you think of that?

Perkins must have smiled wryly when he came to the words, "as I speed along," applied to the book he had now

been anticipating for nearly twenty years, but he made his
customary encouraging reply.

It is of interest to note that Copeland's letter had gone on
to say:

> You asked me in a letter once whether I thought Hem-
> ingway would do well in attempting to write about old
> Spain, — Spain centuries ago. I didn't answer, but I meant
> to answer and say that he didn't seem to me the kind of
> man for that sort of thing. He is tremendously vivid in his
> own time, and among people and things that are within
> sight and sound and personal knowledge. What do you
> think?
>
> Do you ever go to the Harvard Club, and if you do, do
> you ever see anybody that speaks of me?

A final mention of the memoirs occurs in a letter Copeland wrote to Perkins, in August, 1940. He was now past
eighty, and deeply troubled over the situation in Europe.

> Poor England! [he wrote] It looks to me, and it
> probably looks to you, as if England can't be saved. It is a
> time and a situation, isn't it, when we all think of the
> phrase, the mother country, with a feeling that seldom
> comes to us.
>
> Never in my wildest dreams did it occur to me to write
> an autobiography. All that I thought of was Reminis-
> cences; and I will try to write to you about that matter
> when I get a little more energy. A brief coolness brings
> me energy and then departs, carrying the energy with it.

The letter was signed, "No more now from your grateful
and oldest friend, 'Mr. Copeland.' "

Perkins tried to cheer him by telling what he had recently

heard about a lift in British morale, and wrote, "A book of reminiscences is right. I knew, of course, it would not be conventional autobiography, — that it would be about what and whom you saw and heard, rather than directly about you." Perkins's letter began with a literary note he knew Copeland would enjoy:

What kept me from answering you was being struck, all of us here, by that literary blitzkrieg, Ernest Hemingway. For over a week I could do little work, and no letter writing. He was revising his manuscript [*For Whom the Bell Tolls*] in a room in the Barclay which was always filled with veterans of the Spanish war, and newspapermen, and striking looking females. And there was a sideboard with ice, soda, and whiskey. At the same time, the printer was setting up. Well, nobody but an ex-newspaperman could have worked under those circumstances, but Hem managed it.

Among Copeland's papers were found three small sheets of typescript with the heading, "Introduction to Reminiscences." These sentences followed:

You who are my friends will read these selections from my life, even if nobody else does. But many of you live at great distances, and so will like to read something like the "Voyage autour de ma chambre," "A trip round my room," of Zavier de Maistre, the famous Savoyard Frenchman of noble birth. Without attempting his philosophy, I follow, with additions, his plan of letting his readers see some of the objects about him.

His room was "situated in latitude 48° east, according to the measurement of Father Beccaria." My four many-windowed rooms (with a kitchen and sun porch added), are on

the fifth floor of an apartment house in Cambridge. West-
ward they look down on the narrowest part of Concord
Avenue, a canyon between high buildings — but eastward
and northward they "give on" incredible stretches of
houses and red chimneys and trees and sky. A good sight
by day is the cross on the steeple of St. Peter's Church,
shining bright in the sunlight. But the best sight of all,
strangely impressive as the night view is, guess if you can.
Nothing equals the red flash-light, up on a hill, guiding
the aircraft from dusk until daylight.

Beyond that point the reminiscences never progressed.

5

Shortly after his abandonment of the Greek anthology,
Copeland was immensely cheered by his inclusion in Bartlett's *Familiar Quotations*. This came about by his own in-
stigation. There had come into his head a witty variation on
a line from Pope by which he was so delighted that in September 1934 he set down a brief account of its inception:

On Tuesday, August 28th, I was glooming along the
shore of Fresh Pond, realizing that I must exercise before I
could write any more on the terrible little introduction [for
the *Translations*] which was finished only a week ago tonight, in time for the New York mail. Thus glooming, I
found myself muttering without meaning to,
To err is human, to forgive divine. And then in less than
two seconds, without any attempt on my part to compose,
or any thought whatever, the manner of my muttering was
changed, and I found myself reciting, as it were, out of a
book,

To eat is human, to digest divine. I began to laugh, not with a vanity laugh, because I didn't think of the words as mine. Then when I got back to my flat, I rushed to Bartlett, more than half expecting, certainly dreading, to find the words there. But there was no parody of the great line in Pope in English or in any other language; so that this inspiration of mine must always be thought original. Mustn't it?

When he learned that a revised edition of the famous reference work was in progress, under the joint editorship of Christopher Morley and Louella D. Everett, he wrote to Roger L. Scaife of Little, Brown & Co. that he would like to be in Bartlett, and submitted his epigram. "Mr. Scaife," Miss Everett recalls, "sent the letter along to me with the notation, 'Put him in.' It seemed rather skimpy representation, but the only thing I had of Professor Copeland's was his *Reader*. I gleaned five extracts from its Introduction and sent them to Copey, asking if he approved my putting them in along with his epigram. He was enchanted, so they went in the 12th edition."

The additions included two sentences from his tribute to Nathaniel Southgate Shaler: "A man is always better than a book," and "For the common man, the best memorial is some beneficent thing or function that shall bear his name." There was a sentence from a lecture on Dickens: "Where novelists are concerned, because with lyric poets novelists are the most personal of writers, the question of the best book is likely to be as alluring as it is ultimately futile." From his address on Charles Lamb, Miss Everett chose: "Whenever we encounter the typical essayist, he is found to be a tattler, a spectator, a rambler, a lounger, and, in the best sense, a citizen of the world"; also, from his comment on Lamb's indulgence in drink, "To blame him were absurd; to pity were profane."

Copeland wrote to Alfred R. McIntyre, then president of the firm:

I am very tired and mildewed with the weather, but not too tired to thank you for allowing me to come into so much famous company. I expect to be thrown out when the next revised edition is made, with the exception — the line of verse so strangely given to me by somebody from somewhere without a word of notice or explanation. As you know, I had been muttering, 'To err is human, to forgive divine,' and suddenly, the metre remaining with some of the words, the thing was changed to what you see. I prophesy without vanity that it will last like bronze, because eating will always be the fashion, and digestion always remain the eater's ideal.

But he guessed wrong about its permanence, at least in Bartlett, for although all but one of the other quotations have been retained, the line he prized so much is absent from the current edition.

It is amusing to note that when Frank Crowninshield, as editor of *Vanity Fair*, invited Copeland to contribute two queries to a literary questionnaire, he included among the four he offered: "Name the little known American author of the line: 'To eat is human, to digest divine.'" At that time, it had not yet appeared in Bartlett, nor had it been published anywhere else.

CHAPTER FOURTEEN

Footnotes to a Legend

THERE IS, as we all know, often a sharp division between the public and the private man. The face presented to the world, the face whose aspect is so frequently determined by careful assessment of what the world expects and must be given if the established image is to endure, and the face this same man confronts in his solitary hours, or sometimes permits to be glimpsed by others, often bear little likeness one to the other. In those cases where the player has the whole world for his stage, sometimes the public image becomes for him his true personality, and for its maintenance he will sacrifice anything and anybody. The twentieth century has produced an exceptional number of such characters. This was inevitable, when, by modern devices, the means of projecting the public personality were greatly multiplied.

Copeland was not a public man as we ordinarily use the term; he did not figure in great events, and only the eyes of his own world were fastened on him. Nevertheless, in his determination to make himself count, to overcome the handicaps by which he had been confronted in that world, and by his histrionic bent, he had created the image which it recognized as Copey. The urge to do this was innate. As Elizabeth Shepley Sergeant wrote in her perceptive sketch of him:

The old Maine stock, from which he comes, is leisurely and beauty-loving as well as pioneering. Aristocrats of the provinces, as good as anybody and even a little better, they are ever scornful of mediocre performance in life. The ghostly inward whip which they lay upon the shoulders of their descendants scourged Copeland, I feel sure, to prove his mettle in the world, to leap obstacles, by persistent courageous effort. And he certainly owes them the slighting accents with which names not loved, like Byron's, are dismissed from his lips; the caustic touch which seems to throw the light of some inward scorn upon his own peccadillos. These Maine folk are not very easily fooled, even about themselves.

And of his individual contribution to the appreciation of good writing — as apart from his instruction in the practice of the art — she wrote:

Most professors of literature present neatly dissected masterpieces to the minds of their students. Copeland has done very little dissecting. He has poured masterpieces whole into the souls of his hearers, with a peculiar fervour of speech and accent that seem, though so perfectly in control, the discharge of some inner compulsion. What we see, especially inside a book, we may ignore. What we hear, really hear, in that fashion, we *feel*, like a kind of music. Literature and life fuse, or rather, literature becomes the flower and consummation of life. The great writers of the past, the figures of their creation, are living, actual, understandable, ourselves. At their best, Copeland's reading of prose and poetry and his biographical lectures have had a breath of living genius.

It was this quality in Copeland's teaching which had moved Heywood Broun to say that for so many students he had "taken the curse off literature." He had made it seem to them, not something immured in a library, but a vibrant world synonymous with life itself. This insistence upon the human quality was apparent even in the titles of some of his courses: Lives, Times and Manners of Men of Letters, English and American, or Dr. Johnson and His Circle. The books about which he lectured were the work of a man or woman, a part of them, as they were a part of the times in which they had their being. His students must be made to see what manner of people they were, and against what kind of background they had lived and written.

As he projected images of them, so that Johnson and Boswell, Fanny Burney and Jane Austen, Coleridge and Lamb and Wordsworth and Shelley and Scott became living presences in Sever Hall, so too he had projected an image of himself. For the average student who saw him only on the platform at his lecture courses, at his reading performances, or even at the Hollis 15 gatherings where he was still consciously playing a part, there were sides of him never glimpsed. For no matter what the wealth of documents, the plenitude of anecdotes, or the insights psychology provides, most of us hide our innermost motivations from other men, and, even, from ourselves. No man ever exposed himself as fully to the world's gaze as Boswell — not even Rousseau, who was less objective — yet even Boswell, with all his unflinching self-dissection, sometimes leaves us baffled.

The public image Copeland had created was, in spite of his unimposing stature, formidable, as if he had slipped over his slight figure an invisible cloak of magisterial dignity. It was caustic, sardonic, peremptory, ready to sacrifice kindness for a witticism, seemingly sure of itself. It held no hint of his timidity, his lack of physical adventurousness, of those fears by which, like Dr. Johnson, he was gripped. (They were alike, too, in the high degree of moral courage they possessed.)

As a natural actor Copeland's need of public approval was

intense, and matched only by his need for affection. His craving for favorable notices of anything he had done or said was consuming; if he were told of some complimentary reference which had escaped him, he would, if need be, spend hours tracking it down, and delightedly report it to his friends. Vanity is not the word for this thirst he had for approval; Copeland saw himself too clearly ever to be touched by megalomania. He knew the value of his teaching, for he had seen it proved, and it was on its obvious results that he prided himself the most. His clear-eyed assessment of himself appears over and over again in his letters. He did not suffer from the illusions to which truly vain men are prone. What he was fundamentally seeking in his quest for praise was reassurance; it was a childlike need. He wanted praise for the same reason that he wanted love. As sweet to him as the applause at his readings were the attentions of his friends, and there were sure to be reproaches if he felt himself neglected. People who knew only the public image, and had perhaps seen the flashes of cruelty it could inflict, did not know the deep tenderness of which he was capable, the instinctive awareness of another's need, and the immediate impulse to be helpful in whatever way he could.

A few instances should suffice. First, this recollection by Charles Allan Smart: "One May evening in 1925, for some strange reason I received a special note from Copey to appear at the following Wednesday evening. I accepted by note, at once. Then I received a telephone call from New York that my father was seriously ill. I sent another note, or took one, rather, round to Copey's door, and left at once for New York. Within a few days my father was dead, and within another few days, with a defensive black band on my arm, I was in the Yard again, which then seemed, like all the earth, quite empty. Copey picked me up in the Yard, did not somehow notice the black band, thanked me for my second note, and inquired about the health of my father. I burst into tears, by which I was more intensely humiliated than I should be now, of course. Copey then saw the band on my arm, and as I remember it clearly, shaking and red with his own humiliation, led me by the arm to his room, gave me two or three stiff drinks, and walked back and forth in front of me, saying almost nothing, but delivering warmly his feelings. He was no actor that afternoon."

It was with this same concern that in 1895, from his vacation retreat at Campobello, he had written to Mark Howe, on the death of Howe's father:

> Mrs. Locke's shockingly written but sincere and rightly felt testimony to your Father's life and works, has forced upon me again the indecency of my having yet sent you no word of sympathy except by the obliterating telegraph. But nature, "whose common theme is death of fathers," can be your only power of help and pity. She must often have said to your Father and to all his house, in peremptory ways, that a man who has lived more than half a generation beyond the psalmist's term, breathes on in daily, hourly peril of the psalmist's penalty.
>
> So, if the thought of immunity to him does not console you for the loss to yourself, no word of mine will bring even a moment's solace. But I want you very much to leave the *place* of sorrow — there is distraction in that, if not comfort — and come to visit me a week. Either here at Welchpool, which we leave on the 28th day of August, or in Calais after the middle of September. You will never see me in the morning, because I read or work, or think about working; and as I walk between six miles and eight every day, and devote some space of the diurnal course to my mother, you will run no grave risk of seeing too much of me at any time. But you shall have me on demand —

always. Do come, and pray let me know at once your choice of time. These waters are the waters of Lethe, and no man lifts up his eyes to these hills without help. I will be as good to you as I know how, and we will walk — or like Landor you shall walk "alone — upon the eastern uplands." Do come. It is the part of wisdom.

He never needed to be told; he always sensed the other man's difficulty. Several years after college I had dinner with him one evening in Boston; although I was not depressed, I was concerned about something I cannot now remember. We had hardly sat down when Copey said, "Something is troubling you; tell uncle." What I answered I can't recall, but Malcolm Cowley remembers a similar instance of his intuition, in this case with graver cause: "After three years in college, dispersed over five years by wartime interruptions, I was leaving Cambridge with my degree at the beginning of February, 1920. I was married by then, my wife was ill, and I was broke, though I hadn't told anyone how broke I was. I lived under the eaves in a rooming house on Mt. Auburn Street. On the last day of the term, there was a knock at my garret door. It was Copey's young man — he always had an assistant to run errands — with an envelope addressed to me in Copey's angular hand. In the envelope there was a little note — I forget what it said — folded around a ten-dollar bill. That bill, with another five dollars I had (but that was all) carried my wife and me to New York and the beginning of another life."

2

Here is the experience, remembered after nearly half a century, of William M. Tugman, a newspaper editor who has long been one of the leading citizens of Oregon. He had not been one of Copeland's students; he had attended the readings, and went several times to the Hollis Hall evenings, where he grew accustomed to being greeted as "Tugman of the wild eyes." From other professors, he recalls, "this would have brought forth flaming resentment, but to be singled out by Copey conferred a distinction of a sort." After Commencement in 1914, his efforts at finding a job were fruitless, and, short of funds, he was immobilized in Cambridge. There had been what seemed an assured prospect of a junior editorship on the just-founded *New Republic*, but one day he was summoned to the office of Felix Frankfurter, then teaching at the Harvard Law School (where the future Justice began a long, admiring friendship with Copeland) and gently informed that a lack of funds would prevent his appointment. Unfounded expectations had led Tugman to indulge in a spell of "riotous living." He borrowed five dollars, and went over to Springfield, in quest of a job on the *Springfield Republican*, whose reputation as a training school in journalism made young men happy to begin there at eight or nine dollars a week. Arriving unheralded and unannounced, he made his way into the office of the editor and publisher, Samuel Bowles, who pushed him down the stairs and screamed, "Write me a letter, young man! Don't ever intrude again without invitation." A few days later, Tugman visited the offices of the *Christian Science Monitor*, where "a sleek, self-satisfied gentleman patted his paunch, gazed at the ceiling, and suggested that I write to 'some farmer in Kansas for an advance of the fare to come out and help in the harvest — and then submit some copy.'" By this time Tugman was eating by means of selling clothes to Max Keezer and an occasional space rate job for the *Boston Globe*.

And then, one evening, he encountered Copey in Harvard Square. "Ah, it is Tugman of the wild eyes. What are you doing in Cambridge at this time of year?" Tugman told him a little of his misadventures, and Copey said, "Why don't you come to see me tomorrow afternoon at two, young man?" "The bell in Memorial," he recalls, "was striking two the next afternoon as I reached the door. It flew open before I could knock. There was Copey hopping on one leg, trying to poke the other through his pants. "Ah, it's you. Had you been one minute earlier — or later, I would have kicked you down the stairs. Come in."

When he had finished dressing, Copeland asked. "Why didn't I see you in English 12 this year?" Tugman explained that there had been complications about the distribution of his courses. "They said," he began. "They, they," snorted Copeland. "Why didn't you speak to me about it? I would have been happy to have you in the course." "Those words," Tugman remembers, "were balm to an ego which had been trampled on. Nothing else he might have said could have done so much to restore my confidence and self-respect."

Tugman could never forget the two hours that followed. There was no heavily moralizing advice, and the difficulties he had experienced were laughed off. But there was one pre-cept Copeland returned to several times: "The most impor-tant thing is to avoid the second-rate." Suddenly he got up, took down a book, and began to read from Whitman, "Afoot and light-hearted, I take to the open road." "For his lone auditor," Tugman recalled, "Copey read a great many other things during that long hot afternoon up under the eaves of Hollis — some of his favorite passages from the Bi-ble, the 18th Psalm, the parable of the Prodigal; a few gay bits from Mr. Pickwick; some of the more graphic and dra-matic passages from Joseph Conrad; some of the most mov-ing statements of Abraham Lincoln."

It seemed to Tugman that "without stating his purpose, Copey seemed to be trying to give me his notion of the opportunities which might lie ahead, his concept of the first-rate as distinguished from the inferior." When the time came to go. Copey followed him to the door and into the corridor. "Good-bye and good luck," he said, "And, Tugman, I think if I were you I'd write that letter to Mr. Samuel Bowles." He did, that same night, and got the job.

3

Back in 1895, when Copeland was just beginning to exercise his unique influence, another boy, whose name was Arthur Stanwood Pier, sat alone in his room at the top of Holworthy, pondering his future. Commencement was only a few days distant. His inclinations were literary, and he had been on the editorial boards of the *Advocate* and the *Monthly*. His friend Charles Flandrau, at Copeland's suggestion, had taken him once to a Copeland evening, but he did not go again. "I often met Mr. Copeland in the Yard," he recalls, "always with embarrassment. He stopped me once and said querulously, 'You don't like my Wednesday evenings?' I explained that all my evenings were crowded with things I had to do. 'I think you might spare a Wednesday evening some time,' he said, and passed on."

These had been their only contacts, so that on that night shortly before his graduation, Pier was both surprised and confused when, answering a knock on the door, he called "Come in," and Copeland entered. "I was mumbling some sort of welcome when he cut me short: 'I saw a light in your room. I thought I would come over and ask you what you mean to do when you graduate.' 'I am going back to Pittsburgh to study law,' I said. 'My father was a lawyer there. He died in my Sophomore year. His partner is willing that I should read law in his office.' "

Copeland shook his head: "I think that would be a mistake. I should like to write a letter introducing you to a friend of mine. May I use your desk?" He marched across the room, sat down and wrote to Mark Howe, at that time editor of *The Youth's Companion*. Then he said, "I wish you would present this before you go to Pittsburgh."

Pier did so, only to find that Howe, suffering from eye trouble, had just begun an extended leave of absence. So Pier went on to Pittsburgh, where both he and his father's partner soon arrived at a similar conclusion: the law was not for him. Encouraged by Copeland's interest, he had meanwhile been submitting stories to *The Youth's Companion*. They were accepted, and presently came a letter from the acting editor, inviting him to join the staff. The letter to Mark Howe was delivered some months later, at the beginning of their long association.

Copeland was seldom in error about the potentialities of his young friends. Hans Kaltenborn gratefully remembers how he early discerned that Kaltenborn's future lay not in the written, but the spoken word, and there were many others who by his insight were saved from careers otherwise destined to disappointment and frustration. Also there were those who drew surety and strength from his aid in overcoming their self-distrust. He had in him a creative urge deeper than that which animates the art of the actor, one more akin to those other arts deriving their impetus from sources more original and profound. This urge lay at the core of his teaching and of the guidance he gave so many boys in realizing themselves or in grasping the values by which life can be enhanced.

His interest in the kind of life his friends were living, even the physical characteristics of their environment, if he was separated from them by distance, was intense. One of his old friends and a fellow Down-Easter, Robert W. Sawyer, went out to Bend, Oregon, to publish and edit a newspaper there.

Copeland wrote to him, "I can tell that you are in good health and spirits. Why don't you make the struggle and let me know where your house stands, what you see from it, and what are the physical characteristics of the country all around and about Bend? Does the river bulk large and impress itself on the scene? Remember that I am presently going back for six weeks of the Summer School in Cambridge, and that letters from my best friends will then be a particular boon." There was a typical postscript: "I am 61, damn it!" Several months later Sawyer received another letter ending with an equally typical appeal for approval: "Although I am nearly sixty-two years old, I am now doing measurably more work than I was doing ten years ago. Applaud and write to your old friend, Cope."

4

His letters are on the whole more revealing than the fragmentary journal he kept through most of his life. Chiefly it merely recorded his appointments; whenever he gave a reading, he entered a list of the selections chosen. Names and addresses were scattered through it without order of any kind. Only rarely did it assume the nature of a diary. When his mother lay dying early in January of 1916, there was a moving entry. The night before her death he wrote on his return to Hollis: "Roused at last about 8.30. Clasped and unclasped hands, then laid them on my head and cheeks. 'So glad you've come. How I love you! Do you love me?' — I — 'I shan't know how to live without you.' M.— 'But you will' — smiling with radiant constancy. Took a little pleasure in carnations and — earlier — in crimson roses. Rousing later, — 'I can't talk, isn't it funny?' smiling with natural humor."
She died early on Sunday morning, the ninth of January,

and the impact upon him may be judged by the fact that save for fifteen scattered days, the remaining pages of his journal for that year were left blank.

Customarily he made note there of any honor which had been paid him, and of any article about him. Thus in June, 1920, when Bowdoin made him an honorary Litt. D., though he did not attend the ceremonies, he copied down the ascription: "Loyal son of Maine, inspiring teacher of literature, patriotic member of a patriotic family." In that same month there is a long entry concerning an invitation from the Class of 1917 to join them for as much of their Triennial celebration as he might care to attend. The journal records that he spent most of that day writing his answer. It was addressed to the Class Secretary, Edward Allen Whitney:

My dear Mr. Secretary,
Few things in a long life have pleased or honored me more, few things could please or honor me more, than the resolution passed at a recent meeting of the Class of 1917, and transmitted to me by you on the nineteenth of this month.

If I were not unavoidably to be away from Cambridge during the Triennial Reunion, I should gladly, proudly accept the invitation of the Class — an invitation with few precedents — to be its guest in those days.

And because I knew eleven of the men who are not coming back to their triennial, I should ask to be allowed to speak at the dinner. Speaking there for the eleven after the silent toast to all who have gone, I should urge the great company of their living comrades always to be worthy of the Class as it fought and strove in 1917. This means that they shall be eager servants of the country and of civilization, in these great, changing times, — in the new epoch so visibly beginning. A well-known Englishman said to me last fall: "We are sorry for our young people." I am glad for my young people, whatever may be their perplexities or their burdens, because their opportunity is the finest since history began. The Class of 1917 will, I hope and believe, show itself conscious now of the opportunity, and worthy of it through all the years to come.

That would be a short speech, it must be admitted. For the rest of the Triennial Reunion, I should endeavor to be an example to the Class of 1882 in genial, joyous association with the Class of 1917.

Pray accept my thanks, Mr. Secretary, for transmitting the resolution, which will leave me always a debtor.

Yours very truly,
C. T. COPELAND

At least one other class, that of 1913, paid him a similar tribute on the occasion of its Twenty-fifth Reunion dinner. Although he did not come, the familiar voice, saying, "Luck and long life to you; I never wish one without the other," rang out vibrantly over an amplifier.

During vacation periods, the journal often held brief jottings on his walks and rides, usually nothing more than the route taken, sometimes making note of birds he had seen, or of some rarely encountered plant or flower. Now and then the entries disclose his old-fashioned pleasure in finding a four-leaf clover. Walking was his only exercise; in early middle age he would march as much as eight miles, but even at eighty, as an aid to sleep, he would cover two or three. One day at Walpole, New Hampshire, he noted having seen several Baltimore orioles, and added, "Often as I have seen them, they still seem exotic, doubtful because I didn't grow up with them. There was a legend current in Calais when I was a boy, that old Mr. Deming said he had once seen an oriole in one of his trees. But he was a thief; why shouldn't he have been the other dishonest thing?"

In his early years, Kennedy's Hotel in St. Andrews had

been his favorite place of recreation; later he spent part of the summers at the Harbor View Hotel in East Gloucester, relishing the smells of salt and fish and low tide. His old friend Frank W. Buxton, one time editor of the *Boston Herald*, recalls that he liked to sit in the hotel's little cardroom and talk with the painters who, like W. M. Paxton, frequented the place. Beginning in 1918, after the visits to the border had been discontinued, he found a spot to his liking in the Walpole Inn, and there he returned almost every summer for nearly twenty years.

The Walpole area is pleasant New England countryside in an unspectacular way, and when David McCord, on his first visit there, admired it, Copeland said it was "good enough," but did he not notice that down east there was a *strangeness* mixed with beauty? McCord has written of these visits:

Walpole seemed more than good enough to me, and when I had driven past white fronts and colonial dignity, and felt the shade of ancient, mighty trees, and turned the corner beyond the stores and postoffice to the Inn itself, there he was sitting on the veranda; the small, familiar figure, alert and upright, looking abnormally respectable and of the city, and harmlessly approximate to the only tennis court in sight.

On the number of times thereafter that I arrived in the same way, it was always with the feeling of veneration at the first sight of the sleepy town, and a little nervous over the first stop before the Inn inanimate, lest I disturb its gracious withdrawal from a world I sadly appeared to represent. Inside the door I can still remember standing speechless and inappropriate. I doubt if Copey was aware of that. He always welcomed his visitor in a strong voice, taking personal care to see that someone carried bag and coat to a pre-arranged corner room. He would then look at you with that remarkable fixity, and offer certain admonishing remarks about the hour of breakfast and the likelihood of his breakfasting alone. I find in some notes which I kept of such a visit on September 30, 1931, that I was thereupon led into the dining room and shown the drawing room through tightly locked glass doors. "Like Moses," he said, "being shown the Promised Land but not allowed to enter."

Mr. Copeland himself lived in elegant seclusion behind the dangerous door of a large second-floor room in the very center of the Inn. It was always full of trunks and books, but very neat with the faint and reminiscent glamor of Hollis. The light came in through windows, front and rear; and "a great jut of room" out back toward the Green, as he used to explain it, gave the appearance of two rooms made into one. But his visitors never had more than a glimpse of all this; and the talk and business of the social day was carried on below stairs, out in the Walpole fields, and under Walpole sky. At such times he seemed more than ever the indefatigable walker. He once told me in a valetudinarian voice that he was good only for a turn just out of the town. But in city clothes and with bowler hat carefully under his arm (as though he had just crossed into Brattle Street) he walked me two or three miles across the country with the steadiness of a mountaineer bred to leather. It was on that occasion that we paused for a minute somewhere above the town to peer into a little brook that trickled down between some boulders much too big. We looked at it in silence and my thoughts ran to the possibility of fish.

"There are no trout in it," I said.

"There's music in it," said Copey.

5

His one trip abroad was made in the summer of 1928, a two months' visit to England and Scotland. For him this was a pilgrimage; his mind was as filled with historical and literary memories of scenes which had so long lived in his imagination as his rooms in Hollis were crowded with mementos of his life. Now, thanks to the royalties earned by the *Reader*, he felt free to go, and with his nephew Charles Dunbar and his niece, Rose Dunbar Gay, he sailed on the *Adriatic* on the seventh of July. Thornton Wilder, whose *Bridge of San Luis Rey* had been published some months before, was a passenger, and Copeland invited him for liqueurs after lunch on the first day out. It would appear from the notes kept by Mrs. Gay that they were the only celebrities aboard, though there is mention of a nameless bootleg king who sported a jewel-handled cane, bow tie and diamond pin. The stewards had "no time for you, sir," and the barber wouldn't shave him because of his blasphemous remarks about King George.

In London Copeland and his companions were quartered in the Burlington Hotel in Cork Street. On his first day there he made a discovery which was to complicate their trips about the city; he became convinced that there was just one kind of taxicab in which he was truly comfortable — a Beardmore — and thenceforth he would have no other. "How much of this was real," reports his nephew, "how much imagination and how much sheer perversity I never could determine."

He was no sooner settled in than he was off to visit Doctor Johnson's house in Gough Square, and soon after that to see the Doctor's pew in St. Clement Danes. There was a visit to Carlyle's house in Cheyne Row, and one to Bumpus's bookshop in Oxford Street. In the House of Commons he heard Churchill and Stanley Baldwin and Ramsay MacDonald. There was of course the Temple and Goldsmith's grave — and all the usual objectives of a first stay in London. Then came Oxford and Cambridge and Canterbury and the other cathedrals; Bath, Stonehenge, Tintern Abbey, visits with

H. M. Tomlinson and Walter de la Mare. Both men were later to climb the stairs of Hollis.

During his ten days in Scotland nothing seems to have delighted him more than the sight of Abbotsford. From boyhood on he had an unwavering admiration for Sir Walter Scott, both as writer and man. Scott's *Journals* was one of his favorite books, and when, a few weeks before his death, he was taken to the McLean Hospital, he had with him the *Journals*, a novel by Jane Austen, and *The Copeland Reader*. In his last years, when his mind was clouding, he would say that he was the only man ever permitted to handle Sir Walter's books, and one day, pointing to the photograph of Scott's library that hung beside his fireplace, he said in a far-off, reminiscent voice to his visitor, James G. King, "*We* knew him. I only wish we had seen more of him."

With his strong historical imagination, and because he thought of himself as a sentimental Jacobite, it is regrettable that he did not go far enough north in Scotland to stand on the battlefield of Culloden, which still looks much as it did when the Stuart cause ebbed out in Highland blood. He once wrote to a friend:

Another book that you should surely have is Andrew Lang's life of Charles Edward, if only for the wonderful, full, animated account of the Prince's wanderings after Culloden. I don't own it, but I borrow it every year from my nephew, to whose father I presented it some years ago.

Sir Walter Scott, whom you don't love, described himself as "a sentimental Jacobite," by which he meant that he felt the charm although he distrusted the Stuarts, and was sure that Charles Edward would never have made a good king. That, I am clear, is the kind of Jacobite I am. As Theodore Roosevelt said to me, "The lost cause is always the more charming cause," and he might have added that of all lost causes the '45 is the most romantic episode in history.

Whatever else he may have missed, the trip abroad had been a deeply satisfying experience. On the last day of August, together with his nephew and niece, he boarded the *Calgaric* at Liverpool and sailed for home.

6

When Copeland returned to Hollis Hall in September, his official teaching career was over, for in June, after only three years in the Boylston Professorship, he had retired. Unofficially, however, his influence continued. Each fall, usually in the opening week of the college year, he read to the freshmen at the Harvard Union. The Copeland legend was one of the first Harvard traditions of which each incoming class became aware, and many men have testified that these gatherings drew them together, for the time being, at least, in a memorable shared experience; it gave them their first strong sense of belonging. Beginning in 1931, when under the new House plan the Yard dormitories were set aside for the freshmen, he established a new liaison. At the suggestion of Delmar Leighton, the Dean of Freshmen, one evening each week of the college year he received two or three selected members of the entering class, a practice which was continued until he was well past eighty. James G. King, who was present on one of these occasions, writes:

I watched the two boys there that evening, sitting for an hour or so on the edges of their seats, simply polarized by the battery of well-suited, deliberately phrased challenges — all of a constructively provocative nature, about their views of life and conduct in their young contemporary world, that Copeland, then long retired, was throwing at them. For them it was obviously, every moment of it, a most hazardously enjoyable evening. His queries and comments seemed to strike them, more than sixty years his juniors — right between the eyes, as pertaining directly to their own immediate lives and problems, to things important to them, in a way that was fascinating to watch.

The boys enjoyed, too, no doubt, his own forthright and crisply phrased opinions. On any controversial issue he was sure to take an unequivocal stand, as he did in the Sacco-Vanzetti case; although unconvinced of their innocence, he would always maintain that they had not had a fair trial. Lawrence E. Spivak, producer of the TV program, Meet the Press, remembers his vehemence over the Versailles Treaty and his passionate support of the League of Nations:

I had written a piece criticizing the peace treaty of the first World War, and the following was his criticism: "Regarded as a punishment for what the Germans have done the peace terms are mild indeed. But then no punishment could be adequate for the inhuman ferocities of these people. The question is one of wisdom and I will fully admit that in my opinion the Allies have gone too far. They are exacting all at once more than they are likely to be able to get from the Germans. But the League of Nations is so important a matter that I don't want any paper to come into my house which is against it. And the opposition to it on the part of the New Republic shows the path to which fine spun theorizing will always bring people. I stopped the paper during the war because I wanted nothing that makes against the League. You and your teachers in matters political are only a little better than the Tories who are against the League — and much less logical."

Occasionally he indulged in prophecy, and in his later years he was proud of one prediction in particular. When the Senate was stormily considering the nomination to the Supreme Court of his old friend Louis D. Brandeis, he dined one evening in Boston with Felix Frankfurter and several other ardent Brandeis supporters. Afterward he took Frankfurter back to Hollis, where a group of undergraduates had been invited to hear the Law School professor talk in defense of the Brandeis appointment. When Frankfurther had finished, Copeland said, "I am sure that we shall not only see Brandeis a Justice of the Supreme Court, but that" (turning to Frankfurter) "the day will come when you will sit there by his side." It so happened that a week before Brandeis resigned from the Court, Frankfurter took his place on the high bench, and for some time thereafter, in letters to his friends, Copeland would ask, "Tell me what you thought of my prophecy concerning the Brandeis and Frankfurter appointments." And he called the turn when in 1919, at the time of the Boston police strike, he wrote to a friend: "The country will never — at least not in your time — come back to what you and your father call 'normal.' One era is finished, another is beginning. Labor is not going to content itself with higher wages and better conditions of work, but will insist upon a great share of profits and a considerable part in management."

For a few years after his move to the Concord Avenue apartment in 1932, the pattern of his life remained much the same. The readings continued, and the freshmen made their visits; young and older friends occasionally came in for tea and talk. Until he was eighty he served, as he had for many years, on the library committee of the Harvard Union, and also as a trustee of the Massachusetts State Library, the one public office he held, and in which he took great pride. When he left Hollis, he had still twenty years to live, but they were soon to become years of rapidly diminishing activity. As the delusion of financial insecurity grew upon him, he abandoned his summer visits to Walpole and stayed in Cambridge.

Of his former students, the one who saw most of him during these declining years was Walter D. Edmonds, who was then living near Concord Avenue. They lunched together frequently at the nearby Hotel Commander, and of these meetings Edmonds remembers that the time came when "he could not help himself to the pony of brandy that made the meal possible for him, and I would have to hold it to his lips across the table, to the astonishment, sometimes, of other guests. But once the brandy was inside, Copey would revive, and until the last year or so be as good as ever for the half hour we had together." Of his fear of destitution Edmonds recalls that "nothing his nephew Charles Dunbar or I could do would reassure him; and the only partial solution I arrived at was to hide a ten-dollar bill or so in a drawer of his bureau, or in a book, and then take him on a search of the apartment. Discovery of the money always reassured him for as long as I stayed, but I often wondered what anxieties he must have gone through later on."

Another friend who lunched regularly with him at the Commander during these years was Robert Hillyer, who in 1937 was appointed to the Boylston Chair. Their friendship had begun in 1928, when Hillyer returned to Harvard as a member of the English department. As an undergraduate he had not been one of Copeland's students, and he remembers that Copey "frequently alluded to the fact with irony." For fifteen years they would from time to time discuss the projected memoirs, and Copey would often make the excuse that many people might be embarrassed by finding their names in print. To a certain extent, Hillyer believes, he did feel this handicap, "for he had a Victorian niceness in his personal relationship, but more and more he found in it a pretext for not writing the memoirs at all."

7

During his last ten years his housekeeper was a brisk and kindly Scotswoman, Mrs. Isabella Arbuthnott, who was engaged for him by his niece Katharine Dunbar. When she reported for duty and pronounced her name, accenting it on the second syllable, she was startled to hear him firmly insist, "That is not your name. You are Mrs. *Ar*buthnott." At the end of the first week she told Mrs. Dunbar she could not put up with his demanding ways, but the initial difficulties were soon smoothed over, and gradually they became good and understanding friends. He would tease her, as Johnson had teased Boswell, about Scotland; having seen that country's gray and lowering skies, he would say, he could readily understand the cruelties of the Covenanters. But he delighted in her blunt Scottish speech, even though he might bark at her, "You British — you are always confusing the uses of 'shall' and 'will.' " Once she ventured to ask him if he had ever been in love, but all that was forthcoming in answer to that question was "Now, now, Isabel, enough of that." She remembers that he drank very sparingly — a glass of sherry or a thimbleful of brandy — for he had now given up the Chartreuse that had been his favorite liqueur — and as he sipped he would say to her, "I am a drinkard, but not a drunkard."

Even when his mind began to fail badly, and he was living mainly in a blurred remembrance of the past, he dressed with care each day, as he had throughout his life. He would recall at times how he had once set the fashion in the Harvard Yard. Max Perkins while an undergraduate went one day to Hollis 15 for a conference, and found him wearing a handsome new corduroy waistcoat. Admiring it — and partly to divert attention from his theme — Perkins praised this addition to his wardrobe, to Copey's evident pleasure. When he left he saw an identical waistcoat in a Harvard Square shop window, and bought it. The next purchase was made the same afternoon by Perkins's roommate, then by four or five men they dined with that evening. Within a few days the Yard was spotted with corduroy waistcoats. Copeland, ever observant, inquired of Perkins just what had happened, and when he heard the story, said, "Well, I have aspired to a number of things, but I would never have had the audacity to aspire to set the fashion for the Gold Coast."

By the spring of 1952 it became apparent that Copeland was in need of constant nursing attention. There were times now when he did not seem certain of his identity or of his whereabouts. When his mind did function it carried him back always to distant days. He saw himself driving once more up to Clendinnin's Hill with his mother, or rowing slowly down the long reaches of the St. Croix. The day came when he was driven by his Dunbar nephew and niece to the McLean Hospital in Waverly. His mind was very clouded on that journey, and when an orderly came out to assist him, he said to Charles Dunbar, "Who is this young man?" and protested against going with him. Dunbar thought fast, and answered, "Why, uncle, he's the son of an old student of yours, class of 1912." "Well, in that case," said Copeland, "I'll go with him."

That afternoon he rested in his room, but shortly after supper he picked up his copy of the *Copeland Reader*, and walked down the hall to the recreation room. Twenty or more patients were gathered there, playing checkers and backgammon, or chatting together. He found a table near the center of the room, drew up a chair, sat down, coughed, cleaned his spectacles, and then, without any prefatory remark, opened the book and began to read aloud. He went on for about half an hour. When he had finished he looked calmly about, and said in his precise tones to the astonished audience, "I do not wish to appear in any way conceited, but I think you should know that I am Copeland." Amid a spatter of applause he rose, bowed stiffly, and trudged back to his room.

That was the last time he read aloud. He died a few weeks later, on July 24th, 1952, three months past the beginning of his ninety-third year. Robert Cushman, one of his old boys, carried the ashes to Calais, and buried them in the Copeland plot of the Calais Cemetery, which lies on a long and heavily wooded ridge overlooking the countryside loved by this son of the tidewater beyond all others that he knew.

As I remember him, and as he lives in the memory of many others, there were combined in him contradictory elements to an extraordinary degree. He was caustic and tender, demanding and generous, rude and punctilious, timid and courageous, indolent and indefatigable, self-centered and even, sometimes self-forgetting. Out of this strange and baffling ambivalence emerged a man who, I believe, left his imprint upon more lives in their budding period than any other American teacher of his time.

Acknowledgments
and Index

Acknowledgments

IN THE CASE of a more or less informal biography such as this portrait of Charles Townsend Copeland, and because it is the first life of him to be published, it seemed to me desirable to avoid the use of footnotes. Neither have I appended reference notes; I should, however, make specific mention of my reliance upon *Saint Croix: The Sentinel River*, by Guy Murchie, in the American Folkways Series published by Duell, Sloan & Pearce, for much of my information about the early history of the border settlements in the region of Copeland's birth. I drew something also from the information gathered by Mr. J. C. Furnas about the curious relations between the towns of Calais, where Copeland was born, and St. Stephen, which lies directly across the St. Croix, in New Brunswick; this was published in an article he wrote for *The Saturday Evening Post* in the issue for August 31, 1946.

My chief single indebtedness in assembling the material dealing with Copeland's life is to Mr. Charles F. Dunbar, Copeland's nephew and executor of his estate, and to his wife, Katharine Barbey Dunbar, who kindly placed at my disposal all the papers in their possession, and who were helpful in innumerable ways. I am grateful also for the assistance of other relatives: to Copeland's other nephew, Mr. Lowell Townsend Copeland, to his niece, Mrs. Paul McClintock, and to his cousin, Mrs. Richard Wait, who was of particular aid in providing me, through the memories of her mother, with some details of Copeland's boyhood.

I am indebted to the following persons for giving me access to their correspondence with the subject of this biography: Mr. Mark A. DeWolfe Howe, Mr. David McCord, Mr. Robert Hillyer, Mr. Walter D. Edmonds, Mr. Robert W. Sawyer, Mr. Frank W. Buxton, Mr. Charles P. Curtis, Mr. Granville Hicks, Mr. Richard C. Evarts, Mr. Waldo Peirce, Mr. Grant Code and Mr. Corliss Lamont; to Mrs. Robert C. Benchley for letters to her late husband; to Mr. John Mason Brown for a letter from Robert Sherwood to Alexander Woollcott; to Mr. Wallace Meyer, formerly of Charles Scribner's Sons, for access to the files of Copeland's correspondence with that publishing house; to Mrs. Henry Cunningham, both for letters to her and to her grandmother, Mrs. Charles E. Swan, and to Miss Grace Helen Mowat.

My special thanks are due to Mr. T. S. Eliot for his permission to quote from an essay written by him while a member of Copeland's writing course. I am grateful also for the assistance given me by the staff of the Widener Library and of the University Archives at Harvard. I owe to Dean McGeorge Bundy the seldom granted permission to publish the grades received by an alumnus while he was an undergraduate, and I am indebted to former President James B. Conant for information concerning Professor Copeland's academic advancement.

Nearly two hundred Harvard alumni and other friends of Copeland, either by correspondence or in conversation, gave me their impressions and memories of him. Without the generous and interested help they extended, I would have been greatly handicapped. To many of them whom I have quoted at some length, specific acknowledgment has been made in the book itself. Naturally, in the case of a man about whom stories were legion and of wide circulation, there were many

duplications and variations in the letters I received, and ac-
cordingly I hope that I shall be forgiven for not naming
everybody who contributed to the picture I have tried to
make. I should add that in the early months of collecting this
material I had the assistance of Mr. Paul Hollister.

The following books were helpful: *Saint Croix: The Sentinel River* by Guy Murchie; *Three Centuries of Harvard*
and *Development of Harvard University* by Samuel Eliot
Morison; *Fire Under the Andes* by Elizabeth Shepley Ser-
geant; *College in a Yard: Minutes by Thirty-Nine Harvard
Men*, edited by Brooks Atkinson; *Harvard: Four Centuries
and Freedoms* by Charles A. Wagner; *A Venture in Remem-
brance* by Mark A. DeWolfe Howe; *Scenes and Portraits:
Memories of Childhood and Youth* by Van Wyck Brooks;
Harvard Yard in the Golden Age, by Rollo Walter Brown;
My Last Seventy Years by Henry Goddard Leach; *The
Manner Is Ordinary* by John La Farge; *The Harvard Book:
Selections From Three Centuries*, edited by William Bentinck
Smith; *The Middle Span* by George Santayana; *Enchanted
Aisles* by Alexander Woollcott; *Diary of a Harvard Fresh-
man* by Charles M. Flandrau; *Fifty Fabulous Years* by Hans
Kaltenborn; *And Gladly Teach* by Bliss Perry; *Harvard Ce-
lebrities: A Book of Caricatures and Decorative Drawings*
by Frederick Garrison Hall and Edward Revere Little, with
verses by Henry Ware Eliot, Jr.

For permission to quote from some of these my thanks are
due to the following: to the President and Fellows of Harvard
College and the Harvard University Press for excerpts from
Three Centuries of Harvard by Samuel Eliot Morison, and
College in a Yard edited by Brooks Atkinson; to Alfred A.
Knopf, Inc., for passages from *Fire Under the Andes* by Eliza-
beth Shepley Sergeant; to E. P. Dutton & Co. for a passage
from *Scenes and Portraits* by Van Wyck Brooks; to Little,
Brown & Co. for excerpts from *A Venture in Remembrance*

by Mark A. DeWolfe Howe; to Charles Scribner's Sons for an excerpt from *The Middle Span* by George Santayana, and for quotations from the introductions to *The Copeland Reader* and *The Copeland Translations;* to *The Atlantic Monthly* for a passage from Rollo Walter Brown's article entitled "Copey of Harvard."

The files of the *Harvard Crimson, Lampoon,* and *Advocate* supplied some of the material included, and I am grateful for its use. My thanks are due also to Mr. Mark A. DeWolfe Howe for permission to reprint the verses about Copeland which he included in *Personae Gratae*, published for him by the Club of Odd Volumes in Boston. Finally, I wish to thank the *Reader's Digest* for permission to adapt for this book the material included in the article on Copeland I wrote for its issue of May, 1958.

Index

Lowell, Agnes, 12
Lowell, George Albert, 10-11
Lowell, James Russell, 77
Lowell, John, 10
Lowell, Minerva, 10
Lowell, Perceval, 10
Lowell, Reuben, 9, 10, 11-12, 13
Lowell, Reuben B., 10-11
Lowell, Richard, 10
Lowes, John Livingston, 99
Lyman, Theodore, 209

McArthur, Arthur, 40
McCarthy, Eugene F., 62, 71
MacColl, Duncan, 7
McCord, David, 232, 233, 274-275
Macgowan, Kenneth, 99, 135, 150, 151
McIntyre, Alfred R., 260
McKittrick, T. H., 224
MacLeish, Archibald, 121, 142
MacNair, Malcolm, 17
Marliave's, 96
Marlowe, Julia, 76, 77, 82-83
Marquand, John, 152
Marvin, Langdon P., 234, 235
Massey, Raymond, 83
Mattingly, Garrett, 151
Maynard (of Small, Maynard & Co.), 140
Melia, Frank, 234-235, 236
Meredith, George, 77, 88
Meyer, Wallace, 248, 254
Middlemass, Robert, 224
Millet, J. B., 219
Modjeska, Madame Helena, 76, 77, 231
Morison, Samuel Eliot, 16-17, 41, 67, 69, 207
Morley, Christopher, 259
Mounet-Sully, Jean, 126, 132
Munn, Ector O., 116
Munn, James B., 254
Munro, William B., 209

Porcellian (club), 37
Pottinger, David T., 108
Powel, Harford, 150, 151
Power, Tyrone, 83
Pratt, John R., 224
Putnam, Alfred, 146

Quincy, Fanny Huntington, 70-71, 73

"Readings" in Boston, Copeland's reviews of, 83-84
Realism in literature, 90
Reed, John, 120, 150, 156, 186-193, 219
   dedication to Copeland, 191-192
   letter from Bucharest, 212-214
   verses to Copeland, 187
Richards, Theodore C., 99
Riddle, George, 83, 84
Rideout, Henry Milner, 6, 21, 138, 150, 188
   collaborates with Copeland on composition text, 121-124, 136
Rinehart, Frederick R., 151
Rinehart, Stanley M., 151
Robinson, Fred N., 97
Robinson, Japhet, 13
Roethke, Theodore, 121
Rogers, Alan, 224
Roope, W. H., 224
Roosevelt, Archibald, 151
Roosevelt, Kermit, 150
Roosevelt, Nicholas, 150, 184-185
Roosevelt, Theodore, 36, 40, 205, 208, 277
Royce, Josiah, 95

Sacco-Vanzetti case, 279
St. Andrews, Maine, 24, 29, 273
St. Croix River, early history of, 4-6
St. Stephen, New Brunswick, 7-9
Salvini, Tommaso, 76, 77, 81-82
Sammons, Wheeler, 150, 151